fine
Cooking
Appetizers

200 recipes for SMALL BITES with BIG FLAVOR

Editors and Contributors of *Fine Cooking*

The Taunton Press
Inspiration for hands-on living®

The Taunton Press
Inspiration for hands-on living®

The Taunton Press, Inc.
63 South Main Street
PO Box 5506, Newtown, CT 06470-5506
e-mail: tp@taunton.com

Copy editor: Nina Rynd Whitnah
Indexer: Cathy Goddard
Cover design: Kimberly Adis
Cover photographer: Scott Phillips, © The Taunton Press, Inc.
Interior design & layout: Kimberly Adis

Fine Cooking® is a trademark of The Taunton Press, Inc., registered in the U.S.
Patent and Trademark Office.

The following names/manufacturers appearing in *Fine Cooking Appetizers* are
trademarks: 4C®, Amaretto di Saronno®, Best Foods®, Budweiser®, Cholula®,
Cointreau®, Coleman's®, Combier®, Corona®, Crispin®, FAGE Total® yogurt,
Farnum Hill™, Frank's® Red Hot®, Gosling's®, Grand Marnier®, Guinness®,
Hellmann's®, Hendrick's®, Huy Fong Foods®, Jack Daniel's®, Joyva® tahini,
Kahlúa®, Lindemans®, Linie®, Maker's Mark®, Modelo® Especial, Nestlé®, Old
Bay®, Pepperidge Farm®, Pomi®, Post-it®, Pyrex®, Segura Viudas® Brut Reserve,
Sokol Blosser®, Sriracha®, Sugar in the Raw®, Tabasco®, Tuong Ot Toi Viet Nam®,
Warre's® Warrior, Whole Foods Market℠, Worcestershire®

Library of Congress Cataloging-in-Publication Data

Fine cooking appetizers : 200 recipes for small bites with big flavor / from the
editors and contributors of Fine cooking.
    p. cm.
Includes index.
ISBN 978-1-60085-330-2
1. Appetizers. I. Fine cooking.
TX740.F523 2010
641.8'12--dc22
                        2010028598

Printed in the United States of America
10 9 8 7 6 5 4 3 2 1

contents

quick & simple

goat cheese marinated with lemon and herbs

- 1 ¼-lb. log fresh goat cheese, sliced into 6 equal rounds
- 2 tsp. (loosely packed) freshly grated lemon zest
- 2 Tbs. finely chopped drained oil-packed sun-dried tomatoes
- ½ tsp. minced capers
- 1 tsp. coarsely chopped fresh thyme leaves

  Sea salt or kosher salt
- 3 small rosemary sprigs
- ½ cup extra-virgin olive oil; more if needed

  Crostini (recipe p. 65) or good-quality crackers, for serving

What's especially nice about this dish is that many of the ingredients are ones you're likely to already have in the fridge and the pantry. If serving this as part of an hors d'oeuvre spread, include a small knife and encourage people to spread a teaspoon or so of the cheese, as well as some of the marinade ingredients, over a crostini or cracker.

In a small, shallow dish (about 1½-cup capacity, preferably straight-sided, such as a small cazuela), arrange the six pieces of goat cheese in one layer. Don't worry if some of the cheese pieces crumble; just tuck them into the dish. Sprinkle the lemon zest, sun-dried tomatoes, capers, and thyme over the cheese. Sprinkle a little sea salt (fleur de sel is great if you have it) or kosher salt over the cheese, and tuck the rosemary sprigs into the dish. Pour the olive oil over the cheese so that it just covers it (use a little more if necessary). Let the cheese marinate in the refrigerator for 2 to 6 hours (you can serve it sooner, too, but the flavors will build if given a little time to marry). Bring the dish to room temperature (about 45 minutes) before serving.

PER SERVING: 160 CALORIES | 4g PROTEIN | 1g CARB | 15g TOTAL FAT | 5g SAT FAT | 9g MONO FAT | 1g POLY FAT | 15mg CHOL | 400mg SODIUM | 0g FIBER

marinated olives

- 3 cups mixed olives, rinsed and drained well
- 1 cup extra-virgin olive oil
- 4 sprigs fresh thyme
- 3 sprigs fresh rosemary
- 1½ tsp. whole fennel seeds
- 2 strips orange zest
- ¼ tsp. crushed red pepper flakes
- 1 bay leaf
- 1 clove garlic, slivered
- ¼ cup fresh lemon juice

Serve these olives at your next party and later send a jarful home with your guests.

Put the olives in a 1-quart jar. In a small saucepan, combine the oil, thyme, rosemary, fennel seeds, zest, red pepper flakes, bay leaf, and garlic. Heat on very low for 10 minutes. Pour the oil and seasonings over the olives. Add the lemon juice and close the jar. Turn a few times to distribute the seasonings; let cool to room temperature. Store in the refrigerator for no longer than 4 days. Before serving, bring the olives to room temperature and drain off most of the oil.

PER ¼ CUP: 80 CALORIES | 0g PROTEIN | 2g CARB | 8g TOTAL FAT | 1g SAT FAT | 6g MONO FAT | 1g POLY FAT | 0mg CHOL | 290mg SODIUM | 1g FIBER

curried pecans

YIELDS 4 CUPS

- **4 Tbs. unsalted butter**
- **2 Tbs. canola oil**
- **1 Tbs. Madras curry powder**
- **2 tsp. kosher salt**
- **1 tsp. ground cinnamon**
- **¼ tsp. ground cumin**
- **¼ tsp. cayenne**
- **1 lb. (4 cups) shelled pecans**

All nuts burn easily because of their high oil content. Be vigilant and test frequently for doneness. Taste the nuts when they're cool and feel free to adjust the seasonings with a final light dusting of spices, if you like.

1. In a conventional oven: Heat the oven to 300°F. Heat all the ingredients except the nuts in a small saucepan over medium heat to release the flavors and dissolve the salt. Pour the mixture into a large bowl and add the nuts. Toss and stir the nuts to coat them thoroughly. Spread them in a single layer on a foil-lined rimmed baking sheet. Bake for 30 minutes, stirring well every 10 minutes, until the nuts are deeply browned. Slide the foil out of the pan onto a cooling rack and let the nuts cool completely.

2. In a microwave: Put all the ingredients except the nuts in the largest shallow dish that fits in your microwave. Heat on high for 1 minute to release the flavors and melt the butter. Stir to combine. Add the nuts, tossing and stirring to thoroughly coat them. Toast the nuts on high for 6 minutes, stirring well at 2-minute intervals to redistribute the seasonings. Rotate the dish occasionally if your microwave doesn't have a carousel. Spread the nuts on a length of foil to cool.

3. For either method: Store in airtight containers or plastic freezer bags.

PER ¼ CUP: 240 CALORIES | 3g PROTEIN | 4g CARB | 25g TOTAL FAT | 4g SAT FAT | 13g MONO FAT | 7g POLY FAT | 10mg CHOL | 290mg SODIUM | 3g FIBER

steamed mussels with lime and cilantro

SERVES 8

- **4 lb. mussels**
- **2 Tbs. extra-virgin olive oil**
- **1 medium carrot, peeled and cut into small dice**
- **1 large fresh jalapeño, seeded and minced**
- **2 cloves garlic, minced (about 1 Tbs.)**
- **Finely grated zest and juice of 1 lime**
- **½ cup dry white wine or white vermouth**
- **½ cup heavy cream**
- **⅓ cup loosely packed cilantro leaves and tender stems, coarsely chopped**
- **½ to 1 tsp. Asian chile sauce, such as Sriracha, or other hot sauce (optional)**
- **Kosher salt**

Mussels are inexpensive and easy to prepare, yet they're special enough for a party.

1. Rinse the mussels in a colander under cold water, scrub the shells thoroughly, remove the tough, wiry beards, and discard any mussels with broken or gaping shells. While the mussels drain, heat the oil in a large, wide pot over medium-high heat. Add the carrot and jalapeño and sauté, stirring occasionally until they begin to soften and lightly brown, about 2 minutes. Add the garlic and ½ tsp. of the lime zest and continue to sauté until fragrant, 30 seconds. Pour in the wine and raise the heat to high. As soon as the wine boils, add the mussels and cover the pot. Steam the mussels, shaking the pot once or twice, until the shells open, 5 to 6 minutes.

2. Remove the pot from the heat. With a slotted spoon, transfer the mussels to a large bowl and keep warm. Return the pot with the cooking liquid to the heat, add the cream, and boil until the sauce reduces just a bit, 2 to 3 minutes. Add 1½ Tbs. of the lime juice, the cilantro, and the chile sauce, if using. Taste and add more lime juice and salt if needed. Ladle the mussels into wide, shallow bowls, pour some of the sauce over each portion, and serve immediately.

3. Serve with crusty bread or rolls, or jasmine rice.

PER SERVING: 292 CALORIES | 27g PROTEIN | 10g CARB | 14g TOTAL FAT | 5g SAT FAT | 5g MONO FAT | 2g POLY FAT | 84mg CHOL | 801mg SODIUM | 0g FIBER

Check Each Mussel

Give mussels a tap to see if they're alive. If alive, open ones will close when tapped, and the shells of closed ones will not easily separate when slid between thumb and finger. Discard any open mussels that don't close at least partially when you tap them.

smoked salmon and cucumber tea sandwiches

½ cup crème fraîche

3 Tbs. chopped fresh dill

   Kosher salt and freshly
   ground black pepper

½ medium English cucumber

8 large slices pumpernickel
   bread, each cut into four
   2-inch triangles

¼ lb. thinly sliced cold-smoked
   salmon, cut into 16 pieces

Using English cucumbers, which are seedless, makes preparing these sandwiches a snap.

1. In a small bowl, mix the crème fraîche with the dill and season to taste with salt and pepper. (You can refrigerate this mixture, tightly covered, for up to 1 day.)

2. Peel the cucumber. Then, using the peeler, shave 16 wide strips from several sides of the cucumber (discard the seed core). In a medium bowl, toss the cucumber strips with ¼ tsp. salt and let sit until softened, about 10 minutes. Pat dry with paper towels.

3. Spread the crème fraîche generously on one side of each bread triangle (you may not use it all). Top half of the triangles with a folded cucumber strip, a curl of the salmon, and a grind of black pepper. Set the remaining bread on top and serve.

PER SERVING: 150 CALORIES | 6g PROTEIN | 16g CARB | 7g TOTAL FAT | 4g SAT FAT | 2g MONO FAT | 0.5g POLY FAT | 15mg CHOL | 540mg SODIUM | 2g FIBER

manchego marinated in olive oil and herbs

SERVES 8

1 cup extra-virgin olive oil; more if needed

3 large sprigs fresh thyme

2 4-inch sprigs fresh rosemary

1 small dried red chile, cut in half or thirds

½ lb. Manchego (the more aged, the better), rind cut off, cut into ½- to ¾-inch cubes

This is an easy way to make Manchego cheese from the supermarket taste extra special.

1. In a small saucepan, heat the olive oil, thyme, rosemary, and chile over medium heat until the oil is hot (160°F) and looks shimmery, about 2 minutes. Set aside to cool completely at room temperature.

2. Put the Manchego in a glass or ceramic bowl. Pour the olive oil, herbs, and chile on top. Add more oil to cover, if needed. Cover and refrigerate for at least 4 hours and up to 3 days. Remove from the refrigerator a few hours before serving to return the oil to room temperature.

3. To serve, transfer everything to a pretty bowl, with toothpicks alongside for spearing the cheese.

PER SERVING WITH 2 TBS. OIL: 200 CALORIES | 7g PROTEIN | 0g CARB | 19g TOTAL FAT | 8g SAT FAT | 7g MONO FAT | 1g POLY FAT | 130mg CHOL | 170mg SODIUM | 0g FIBER

grilled bread with garlic, olive oil, prosciutto, and oranges

YIELDS ABOUT 24 TOASTS

1 loaf chewy, country-style bread

10 to 20 cloves garlic, peeled

4 to 5 oranges, peel and pith cut away, very thinly sliced, seeds removed

½ lb. prosciutto, preferably Parma, sliced paper-thin

Extra-virgin olive oil for drizzling

The combination of salty ham and tart-sweet oranges is unexpectedly delicious, especially when the whole thing is bathed in a full-bodied, earthy extra-virgin olive oil.

1. Prepare a wood or charcoal fire, or set a gas grill on high (you can also use a broiler). Wipe the grill rack clean and rub with oil.

2. Slice the bread a generous ¼ inch thick (cut the slices in half if they're large). When the coals are hot but no longer flaming, put the bread on the rack and grill until lightly browned, 1 to 2 minutes. Turn and grill the other side. Transfer to a plate or basket and cover to keep warm. Arrange the garlic cloves, oranges, and prosciutto on a platter and serve with the olive oil.

3. Each diner should rub a piece of toast with a garlic clove, drizzle the toast with olive oil, and add a slice each of orange and prosciutto.

PER SERVING: 100 CALORIES | 6g PROTEIN | 13g CARB | 3g TOTAL FAT | 0.5g SAT FAT | 1.5g MONO FAT | 0.5g POLY FAT | 10mg CHOL | 480mg SODIUM | 1g FIBER

saucy grilled chicken wings
with asian-style barbecue sauce

saucy grilled chicken wings

SERVES 4 TO 6

2 lb. chicken wings (about 10 whole wings), split at the wing joints (discard the wing-tips or save for stock)

Kosher salt and freshly ground black pepper

Oil for the grill

Asian-Style Barbecue Sauce (recipe below)

It's easy enough to double or triple this recipe. Just be sure to do the same with the accompanying sauce.

1. Heat a gas grill to medium high or prepare a medium-hot charcoal fire. Season the wings with 1 tsp. salt and ¼ tsp. pepper.

2. Rub the grill grate with oil. Grill the wings, covered on a gas grill or uncovered over a charcoal fire, flipping every couple of minutes, until they're browned and crisp and completely cooked through, about 20 minutes; if there are flare-ups, move the wings to another part of the grill. If the wings begin to burn at any point, reduce the heat to medium or transfer the wings to a cooler part of the grill.

3. As the wings are done, transfer them to a large bowl. Stir the sauce and toss with the wings. Serve immediately on a platter and with plenty of napkins.

PER SERVING: 118 CALORIES | 14g PROTEIN | 7g CARB | 4g TOTAL FAT | 1g SAT FAT | 1g MONO FAT | 1g POLY FAT | 37mg CHOL | 926mg SODIUM | 0g FIBER

asian-style barbecue sauce

YIELDS ENOUGH FOR 2 LB. WINGS

¼ cup tomato ketchup

2 Tbs. soy sauce

1 Tbs. light brown sugar

1 Tbs. rice vinegar

Large pinch of crushed red pepper flakes

4 scallions (both white and green parts), trimmed and thinly sliced

In a small bowl, whisk the ketchup, soy sauce, brown sugar, rice vinegar, red pepper flakes, and half of the scallions. Reserve the remaining scallions to sprinkle on the wings after tossing.

baked herbed feta

- 1 ¾-inch-thick slab feta

  Pinch of crushed red pepper flakes

  Pinch of dried oregano

- 1½ to 2 Tbs. extra-virgin olive oil

  Crusty bread or toasted pita chips (recipe p. 87), for serving

  2 or 3 lemon wedges

Gently heating some sliced feta sprinkled with herbs makes an easy and satisfying predinner nosh.

1. Heat the oven to 350°F. Put the feta on a sheet of foil. Sprinkle the red pepper flakes and oregano evenly over the cheese. Drizzle with about 1 Tbs. of the olive oil. Wrap the feta in the foil, put the package in a small baking dish, and bake until softened but not mushy, about 10 minutes.

2. Unwrap the foil at the table and drizzle with a little more olive oil if you like. Serve with the bread or toasted pita chips and have lemon wedges available for those who want to squeeze on a bit of fresh lemon juice.

PER SERVING: 140 CALORIES | 4g PROTEIN | 1g CARB | 13g TOTAL FAT | 5g SAT FAT | | 6g MONO FAT | 2g POLY FAT | 25mg CHOL | 315mg SODIUM | 0g FIBER

endive spears with sweet potato, bacon, and chives

- 3 slices bacon, thinly sliced crosswise

- 1 small sweet potato, peeled and cut into ¼-inch dice (about 1½ cups)

  Kosher salt and freshly ground black pepper

- 3 Tbs. thinly sliced fresh chives

- 2 medium heads Belgian endive

- ¼ cup crème fraîche or sour cream

Curved endive leaves make a crisp, fresh counterpoint to the sautéed bacon and sweet potatoes.

1. Cook the bacon in a 10-inch nonstick skillet over medium heat until it has rendered some of its fat, about 3 minutes. Add the sweet potato and ¼ tsp. each salt and pepper. Cook, stirring, until the sweet potato is tender and the bacon starts to crisp, 6 to 8 minutes. Stir in 2 Tbs. of the chives and season with more salt and pepper to taste. Let cool for a couple of minutes.

2. Slice the bottom ½ inch off the endive heads so some of the outer leaves break free. Cut another ½ inch off and break some more leaves free. Keep going until all the larger leaves are free. (You should have about 20.) If you like, trim the leaves so they're all the same length. Save the remaining endive for a salad.

3. Set the endive leaves on a large platter. Spoon the sweet potato mixture near the base of the leaves. Top each with a dollop of the crème fraîche and then sprinkle with the remaining chives. Serve immediately or let sit for up to 20 minutes before serving.

PER SERVING: 50 CALORIES | 1g PROTEIN | 3g CARB | 4g TOTAL FAT | 2g SAT FAT | 1.5g MONO FAT | 0g POLY FAT | 10mg CHOL | 100mg SODIUM | 1g FIBER

greek salad skewers

SERVES 4 TO 6

¼ **English cucumber**

Kosher salt and freshly ground black pepper

¼ **lb. feta cheese, cut into 16 small cubes**

8 **pitted kalamata olives, halved**

8 **ripe grape or cherry tomatoes, halved**

2 **Tbs. extra-virgin olive oil**

Break out your fancy cocktail picks for this cute appetizer (although toothpicks work just as well).

Cut four ½-inch-thick diagonal slices from the cucumber and then quarter each slice. Set the cucumber pieces on a large serving platter and season with ¼ tsp. each salt and pepper. Top each with a piece of feta and then an olive half. Stab a toothpick through a tomato half and then thread through one of the cucumber stacks, pushing the toothpick down to secure it. Drizzle with the olive oil, sprinkle with some more black pepper, and serve.

PER SERVING: 110 CALORIES | 3g PROTEIN | 3g CARB | 10g TOTAL FAT | 3.5g SAT FAT | 5g MONO FAT | 1g POLY FAT | 15mg CHOL | 240mg SODIUM | 0g FIBER

Make Ahead

These skewers will keep at room temperature for up to 1 hour.

sweet and spicy roasted nuts

YIELDS 3½ CUPS

- 1 lb. mixed unsalted almonds, pecans, and cashews
- 1½ Tbs. light brown sugar
- 2 tsp. chopped fresh thyme
- ½ tsp. chipotle powder
  Kosher salt
- 2 Tbs. unsalted butter, melted

Here, the mix of brown sugar and chipotle hits all the right sweet-hot notes.

1. Position a rack in the center of the oven and heat the oven to 400°F. Spread the nuts on a large rimmed baking sheet and roast until they start to brown, about 10 minutes.

2. While the nuts are roasting, combine the sugar, thyme, chipotle powder, and 1 tsp. salt in a small bowl. Transfer the nuts to a large bowl, add the butter, and toss well. Add the sugar mixture and toss again to coat evenly. Season with more salt to taste, transfer to small bowls, and serve while still warm.

PER ¼ CUP: 220 CALORIES | 5g PROTEIN | 9g CARB | 20g TOTAL FAT | 3g SAT FAT | 11g MONO FAT | 4.5g POLY FAT | 5mg CHOL | 85mg SODIUM | 3g FIBER

Make Ahead

These nuts are also good at room temperature and will keep in an air-tight container for at least 3 days.

grilled brie sandwiches with apricot jam

SERVES 4 TO 8

- 4 tsp. salted butter, at room temperature
- 8 slices French bread, cut on an angle ¼ inch thick
- 3 Tbs. apricot jam
- 5 oz. ripe Brie or Camembert, rind removed; cheese sliced while cold (leave the slices at room temperature for easier spreading)

For smaller bites, cut the sandwiches into quarters.

1. Butter all the bread slices on one side only. Put them all, buttered side down, on a cutting board. Spread 4 of the slices with a thin layer of jam (about 2 tsp. per slice). Spread the cheese on the other 4 slices. Pair the jam slices with the cheese slices.

2. Heat a large nonstick pan over medium-high heat for 2 minutes. Put as many sandwiches as will fit in the pan without crowding, cover, and cook until the cheese has just begun to melt and the bread is golden brown, about 2 minutes. Remove the lid and turn the sandwiches, pressing each one firmly with a spatula to flatten it slightly. Cook the sandwiches uncovered until the bottom is golden brown, about 1 minute. Turn them once more and press with the spatula again to recrisp the bread, about 30 seconds. Cut the sandwiches in half and serve immediately.

PER SERVING: 240 CALORIES | 9g PROTEIN | 19g CARB | 14g TOTAL FAT | 9g SAT FAT | 4g MONO FAT | 1g POLY FAT | 45mg CHOL | 380mg SODIUM | 1g FIBER

sweet and spicy
roasted nuts

smoked salmon and dill mascarpone toasts

4 slices (about 4½ x 3½ inches) country white bread (such as Pepperidge Farm®)

1 Tbs. unsalted butter, melted

Kosher salt and freshly ground black pepper

8 oz. mascarpone

2 Tbs. chopped fresh dill, plus 16 small fronds for garnish

Finely grated zest and juice of 1 lemon

½ medium fennel bulb (about 8 oz.), cut in half through the core and cored

4 oz. sliced cold-smoked salmon, cut into 16 even pieces

Make the breads a day ahead of serving (store in an airtight container) to save time.

1. Position a rack 6 inches from the broiler and heat the broiler on high. Set the bread on a baking sheet, brush 1 side with the melted butter, and season with salt and pepper. Broil the bread until golden brown and crisp on top, 1 to 2 minutes. Flip and cook the other side until golden, about 1 minute. While the bread is still hot, slice off the edges. Let cool slightly.

2. In a medium bowl, mix the mascarpone, chopped dill, 1 tsp. lemon zest, and 2 tsp. lemon juice. Season with salt, pepper, and more lemon juice or zest to taste. Using a vegetable peeler, peel the fennel into long, thin strips by pressing firmly against it; season the strips with salt. (You can do all this ahead and refrigerate; bring to room temperature before assembling.)

3. To assemble, spread the toasts with some of the mascarpone and then cut each toast into 4 even rectangles. Top each square with a couple of pieces of the fennel, a curl of the salmon, a dill frond, and a few grinds of pepper.

PER SERVING: 100 CALORIES | 3g PROTEIN | 6g CARB | 8g TOTAL FAT | 4g SAT FAT | 2g MONO FAT | 0g POLY FAT | 20mg CHOL | 260mg SODIUM | 1g FIBER

endive with apple, blue cheese, and toasted hazelnuts

YIELDS ABOUT 20

- ½ large tart-sweet red apple, such as Braeburn or Gala, unpeeled and cut into ⅛-inch dice
- ⅔ cup crumbled blue cheese (about 1½ oz.)
- ⅔ cup finely chopped celery (1 large rib)
- 1½ Tbs. mayonnaise
- 1½ tsp. fresh lemon juice
-    Kosher salt
- 3 Belgian endives, leaves separated; smallest saved for another use
- ½ cup hazelnuts, toasted and coarsely chopped

The lemon juice in the apple filling slows down browning, so you can make the apple mixture ahead and then quickly assemble this nibble once guests have arrived.

1. In a medium bowl, combine the apple, blue cheese, celery, mayonnaise, and lemon juice. Stir gently to combine. Season to taste with salt.

2. To assemble, mound a small spoonful of the apple mixture onto each endive leaf. Sprinkle with the hazelnuts and serve.

PER SERVING: 30 CALORIES | 1g PROTEIN | 1g CARB | 2.5g TOTAL FAT | 1g SAT FAT | 1g MONO FAT | 0.5g POLY FAT | <5mg CHOL | 125mg SODIUM | 0g FIBER

fresh ricotta with lemon, black pepper, and mint

YIELDS ABOUT 1 CUP

- 10 oz. fresh whole-milk ricotta cheese (1⅓ cups)
- 1 tsp. finely chopped lemon zest
-    Kosher salt
-    Freshly cracked black pepper
-    Extra-virgin olive oil for drizzling
- 1 or 2 sprigs fresh mint, leaves picked and finely chopped
-    Bruschetta (recipe p. 72) or crostini (recipe p. 65), for serving

Don't substitute part-skim ricotta for whole-milk ricotta, which is (no surprise) much richer in flavor and texture.

In a small bowl, combine the ricotta, lemon zest, and salt. Spread on top of garlic-rubbed bruschetta or crostini. Season with a few twists of pepper, drizzle with the olive oil, and scatter the mint on top.

PER 1 TBS.: 40 CALORIES | 2g PROTEIN | 1g CARB | 3.5g TOTAL FAT | 1.5g SAT FAT | 1.5g MONO FAT | 0g POLY FAT | 10mg CHOL | 250mg SODIUM | 0g FIBER

almonds with parmesan, rosemary, and fennel

Olive oil for the pan

1 **Tbs. chopped fresh rosemary leaves**

2 **tsp. salt**

1 **tsp. fennel seed**

¼ **tsp. freshly ground black pepper**

2 **egg whites**

½ **cup finely grated Parmesan cheese**

½ **lb. (1½ cups) blanched almonds**

½ **lb. (1½ cups) skin-on almonds**

A combination of blanched and skin-on almonds gives this mix great eye appeal.

1. Heat the oven to 300°F. Line a jellyroll pan with foil and spray or brush lightly with olive oil.

2. Grind the rosemary, salt, fennel seed, and pepper in a spice mill to a fine powder, or mince the rosemary and grind the mixture in a mortar and pestle. In a large bowl, whisk the egg whites until they foam. Add the spices and cheese. Whisk again to combine. Add the nuts, stirring and tossing to thoroughly coat them. Spread them in a single layer on the foil-lined pan. Bake for 45 minutes, stirring every 15 minutes to redistribute the coating. The nuts will stick to the foil at first and need to be gently pried loose to expose them evenly to the heat. Slide the nuts, on the foil, onto a rack to cool.

3. Store in screw-top jars or airtight tins; plastic may cause the crisp coating to soften.

PER ¼ CUP: 240 CALORIES | 11g PROTEIN | 8g CARB | 20g TOTAL FAT | 2g SAT FAT | 13g MONO FAT | 5g POLY FAT | 5mg CHOL | 480mg SODIUM | 4g FIBER

Instant Starters

For impromptu entertaining or easy hors d'oeuvres, keep a few of these delicious starters on hand.

Marcona Almonds from Spain are sweet and rich, with an extraordinary crunch more like a macadamia nut than an almond. Our favorite kind of these almonds, which are wider and flatter than their American counterparts, are fried in extra-virgin olive oil and then sprinkled liberally with salt. Serve them as a predinner nosh with some olives and a glass of sherry. Available at Whole Foods Markets℠ or Tienda.com.

Membrillo (Spanish Quince Paste) has a concentrated fruit flavor and honey-like sweetness that makes it the perfect foil for cheese. Do as the Spanish do: Cut it into slivers and serve it with a well-aged cheese like manchego or Cheddar. Quince paste also spreads nicely over a piece of crusty bread as a tea-time snack. Available at Tienda.com.

Taku Smokeries' Smoked Salmon is pleasantly lean and has a clean taste that the Alaska-based company attributes to its catch of wild (nonendangered) Pacific salmon. Drape the cold-smoked slices over canapés or serve the hot-smoked salmon with lemon wedges, capers, and a touch of sour cream spiked with horse-radish. Available at Takusmokeries.com.

Point Reyes "Original Blue" Cheese may be just the cheese to tempt those who aren't lovers of blues. The Giacomini family produces the cheese on their coastal Northern California farm from raw milk and then ages it for at least six months. The result is a cheese full of salty, tangy, and earthy notes, with a creaminess not often found in cow's milk blues. Available at cheese shops and at Pointreyescheese.com.

Sokol Blosser's® Evolution Wine blends nine grape varietals into one wine, making it a great conversation piece. But this Oregon white wine's balanced acidity and fruitiness far outshine its curiosity factor. This clean, refreshing wine is a perfect apéritif to accompany strong flavors like spiced nuts or smoked salmon.

olive oil–fried
almonds

prosciutto-wrapped greens

SERVES 8

- 3 Tbs. extra-virgin olive oil
- 2 tsp. red-wine vinegar
- 2 tsp. fresh lemon juice
- ½ tsp. Dijon mustard
- ¼ lb. mesclun or arugula, washed and spun dry

  Kosher salt and freshly ground black pepper
- 2 Tbs. freshly grated Parmigiano-Reggiano
- 12 thin slices prosciutto

These pretty bundles can be assembled in minutes, and the recipe is easily doubled.

1. In a small bowl, whisk the olive oil, vinegar, lemon juice, and mustard. Put the mesclun or arugula in a medium bowl and season with a generous pinch of salt and pepper. Add the Parmigiano to the greens and gently toss with just enough of the vinaigrette to coat the greens lightly. Taste for salt and pepper.

2. Set a slice of prosciutto on a work surface and put a small handful of greens at the narrow end of the meat (if the prosciutto is very long, cut each piece in half crosswise before using). Squeeze the greens together and roll the prosciutto into a tight log. Cut the log into 2-inch pieces on the diagonal (two or three pieces, depending on the width of the prosciutto). Repeat with the remaining prosciutto and greens and serve.

PER SERVING: 90 CALORIES | 5g PROTEIN | 1g CARB | 8g TOTAL FAT | 2g SAT FAT | 5g MONO FAT | 1g POLY FAT | 15mg CHOL | 600mg SODIUM | 0g FIBER

olive oil–fried almonds

YIELDS 2 CUPS

- 2 cups blanched almonds
- 1 cup extra-virgin olive oil
- 8 large fresh sage leaves
- 2 Tbs. fresh rosemary leaves
- 1 Tbs. fresh thyme leaves
- 1 tsp. sea salt

The almonds and herbs are crisp, salty, and sure to whet your appetite.

1. Set a metal strainer over a large heatproof bowl to quickly drain the almonds at the end of cooking. Put the almonds and olive oil in a 3- or 4-qt. saucepan with a lid (the nuts and oil should fill no more than one-third of the pot). Set the pot over medium heat, stirring almost constantly until the almonds are lightly golden, 3 to 10 minutes, depending on your stove and pot. Toss in the sage, rosemary, and thyme simultaneously and cover the pot immediately with the lid to prevent the oil from spattering. Remove the pot from the heat. The herbs will make a popping sound as they cook.

2. After the popping dies down, remove the lid and immediately pour the almonds into the strainer. Spread the drained almonds on a rimmed baking sheet and toss with the salt. When they're thoroughly cooled, store them in an airtight plastic container at room temperature.

PER SERVING: 243 CALORIES | 8g PROTEIN | 7g CARB | 22g TOTAL FAT | 2g SAT FAT | 14g MONO FAT | 5g POLY FAT | 0mg CHOL | 298mg SODIUM | 4g FIBER

cherry tomatoes stuffed with mozzarella and basil

YIELDS ABOUT 3 DOZEN

- ½ lb. fresh mozzarella, cut into tiny dice (to yield about 1 ¼ cups)
- 3 Tbs. extra-virgin olive oil
- ⅓ cup coarsely chopped fresh basil leaves
- ½ tsp. freshly grated lemon zest (from about a quarter of a lemon)
- Kosher salt and freshly ground black pepper
- 1 pt. (about 18) cherry tomatoes, rinsed and stems removed

This is a spin-off of the classic tomato, mozzarella, and basil salad, called Insalata Caprese. These little stuffed tomatoes deliver all the great flavors of that salad but in a much cuter package.

1. In a medium bowl, stir the cheese, oil, basil, zest, ½ tsp. salt, and ¼ tsp. pepper. Refrigerate for at least 2 hours and up to 4 hours before assembling.

2. When ready to assemble, slice each tomato in half (either direction is all right) and scoop out the insides with a melon baller or a teaspoon. Sprinkle lightly with salt. Invert onto a paper towel and let the tomatoes drain for 15 minutes.

3. Fill each tomato half with 1 scant tsp. of the cheese mixture. Arrange on a serving tray. Serve immediately or wrap and refrigerate for up to 2 hours.

PER SERVING: 180 CALORIES | 10g PROTEIN | 4g CARB | 14g TOTAL FAT | 6g SAT FAT | 7g MONO FAT | 1g POLY FAT | 20mg CHOL | 390mg SODIUM | 1g FIBER

how to slice and mince basil

FINE SHREDS Stack leaves atop one another and roll into a tight tube. (For smaller leaves, bunch as tightly together as possible before cutting.) Cut the rolled leaves using a single swift, smooth stroke for each slice. The width is up to you. This is known as a chiffonade.

MINCED Turn the chiffonade slices (keeping them together with a gentle pinch) and make a few perpendicular cuts as wide or as narrow as you like. Don't go back over the basil as you might when finely chopping parsley.

sautéed chorizo with red wine

SERVES 8

- **3** Tbs. extra-virgin olive oil
- **1½** lb. cured but soft chorizo, cut into ½-inch-thick slices
- **⅓** cup dry red wine
- Good country bread, cut into large cubes

You'll need a softer cured chorizo here, not the very firm types that are meant to be eaten without cooking.

Heat the olive oil in a large, 12-inch skillet over medium heat. Add the chorizo slices and cook until they begin to turn a deep brown on one side, 3 to 5 minutes. Stir and continue to cook, stirring occasionally, until the chorizo is deeply browned all over, about another 5 minutes. Carefully add the wine (be ready in case it flames) and let it simmer, scraping the pan to deglaze it, until it has reduced somewhat but is still saucy, 1 to 3 minutes. Pour the chorizo and juices into a dish. Serve with the bread for dipping into the sauce.

PER SERVING: 440 CALORIES | 21g PROTEIN | 2g CARB | 38g TOTAL FAT | 13g SAT FAT | 19g MONO FAT | 3.5g POLY FAT | 75mg CHOL | 1050mg SODIUM | 0g FIBER

What Is Chorizo?

Consisting of pork, pimentón (smoked paprika), and garlic, chorizo is a spicy sausage of Spanish origin. Some dry-cured chorizo are hard and ready to eat; others are softer (though not raw, the way you may find bulk Mexican chorizo) and benefit from a little cooking. You want the softer kind for the recipe above. Look for imported Spanish or domestic Spanish-style chorizo.

cucumber rounds with hummus and yogurt

YIELDS ABOUT 40

- **1** 15-oz. can chickpeas, rinsed and drained
- **1** large clove garlic, coarsely chopped
- **3** Tbs. fresh lemon juice
- **3** Tbs. tahini (mixed well before measuring)
- **2** Tbs. extra-virgin olive oil
- **1** tsp. ground cumin
- Kosher or sea salt
- **1** large seedless cucumber
- **¼** cup plain yogurt, well stirred
- **2** Tbs. sesame seeds, toasted until golden brown

No cooking required here—once you've made the hummus, just assemble these easy bites and serve.

1. Put the chickpeas, garlic, lemon juice, tahini, olive oil, cumin, ¼ tsp. salt, and 2 Tbs. water in a food processor. Process until the mixture is smooth, about 2 minutes.

2. Use a vegetable peeler to peel the cucumber skin lengthwise at ¼-inch intervals to create a striped pattern. Slice the cucumber crosswise into ¼-inch rounds and set them on a platter.

3. To assemble, lightly salt the cucumber rounds. Top each round with a generous teaspoon of hummus, and top the hummus with a small dollop of the yogurt. Sprinkle with sesame seeds.

PER SERVING: 25 CALORIES | 1g PROTEIN | 2g CARB | 1.5g TOTAL FAT | 0g SAT FAT | 1g MONO FAT | 0.5g POLY FAT | 0mg CHOL | 60mg SODIUM | 1g FIBER

green olive tapenade toasts

YIELDS 2⅔ CUPS TAPENADE;
SERVES 8

- **2** whole salt-packed anchovies or 4 oil-packed anchovy fillets
- **2** cups (1 lb.) fruity green French-style olives, pitted
- **¼** cup salt-packed capers, rinsed and finely chopped
- **6** medium cloves garlic, minced
- **½** cup extra-virgin olive oil; more for brushing
- **4** tsp. grappa (optional)
- **1** baguette or other good French bread, cut diagonally into ½-inch-thick slices

If salt-packed anchovies and capers aren't available, use brine-packed capers and oil-packed anchovy fillets, choosing the meatiest ones.

1. If using salt-packed anchovies, rinse them well with cold water. With the belly side up, run your finger from the head end down through the tail, removing the viscera and exposing the backbone. Lift out the bones. Soak the fillets in cold water for about 20 minutes and pat dry.

2. Mince the anchovies. With a chef's knife or in a food processor, chop the olives to a slightly coarse texture. In a bowl, mix the olives, minced anchovies, capers, garlic, olive oil, and grappa, if using. Taste. Let sit for 1 hour to let the flavors develop.

3. Prepare a charcoal or wood fire. Brush the baguette slices with olive oil and grill on both sides. (You can grill the bread in a broiler or on the stovetop using a ridged pan, if that's easier.) Spread the tapenade on the toast.

PER SERVING: 280 CALORIES | 5g PROTEIN | 16g CARB | 22g TOTAL FAT | 3g SAT FAT | 17g MONO FAT | 2g POLY FAT | 5mg CHOL | 1,770mg SODIUM | 2g FIBER

Pitting Olives

Many appetizers call for pitted olives, but there's no need to purchase a fancy olive-pitting tool. Instead, use a chef's knife or a small skillet or saucepan. The action is the same for both tools: Apply pressure with the bottom of the pan or the side of the knife until the olive splits, exposing the pit enough that it can be plucked away by hand.

prosciutto-wrapped mozzarella and basil

SERVES 8

- 8 thin slices prosciutto (preferably imported), halved lengthwise
- 8 large basil leaves, torn in half
- 8 small fresh mozzarella balls (about 1 inch in diameter), halved
- 8 ripe grape tomatoes or cherry tomatoes, halved

   Kosher salt and freshly ground black pepper
- 2 Tbs. extra-virgin olive oil

These clever appetizers wrap all the classic Italian flavors into a single bite.

Arrange 8 slices of prosciutto flat on a cutting board and put a piece of basil on one end of each slice. Top each piece of basil with a piece of mozzarella and a tomato half, matching the cut sides to make a ball. Season very lightly with salt and generously with pepper and then roll up the balls in the prosciutto. Secure each with a toothpick and set on a platter. Repeat with the remaining ingredients. Drizzle with the olive oil and serve.

Make Ahead

These keep at room temperature for up to 1 hour before serving.

PER SERVING: 180 CALORIES | 11g PROTEIN | 1g CARB | 15g TOTAL FAT | 7g SAT FAT | 5g MONO FAT | 0.5g POLY FAT | 45mg CHOL | 540mg SODIUM | 0g FIBER

spicy maple walnuts

YIELDS 4 CUPS

- 4 Tbs. unsalted butter
- ⅓ cup pure maple syrup
- 6 quarter-size slices fresh ginger, halved
- 1 Tbs. water
- 1 tsp. ground ginger
- 1 tsp. salt
- ¼ tsp. Tabasco®, or to taste
- 1 lb. (4 cups) shelled walnuts

These nuts continue to toast a bit from the intense heat of the glaze, so don't overbake them. Leave the ginger slices in the nut mixture for a delicious surprise. If you like, try substituting pecans or hazelnuts for the walnuts.

1. In a conventional oven: Heat the oven to 300°F. Combine all the ingredients except the nuts in a small saucepan and slowly simmer over low heat for 2 to 3 minutes. Put the nuts in a bowl, pour the glaze over them, and stir and toss to coat them with the glaze. Line a jellyroll pan with foil and spread the nuts in a single layer on it. Bake for 30 to 40 minutes, stirring at 15- and then 10-minute intervals. When the nuts look light and almost dry as you toss them, they're done. Don't touch them; the caramelized sugar is extremely hot. Slide the foil onto a rack and let the nuts cool completely.

2. In a microwave: Put the butter in the largest shallow dish that fits in your microwave. Heat on high for 1 minute to melt the butter. Add the remaining ingredients except the nuts and heat for 3 minutes on high. Stir to combine. Add the nuts, stirring and tossing to coat them with the glaze. Microwave on high for up to 9 minutes, stirring at 2-minute and then 1-minute intervals to redistribute the coating and prevent scorching. When all the liquid has caramelized, they're done. Don't touch them; the caramelized sugar is extremely hot. Carefully slide the nuts onto a foil-lined rack to cool.

3. For either method: Store in airtight containers or plastic freezer bags.

PER ¼ CUP: 230 CALORIES | 4g PROTEIN | 9g CARB | 21g TOTAL FAT | 4g SAT FAT | 3g MONO FAT | 13g POLY FAT | 10mg CHOL | 150mg SODIUM | 2g FIBER

toasted spiced cashews

YIELDS 4 CUPS

4 cups unsalted cashews (about 1¼ lb.)

1 large egg white, beaten slightly

¼ cup granulated sugar

4 tsp. garam masala

1½ tsp. kosher salt

½ to 1 tsp. cayenne pepper

This recipe uses garam masala, an Indian spice blend. You can make these cashews up to a day ahead.

1. Position a rack in the center of the oven and heat the oven to 325°F.

2. In a large bowl, toss the cashews with the egg white, coating the nuts evenly. Add the sugar, garam masala, salt, and cayenne. Toss again to combine.

3. Line a large rimmed baking sheet with parchment. Spread the nuts on the baking sheet and roast, stirring every 5 to 10 minutes and breaking up clumps if they form, until nicely browned, 25 to 35 minutes. Break up any clumps again while the nuts are still warm. When the nuts have cooled, put them in a serving bowl, and cover if making ahead.

PER SERVING: 210 CALORIES | 6g PROTEIN | 15g CARB | 16g TOTAL FAT | 3g SAT FAT | 9g MONO FAT | 2.5g POLY FAT | 0mg CHOL | 115mg SODIUM | 1g FIBER

What Is Garam Masala?

Garam masala is a fragrant mix of toasted, ground spices that in India varies from cook to cook. It seems that there are infinite variations, many of which contain cinnamon, cumin, cloves, nutmeg, mace, coriander, cardamom, and black pepper. Traditionally, garam masala is made at home from scratch, but these days, you can buy it in the spice section of well-stocked supermarkets.

prosciutto with marinated melon

SERVES 8 TO 10

1 medium (4-lb.) ripe honeydew melon (or any kind of melon except watermelon)

Juice of ½ lime

½ tsp. crushed red pepper flakes

Kosher salt

4 mint leaves, torn into small pieces

6 oz. paper-thin slices prosciutto di Parma or prosciutto San Danielle

1 Tbs. extra-virgin olive oil

This classic Italian starter has a great balance of salty and sweet flavors.

Cut off the stem and blossom ends of the melon. Stand the melon on one cut end and slice off the remaining rind. Cut the melon in half lengthwise from stem to blossom end and scoop out the seeds. Halve each melon half, so that you have four long wedges. Slice the wedges crosswise about ¼ inch thick. Gently toss the melon in a bowl with the lime juice, red pepper flakes, ¼ tsp. salt, and half of the mint. Arrange on a platter, drape the prosciutto on top, and drizzle with the olive oil. Sprinkle with the remaining mint and serve immediately.

PER SERVING: 90 CALORIES | 7g PROTEIN | 8g CARB | 3.5g TOTAL FAT | 1g SAT FAT | 2g MONO FAT | 0.5g POLY FAT | 15mg CHOL | 690mg SODIUM | 1g FIBER

passed & plated

hearts of palm and radish coins with shrimp

YIELDS 24

3 to 4 **hearts of palm (1 to 1½ inches wide), rinsed and cut into ¼-inch-thick coins (you'll need 24)**

2 **Tbs. plus ¼ tsp. fresh lime juice**

2 **Tbs. extra-virgin olive oil**

Pinch of granulated sugar

Kosher salt

1 **Tbs. mayonnaise, preferably Hellmann's® or Best Foods® brand**

¼ **tsp. coriander seeds, toasted and coarsely ground in a mortar**

¼ **tsp. freshly grated lime zest**

Pinch of cayenne

Freshly ground black pepper

48 **small peeled, deveined, and cooked shrimp (71 to 90 per lb. or 100 to 150 per lb.)**

5 to 6 **radishes (1 to 1½ inches wide), sliced into ¼-inch-thick coins (you'll need 24)**

24 **fresh cilantro leaves, for garnish**

These appetizers look most adorable when the hearts of palm and radishes are roughly the same diameter, so the rounds are of equal size.

1. Lay the palm coins in a single layer in a nonreactive dish. Drizzle with 2 Tbs. of the lime juice, 3 Tbs. water, and the olive oil. Sprinkle evenly with sugar and a generous pinch of salt. Shake the dish to coat the palm coins and let sit while preparing the remaining ingredients.

2. In a medium bowl, mix the remaining ¼ tsp. lime juice with the mayonnaise, coriander seeds, lime zest, cayenne, a generous pinch of salt, and a pinch of pepper. Toss the shrimp with the mayonnaise and season to taste with salt and pepper.

3. Carefully drain the hearts of palm and pat dry with paper towels. Top each radish coin with a palm coin of similar size, 2 shrimp, and a cilantro leaf.

PER SERVING: 30 CALORIES | 2g PROTEIN | 1g CARB | 2g TOTAL FAT | 0g SAT FAT |
1g MONO FAT | 0G POLY FAT | 15mg CHOL | 65mg SODIUM | 0g FIBER

mini tuna burgers with mint-caper aïoli

SERVES 6 TO 8;
YIELDS ABOUT 18

- 1 large egg, separated
- 2 Tbs. capers, rinsed
- 1 large clove garlic, coarsely chopped
- 1 Tbs. fresh lemon juice
- Kosher salt and freshly ground black pepper
- ½ cup extra-virgin olive oil; more for brushing
- 2 Tbs. chopped fresh mint, plus 18 large leaves, for garnish
- 1 lb. tuna steak, cut into 1-inch chunks
- 3 regular pitas, each cut into 6 triangles

Make the aïoli with a pasteurized egg if you prefer not to use raw eggs.

1. In a food processor, combine the egg yolk, capers, garlic, lemon juice, ¼ tsp. salt, and ⅛ tsp. pepper; purée until smooth. With the motor running, slowly drizzle the oil through the feed tube to form an emulsion. Stop the motor, add the chopped mint, and pulse to combine. Spoon ¼ cup of the aïoli into a small bowl.

2. Add the tuna and egg white to the food processor bowl and pulse until just chopped. Line a baking sheet with waxed paper or parchment. Drop 18 rounds of the tuna mixture by heaping tablespoons onto the baking sheet. Use your hands to shape the mounds into mini burgers about ⅓ inch thick.

3. Heat a gas grill to high or prepare a hot charcoal fire (or prepare a stove-top grill pan). Brush one side of the tuna burgers with oil and season with salt and pepper. Gently flip the burgers and season the other side. Put the pita triangles on another baking sheet, brush both sides with oil, and sprinkle both sides with a little salt and pepper. Grill the pitas on both sides until lightly browned and a little crisp but still pliable, 1 to 2 minutes total. Transfer to a platter.

4. Grill the burgers (covered on a gas grill, uncovered on a charcoal grill) on one side until they have nice grill marks, about 2 minutes. Flip the burgers, loosening them with a metal spatula if necessary, and grill the other side until marked and just cooked through, about another 2 minutes.

5. While the burgers are cooking, spread a little of the reserved aïoli inside each pita. As the burgers come off the grill, tuck 1 into each pita, along with a mint leaf, and serve immediately.

PER SERVING: 280 CALORIES | 16g PROTEIN | 14g CARB | 18g TOTAL FAT | 3g SAT FAT | 11g MONO FAT | 2.5g POLY FAT | 50mg CHOL | 260mg SODIUM | 2g FIBER

warm cheese and mushroom toasts

SERVES 8

- 2 Tbs. unsalted butter
- 1 large shallot, finely diced (about ¼ cup)
- Kosher salt
- 10 oz. mixed fresh mushrooms (like shiitake, cremini, and oyster), trimmed and thinly sliced
- 16 ½-inch slices baguette, cut on a sharp diagonal so they're about 3 inches long
- 1½ cups grated Gruyère (about 4 oz.)

Sautéed mixed mushrooms pack complex flavor into these small bites.

1. Melt the butter in a large, heavy-duty skillet over medium heat. Add the shallot, season with ½ tsp. salt, and cook, stirring, until softened, about 3 minutes. Raise the heat to high, add the mushrooms and another ½ tsp. salt, and cook, stirring frequently, until softened and browned, 3 to 5 minutes longer. (At this point, you can cool to room temperature and refrigerate, tightly wrapped, for up to 1 day. Bring to room temperature before using.)

2. Position a rack about 8 inches from the broiler element and heat the broiler to high. Arrange the bread slices on a large rimmed baking sheet. Broil until lightly toasted, 2 to 4 minutes, rotating the pan as needed for even toasting. Flip the bread, mound 1 heaping Tbs. of the mushrooms on each piece, and sprinkle with the Gruyère. Broil until the cheese is melted and lightly browned, 4 to 7 minutes. Serve immediately.

PER SERVING: 130 CALORIES | 7g PROTEIN | 4g CARB | 9g TOTAL FAT | 6g SAT FAT | 3g MONO FAT | 0g POLY FAT | 30mg CHOL | 220mg SODIUM | 1g FIBER

crisp and spicy chicken tenders with blue cheese dipping sauce

SERVES 4

2½ cups panko (Japanese breadcrumbs)

Kosher salt and freshly ground black pepper

1½ lb. chicken tenders

¾ cup mayonnaise

1 Tbs. hot pepper sauce (like Frank's® Red Hot®)

¼ tsp. cayenne

¾ cup crumbled blue cheese (about 4 oz.)

½ cup sour cream

3 Tbs. milk

Reminiscent of buffalo wings, these are wonderfully crunchy, thanks to panko.

1. Pour the panko into a shallow dish (like a pie plate) and toss with ¾ tsp. salt and ¼ tsp. pepper.

2. Trim off any exposed tendon ends from the wide tips of the chicken tenders, if necessary. In a medium bowl, whisk ¼ cup of the mayonnaise with the hot sauce, cayenne, and ⅛ tsp. salt. Add the chicken and toss with your hands to coat well. Coat each chicken tender in the panko and arrange in a single layer on a heavy-duty rimmed baking sheet. Refrigerate while you heat the broiler and make the sauce.

3. Position a rack 6 inches from the broiler element and heat the broiler on high for at least 10 minutes. Meanwhile, combine the remaining ½ cup mayonnaise with the blue cheese, sour cream, milk, ½ tsp. salt, and a few grinds of pepper in a medium bowl. Whisk until well combined and only small bits of cheese remain intact.

4. Broil the tenders, flipping once, until they're crisp and golden brown in spots on the outside and cooked through, 4 to 6 minutes per side (rotate the pan as needed for even browning). Transfer the tenders to a platter or to individual plates and serve with the dipping sauce.

PER SERVING: 710 CALORIES | 43g PROTEIN | 18g CARB | 51g TOTAL FAT | 14g SAT FAT | 5g MONO FAT | 1.5g POLY FAT | 140mg CHOL | 1190mg SODIUM | 1g FIBER

chicken tostadas pequeñas

Vegetable oil

Juice of 2 limes; more if necessary

½ **cup lightly packed chopped fresh cilantro**

Kosher salt and freshly ground black pepper

6 **to 8 oz. boneless, skinless chicken breast (about 1 breast)**

6 **8-inch flour tortillas**

2 **Tbs. crème fraîche or sour cream**

½ **tsp. ground cumin, lightly toasted in a dry skillet**

½ **cup finely chopped tomatillo**

½ **cup finely shredded lettuce**

¼ **cup finely diced red pepper**

Instead of the tomatillo salsa suggested here, you can use your own favorite recipe or good-quality prepared salsa. You can also use store-bought tortilla chip "scoops" in place of the baked tortillas. Just assemble as close to serving time as possible so that the chips don't get too soggy.

1. To make the chicken, mix ¼ cup vegetable oil, 3 Tbs. of the lime juice, ¼ cup of the cilantro, salt, and pepper. Add the chicken and marinate, refrigerated, for at least 2 hours and up to 24. Grill or broil until done, about 5 minutes each side. Cool, chop fine, and set aside.

2. Meanwhile, make the tortilla cups. With a 2½-inch cookie cutter, cut 40 circles from the tortillas (you'll get about 7 per tortilla). Heat the oven to 350°F. Brush each tortilla with a little oil, press into mini muffin tins, and salt lightly. Bake until golden brown, 8 to 10 minutes. (A regular mini muffin pan rather than a nonstick one is a bit easier to work with. Some of the tortillas may pop out a bit and bake into disks, rather than cups, but you can still use them.) Let cool and store in an airtight container.

3. To make the cumin sauce, mix the crème fraîche, cumin, and 1 Tbs. of the lime juice, then season to taste with salt and pepper.

4. To make the salsa, mix the tomatillo with 2 Tbs. chopped cilantro, and 2 Tbs. of the lime juice, then season to taste with salt and pepper.

5. To assemble, toss the chicken with about 2 Tbs. chopped cilantro, 2 Tbs. of the lime juice, and salt and pepper to taste. Fill each cup with a little chicken, a pinch of shredded lettuce, a spoonful of the salsa, a drizzle of the cumin sauce, and a sprinkle of diced red pepper. Serve immediately.

PER SERVING: 35 CALORIES | 1g PROTEIN | 2g CARB | 2g TOTAL FAT | 0.5g SAT FAT | 0.5g MONO FAT | 1g POLY FAT | 5mg CHOL | 70mg SODIUM | 0g FIBER

cheese sablés

- **9** oz. (2 cups) unbleached all-purpose flour
- **1** tsp. table salt
- **⅛** tsp. cayenne
- **⅛** tsp. baking powder
- **7** oz. (14 Tbs.) cold unsalted butter, cut into chunks
- **3½** oz. (1 ½ cups) finely grated sharp Cheddar
- **1½** oz. (½ cup) finely grated Parmigiano-Reggiano
- **1** large egg, lightly beaten
- **½** cup finely chopped pecans or walnuts (optional)
- **1** large egg yolk mixed with a pinch of paprika and ½ tsp. water to make a glaze
- **Kosher or sea salt**

These are great with drinks and go especially well with dry and off-dry sparkling wines. The dough will keep for 2 days in the refrigerator and for months in the freezer (thaw it in the fridge before using).

1. Put the flour, salt, cayenne, and baking powder in a food processor; pulse to combine. Add the butter and pulse again until the butter is in small pieces, six to eight 1-second pulses. Add the cheeses, pulse, and finally, add the egg and pulse until the mixture just starts to come together.

2. Dump the dough on an unfloured surface. If you're using nuts, sprinkle them on the pile of dough. Knead by lightly smearing the ingredients together as you push them away from you with the heel of your hand until the dough is cohesive. Shape the dough into a flat disk, wrap in plastic, and chill for an hour or two to let the butter firm.

3. Position racks in the top and bottom thirds of the oven. Heat the oven to 400°F. On a lightly floured surface, roll out the dough to about ¼ inch thick. Stamp out shapes or cut shapes with a knife. Arrange 1 inch apart on 2 ungreased baking sheets. Reroll scraps once and stamp again. Brush with the glaze and sprinkle lightly with kosher or sea salt.

4. Bake until golden brown and thoroughly cooked inside, about 14 minutes, rotating the sheets from front to back and top to bottom about halfway through. To test, break a sablé in half to see if the center still looks doughy. If so, cook for a few more minutes, but be careful not to overbake. Let cool on a rack and store only when completely cool.

PER CRACKER: 70 CALORIES | 2g PROTEIN | 4g CARB | 5g TOTAL FAT | 3g SAT FAT | 1.5g MONO FAT | 0g POLY FAT | 25mg CHOL | 115mg SODIUM | 0g FIBER

crabmeat-avocado quesadillas

YIELDS SIXTY 2-INCH QUESADILLAS

FOR THE MANGO SALSA

- **1** ripe mango, peeled, pitted, and diced into ¼-inch cubes
- **½** red bell pepper, seeded, and finely chopped
- **1** large ripe tomato, peeled, seeded, and diced
- **2** Tbs. finely chopped fresh chives
- **2** Tbs. chopped fresh cilantro
- **2** Tbs. fresh lime juice
- **1** fresh jalapeño, seeded and finely chopped

  Kosher salt and freshly ground black pepper

FOR THE QUESADILLAS

- **12** 8-inch flour tortillas
- **1½** cups cooked crabmeat, picked over to remove any bits of shell
- **1½** cups shredded Monterey Jack
- **2** ripe Hass avocados, pitted, peeled, and mashed
- **⅓** cup finely chopped scallion
- **⅓** cup lightly packed, finely chopped, fresh cilantro leaves
- **2** Tbs. fresh lime juice

  Kosher salt and freshly ground black pepper

  Grapeseed or canola oil for frying

This recipe makes individual two-bite hors d'oeuvres, but you can make a full-sized quesadilla and simply cut it into wedges after frying—not as pretty, but quicker.

MAKE THE SALSA

Combine all of the salsa ingredients and let stand at least an hour at room temperature so the flavors can develop. Chill until ready to serve.

MAKE THE QUESADILLAS

1. With a 2-inch cookie cutter, cut out 120 circles from the tortillas (you'll get about 10 per tortilla).

2. In a large bowl, gently mix the crab, cheese, avocados, scallion, cilantro, lime juice, salt, and pepper. Spread the crab mixture onto 60 of the tortillas (about 1 Tbs. each) and top with the other tortillas. (You can assemble these a couple of hours ahead; refrigerate them until ready to fry.)

3. To cook, heat a little oil in a nonstick sauté pan over medium heat and cook the quesadillas in batches until lightly browned and the cheese is melting, about 2 minutes per side. Serve warm with a bit of salsa on top.

PER SERVING: 50 CALORIES | 2g PROTEIN | 4g CARB | 3.5 TOTAL FAT | 1.5g SAT FAT | 1.5g MONO FAT | 0.5g POLY FAT | 5mg CHOL | 85mg SODIUM | 1g FIBER

> If you have a portable burner, consider setting up a station to cook these during the party. Guests love to gather round and eat the food right as it comes out of the pan, and the action of the cooking can make the party feel that much more lively.

smoked salmon and pea fritters with scallion sour cream

YIELDS ABOUT 18 FRITTERS

- 1 **cup sour cream**
- 1 **bunch scallions, thinly sliced (white and green parts kept separate)**
- 2 **Tbs. capers, drained, rinsed, and roughly chopped**
- 2 **large eggs**
- ¾ **cup whole milk**
- ¼ **lb. hot-smoked salmon, cut into ¼-inch dice (about ¾ cup)**
- 1 **cup frozen peas (about 5 oz.)**
- 5½ **oz. (1¼ cups) all-purpose flour**
- 2 **tsp. baking powder**
  Kosher salt
- ¼ **tsp. ground white pepper**
- 1½ **cups vegetable oil**

These delectable fritters are perfect party food. The sour cream dip has just enough tanginess to cut through the richness of the salmon.

1. Position a rack in the center of the oven and heat the oven to 200°F.

2. In a medium bowl, mix the sour cream with the scallion greens and capers.

3. In a large bowl, whisk the eggs until frothy. Whisk in the milk. Stir in the salmon, peas, and the white parts of the scallions. Add the flour, baking powder, ½ tsp. salt, and the white pepper to the egg mixture and whisk until well combined.

4. Pour the oil into a 10-inch skillet that's 2 inches deep (the oil should be about ½ inch deep) and heat over medium-high heat until shimmering hot. (A good way to tell if the oil is hot enough is to drop a 1-inch cube of bread in the oil; it should turn golden brown in about 30 seconds.) Add the batter to the oil 1 heaping Tbs. at a time. Cook the fritters in batches of 6 (don't crowd the pan) until golden brown on the first side, 2 to 3 minutes. Using a slotted spatula or spoon, turn and cook until the second side is golden brown, about 2 minutes. Transfer the fritters to a rimmed baking dish lined with paper towels and keep warm in the oven. Cook the remaining fritters. Serve hot with the scallion sour cream.

PER SERVING: 160 CALORIES | 4g PROTEIN | 9g CARB | 12g TOTAL FAT | 3g SAT FAT | 4.5g MONO FAT | 4g POLY FAT | 35mg CHOL | 250mg SODIUM | 1g FIBER

meatballs in spicy peanut curry sauce

½ cup all-purpose flour

Kosher salt and freshly
ground black pepper

1 lb. ground beef, medium
lean (80% or 85%)

2 Tbs. vegetable oil;
more if needed

4 cloves garlic, coarsely
chopped

1 Tbs. red curry paste;
more to taste

1 cup canned coconut milk
(refrigerate the can, don't
shake it, and use the thick
cream from the top)

2 Tbs. chunky peanut butter

2 tsp. fish sauce (nam pla);
more to taste

1½ Tbs. granulated sugar;
more to taste

1 tsp. chopped fresh mint
or basil, for garnish

Thick canned coconut milk tames the fire in this curry.

1. Put the flour on a plate. Sprinkle 1½ tsp. salt and ¼ tsp. pepper on the beef and mix well. Shape the beef into small, firm balls about 1 inch in diameter; you'll get 32 to 40. Roll the meatballs in the flour, dusting off the excess.

2. Line a plate with paper towels. In a wok or frying pan, heat the oil on high until it's hot. Fry the garlic until browned, about 1 minute; remove the garlic and set aside. Add the meatballs (in batches, if necessary) and sear them on high heat, stirring and tilting the pan, until they're browned evenly and cooked through, about 5 minutes. Using a slotted spoon, transfer the meatballs to the paper towel–lined plate to drain.

3. If no oil remains in the pan, add another 2 tsp. and fry the red curry paste so it releases its aromas, about 2 minutes, stirring with a wooden spoon to prevent sticking. Add the reserved garlic and the cream of the coconut milk and then stir in the peanut butter. Cook and stir to get a smooth, uniform consistency, about 1 minute. Taste and add fish sauce, sugar, or more curry paste to taste; the sauce shouldn't be too sweet.

4. Return the meatballs to the pan with the sauce and simmer over low heat until they're hot, about 2 minutes. Transfer to a serving dish and garnish with the mint or basil sprinkled on top.

PER MEATBALL: 50 CALORIES | 3g PROTEIN | 3g CARB | 3.5g TOTAL FAT | 2g SAT FAT | 1g MONO FAT | 0.5g POLY FAT | 5mg CHOL | 110mg SODIUM | 0g FIBER

how to make a rich, silky curry sauce

Coconut milk is the critical behind-the-scenes ingredient. Refrigerate the can so the cream rises and hardens, making it easy to scoop out.

Peanut butter and coconut milk melt into the curry paste, making a smooth, unctuous sauce.

Rolling the meatballs around right in the pan warms them up and ensures a complete coating of sauce.

crab and scallion stuffed shrimp

- 3½ Tbs. unsalted butter; more for the baking sheet
- ½ cup thinly sliced scallions (white and light green parts)
- Kosher salt
- ½ tsp. Worcestershire® sauce
- 2 drops Sriracha® hot sauce (or other Asian chile sauce)
- ⅓ cup mayonnaise
- 2 Tbs. coarsely chopped fresh parsley, plus 20 whole leaves or small sprigs
- 1½ tsp. fresh lemon juice
- 1 tsp. finely grated lemon zest
- ½ tsp. Dijon mustard
- Freshly ground black pepper
- ½ lb. backfin crabmeat, drained and picked over for shells
- 1¼ cups fine fresh breadcrumbs
- 16 jumbo shrimp (16 to 20 per lb.), butterflied (see the sidebar, below)
- 1 small head frisée, torn into bite-size pieces
- 1½ tsp. extra-virgin olive oil

For this recipe, avoid shrimp that's already been deveined because it's been slit down the back and can't be butterflied properly.

MAKE THE STUFFING

1. In a small saucepan, melt 2 Tbs. of the butter over medium-low heat. Add the scallions and a pinch of salt and cook, stirring, until softened, 3 to 4 minutes (don't let them brown). Take the pan off the heat and stir in the Worcestershire sauce and hot sauce. Let cool to room temperature.

2. In a medium bowl, combine the mayonnaise, 1 Tbs. of the chopped parsley, 1 tsp. of the lemon juice, the lemon zest, the mustard, ¼ tsp. salt, and a few grinds of pepper. Stir in the cooled scallion mixture. Add the crab and mix gently but thoroughly.

3. In a 10-inch skillet, melt the remaining 1½ Tbs. butter over medium heat. Add the breadcrumbs and cook, stirring, until light golden brown, about 4 minutes. Transfer to a medium bowl and mix in the remaining 1 Tbs. chopped parsley and ¼ tsp. salt.

STUFF AND BAKE THE SHRIMP

1. Line a rimmed baking sheet with parchment and rub lightly with butter. Arrange the butterflied shrimp on the baking sheet. Using a spoon or your hands, mound 1 heaping Tbs. of the crab mixture onto each shrimp. Sprinkle and pat the breadcrumbs over the crab. Flip the tail of each shrimp up and over the crab.

2. Position a rack in the center of the oven and heat the oven to 400°F. Bake until the shrimp are cooked through, the crabmeat is hot, and the crumbs are golden brown, 12 to 14 minutes.

MAKE THE SALAD

While the shrimp are in the oven, toss the frisée and the whole parsley leaves with the remaining ½ tsp. lemon juice, the olive oil, and a pinch of salt. On 8 small plates, arrange a small pile of the salad and 2 shrimp. Serve right away.

PER SERVING: 210 CALORIES | 15g PROTEIN | 6g CARB | 14g TOTAL FAT | 4.5g SAT FAT | 4g MONO FAT | 4.5g POLY FAT | 125mg CHOL | 370mg SODIUM | 1g FIBER

how to butterfly shrimp

By butterflying the shrimp from underneath, you'll be able to flip the tails up on the shrimp before baking, giving them a jaunty look. The technique is simple, but it's a good idea to buy a few extra shrimp in case you rip one or two while getting the hang of it. Don't buy "easy-peel" shrimp, because they've already been deveined from the top side and won't work for this technique. Start by rinsing the shrimp and peeling them down to the section closest to the tail.

With a paring knife, slit the underside of a shrimp down the middle, cutting almost but not all the way through to expose the vein that runs along the top of the shrimp.

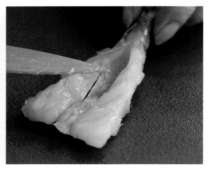

Open the shrimp like a book and use the knife to lift out the vein.

pan-fried halloumi with fennel, olive, and mint compote

SERVES 6

3 Tbs. extra-virgin olive oil

½ medium fennel bulb, cored and cut into ¼-inch dice (about 1¼ cups)

½ medium yellow onion, cut into ¼-inch dice (about ¾ cup)

Kosher salt and freshly ground black pepper

12 pitted Kalamata olives, slivered (about ⅓ cup)

1 tsp. finely grated lemon zest

⅓ cup minced fresh mint

1 ½-lb. package halloumi cheese, cut into ¼-inch- to ⅜-inch-thick slices (see the sidebar below for more about halloumi)

Serve this with slices of warm crusty bread.

1. Heat 2 Tbs. of the oil in a heavy, 10-inch sauté pan over medium heat until hot. Add the fennel and onions and cook gently, stirring occasionally, until the vegetables begin to soften (but don't let them brown), 4 to 5 minutes. Reduce the heat to medium low, add ¼ tsp. salt and ¼ tsp. pepper and continue to cook until the vegetables soften completely, another 3 to 5 minutes. Turn the heat to low and stir in the olives, lemon zest, mint, and the remaining 1 Tbs. oil. Remove from the heat and cover to keep warm.

2. Set a large (preferably 12-inch) nonstick skillet over medium-high heat (no oil is necessary) until hot, about 1 minute. Working in batches if necessary to avoid crowding the pan, cook the halloumi until golden in spots, about 2 minutes. Flip and cook until the second side of each slice is golden, about 2 minutes more. Reduce the heat as needed if the halloumi is browning too fast.

3. Shingle the halloumi on a serving platter. Stir the compote and spoon half of it over the halloumi. Serve immediately with the remaining compote on the side.

PER SERVING: 210 CALORIES | 9g PROTEIN | 5g CARB | 18g TOTAL FAT | 8g SAT FAT | 6g MONO FAT | 1g POLY FAT | 25mg CHOL | 560mg SODIUM | 1g FIBER

What Is Halloumi?

Traditionally made from goat's milk and sheep's milk and hailing from Cyprus, this cheese has a great chewy texture and a mellow yet briny flavor that hints of mint. But the really interesting thing about halloumi is that when heated, it softens but doesn't melt. When pan-fried, for example, it gets a tasty brown crust and a soft gooey center.

crisp parmesan chicken fingers
with marinara dipping sauce

SERVES 4

FOR THE DIPPING SAUCE

2	Tbs. olive oil
1	large clove garlic, minced
¼	tsp. dried oregano, crushed
¼	tsp. crushed red pepper flakes
1	28-oz. can crushed tomatoes
	Kosher salt
2	Tbs. chopped fresh basil
	Freshly ground black pepper

FOR THE CHICKEN

1	lb. chicken tenderloins
½	cup all-purpose flour
3	large eggs
¼	cup finely grated Parmigiano-Reggiano
	Kosher salt and freshly ground black pepper
2¼	cups fresh, coarse white breadcrumbs
1	cup peanut oil

These crisp chicken fingers are addictive. The sauce can be made a day ahead, refrigerated, and then gently reheated before serving.

MAKE THE DIPPING SAUCE

Heat the oil, garlic, oregano, and red pepper flakes in a medium saucepan over medium-low heat until the garlic is sizzling and very fragrant, 2 to 4 minutes. Add the crushed tomatoes and ½ tsp. salt. Increase the heat to medium and bring the sauce to a simmer. Reduce the heat to medium low or as needed to keep the sauce bubbling lazily, and cook, stirring occasionally, for 15 minutes. Add the basil and continue to cook until the sauce is full flavored and thick, about 5 minutes. Season to taste with a few grinds of pepper and more salt, if needed.

MAKE THE CHICKEN

1. If necessary, trim the chicken by cutting away any exposed white tendon from the wide tips of the tenderloins. Slice the tenderloins in half lengthwise to make long, slender strips (some small tenderloins may not need to be sliced).

2. Arrange three wide, shallow dishes, such as pie plates, in a row on the counter. Put the flour in the first dish. In the second dish, beat the eggs, Parmigiano, ¼ tsp. salt, and a couple of grinds of pepper. In the third dish, mix the breadcrumbs with ¾ tsp. salt and a few grinds of pepper. Have ready a baking sheet or other tray. Dredge the chicken tenderloins first in the flour, shaking off any excess, then in the egg mixture, and finally, in the breadcrumbs, pressing to help the crumbs adhere. After you finish each tenderloin, lay it on the baking sheet. When all the tenderloins are done, put the baking sheet in the refrigerator uncovered for at least 10 minutes (and up to 4 hours) to help the breading firm up.

3. When ready to fry the chicken, heat the oven to 200°F. Have ready a baking sheet lined with paper towels. Heat the oil in a 10-inch nonstick skillet over medium heat until the oil bubbles instantly when you dip a tenderloin into it. Working in batches so as not to crowd the pan, fry the chicken until golden brown and cooked through, about 2 minutes per side. Adjust the heat as necessary to keep the oil from getting so hot that the chicken overbrowns before the inside cooks. As each batch finishes cooking, transfer the pieces to the towel-lined baking sheet and keep them warm until all are cooked.

PER SERVING: 340 CALORIES | 32g PROTEIN | 28g CARB | 12g TOTAL FAT | 2g SAT FAT | 7g MONO FAT | 2.5g POLY FAT | 95mg CHOL | 750mg SODIUM | 5g FIBER

seared tuna tostadas

SERVES 8

FOR THE WASABI PASTE

¼ cup wasabi powder

¼ cup water

FOR THE WONTON TOSTADAS

Vegetable oil for frying

8 wonton wrappers, cut into quarters (about 2-inch squares)

FOR THE SALSA

1 lb. (about 4) plum tomatoes, peeled, seeded, and diced

4 fresh shiso leaves (or 1 Tbs. fresh cilantro), chopped

2 scallions, chopped

2 cloves garlic, minced

2 tsp. rice vinegar

Kosher salt and freshly ground black pepper

FOR THE TUNA

1 Tbs. soy sauce

1 Tbs. Asian sesame oil

1 tsp. slivered fresh ginger

Freshly ground black pepper

1 lb. very fresh tuna steaks (ahi is best), cut into rectangular logs about 1¾ inches thick and 5 inches long

1 Tbs. vegetable oil

FOR THE GARNISH

½ cup crème fraîche or sour cream

⅓ cup chopped scallions

Wasabi powder and fresh shiso (also called perilla and Japanese basil) are available at Asian food markets. In an airtight container, the fried wontons will stay crisp for a week. The wasabi needs to be made at least 2 days ahead so the bitterness of the powder fades; it will keep for up to a month. The salsa will hold for a couple of days in the fridge.

MAKE THE WASABI PASTE

At least 2 days before serving, mix the wasabi powder with the water to form a soft paste. Refrigerate.

MAKE THE WONTON TOSTADAS

In a deep skillet, add oil to a depth of ½ inch. Heat the oil to 380°F—a cube of bread will turn golden in 15 seconds. (If the oil isn't hot enough, the tostadas will absorb too much oil and get soggy and greasy after just a few hours.) Fry a few of the wonton squares at a time until they're crisp and evenly golden on both sides, turning them during cooking if necessary, about 5 to 10 seconds. Lift out with tongs and drain on paper towels.

MAKE THE SALSA

In a bowl, stir the tomatoes, shiso (or cilantro), scallions, garlic, and vinegar. Season with salt and pepper.

PREPARE THE TUNA

In a bowl, combine the soy sauce, sesame oil, ginger, and pepper. Marinate the tuna in this sauce for 15 minutes or up to 2 hours, turning it halfway through. Heat a cast-iron skillet over high heat with 1 Tbs. oil. When the oil is very hot—it will be smoking—put the tuna logs in the pan and sear, 20 to 30 seconds on each side; they should be seared outside and rare inside. Slice the logs into ¼-inch pieces.

TO ASSEMBLE

Put a piece of tuna on a wonton. Spread a touch of wasabi paste on the tuna (not too much—it's very hot). Top with a spoonful of salsa. Garnish with a bit of crème fraîche and scallions.

PER SERVING WITH 2 TBS. SALSA: 100 CALORIES | 6g PROTEIN | 8g CARB | 4.5g TOTAL FAT | 1.5g SAT FAT | 2g MONO FAT | 0.5g POLY FAT | 15mg CHOL | 180mg SODIUM | 1g FIBER

smoked salmon on belgian endive with crème fraîche and chives

YIELDS ABOUT 40

- **4** large heads Belgian endive
- **⅓** cup crème fraîche
- **¼** lb. thinly sliced smoked salmon, cut crosswise into ¼-inch-wide strips

  Freshly ground black pepper
- **½** medium lemon
- **1** small bunch fresh chives, sliced diagonally into ¼-inch segments

To get ahead, you can prep everything in advance, but assemble just before serving.

1. Discard any damaged outer endive leaves. Trim the root end and separate the leaves. You should end up with 35 to 40 large leaves (save the small inner leaves for a salad). Arrange the leaves on a baking sheet.

2. Put the crème fraîche in a squeeze bottle or a small piping bag (or you can also make a piping bag by trimming one corner of a small zip-top bag). Pipe a small dollop of crème fraîche on each endive leaf. Gently arrange a small pile (about 4 strips) of the sliced salmon on top of the crème fraîche. Season the salmon with some black pepper and a little squeeze of lemon juice. Sprinkle a few chives on top (you may not need them all), arrange the leaves on a platter, and serve.

PER SERVING: 15 CALORIES | 1g PROTEIN | 1g CARB | 1g TOTAL FAT | 0g SAT FAT | 0g MONO FAT | 0g POLY FAT | 0g CHOL | 60mg SODIUM | 0g FIBER

Belgian endive looks lovely and is easy to grab. Other good toppings for it include crème fraîche with caviar or crumbled blue cheese with diced apple and walnuts.

silky leek and celery root soup

- **3 Tbs. unsalted butter**
- **2 medium leeks (white and light green parts only), trimmed, halved lengthwise, cut crosswise into thin half-moon slices, rinsed thoroughly, and drained**
- **1 medium yellow onion, thinly sliced**
- **Kosher salt**
- **1½ lb. celery root (about 1 large)**
- **¾ cup crème fraîche**
- **¼ cup heavy cream; more as needed**
- **Freshly ground black pepper**
- **¼ cup thinly sliced fresh chives**

A sip of soup is a comforting surprise at a cocktail party. For the best flavor, make this soup a day in advance.

1. In a 4-quart or larger heavy-based pot, melt the butter over medium-low heat. Add the leeks, onion, and a generous pinch of salt and cook, stirring occasionally, until very soft and lightly golden but not brown, 15 to 20 minutes. Reduce the heat to low if you see signs of browning.

2. Meanwhile, peel the celery root with a sharp knife (expect to slice quite a bit off the exterior as you trim). Halve the peeled celery root lengthwise and cut each half into 1-inch-thick wedges. Cut each wedge crosswise into ¼-inch slices. You should have about 5 cups.

3. Add the celery root, 1 tsp. salt, and ½ cup water to the leeks. Cover and cook until the celery root is tender, 10 to 15 minutes. (Check occasionally; if all the water cooks off and the vegetables start to brown, add another ½ cup water.) Add 4½ cups water, bring to a simmer, and continue to cook another 20 minutes. Let cool slightly.

4. Purée the soup (with a hand blender or in small batches in a stand blender) to a very smooth, creamy consistency. Let cool completely and then store in the refrigerator at least overnight or for up to 2 days.

5. About an hour before serving, put the crème fraîche in a small bowl and stir in enough of the heavy cream so that the mixture reaches the consistency of yogurt. Leave the cream mixture at room temperature until you are ready to serve the soup. (If the cream is too cold, it will cool the soup.)

6. Reheat the soup. (If it's too thick, gradually thin it with as much as 1 cup water.) Taste and add more salt as needed. Ladle the soup into small espresso cups or shot glasses. Top each portion with a small spoonful of crème fraîche (it should float on top of the soup). Finish each cup with a pinch of black pepper and a sprinkle of chives.

PER SERVING: 70 CALORIES | 1g PROTEIN | 4g CARB | 5g TOTAL FAT | 3g SAT FAT | 1.5g MONO FAT | 0g POLY FAT | 15mg CHOL | 85mg SODIUM | 1g FIBER

sesame coins

YIELDS ABOUT 3 DOZEN
1½-INCH COINS

5¾ oz. (1¼ cups)
     all-purpose flour

  1 tsp. table salt

  ¼ tsp. coarsely ground
     black pepper

  ¼ lb. (½ cup) unsalted butter,
     cut into ½-inch pieces, chilled

  1 large egg yolk

  1 Tbs. Dijon mustard

  2 Tbs. sesame seeds, toasted

     Kosher salt for sprinkling
     (optional)

Make Ahead

Freeze unbaked logs,
well wrapped in plastic
wrap, for up to a month;
thaw on the counter for
an hour or overnight in
the fridge before slicing
and baking. Or wrap
baked, cooled coins
and stash them in the
freezer. Refresh them
in a 325°F oven for a few
minutes before serving.

Sesame seeds add a toasty flavor as well as some texture.

1. Combine the flour, salt, and pepper in a food processor. Process until just blended. Add the butter pieces and pulse until the dough resembles coarse crumbs. Stir the yolk and mustard with a fork and drizzle over the flour mixture. Pulse until the dough begins to form moist crumbs that are just beginning to clump together. Add the sesame seeds and pulse very briefly (just two or three quick pulses will do the trick; any more and the seeds will break down too much).

2. Pile the moist crumbs on an unfloured work surface. With the heel of your hand, push and gently smear the crumbs away from you until they start to come together in a cohesive dough. Using a pastry scraper or a metal spatula, lift up one edge of the dough and fold it into the center (the dough will still be rough, so don't expect a neat, smooth fold). Repeat with the opposite edge, like folding a letter. Turn the dough 45 degrees. Give the dough another smearing and shape it into a 12-inch log that's 1¼ inches in diameter. Wrap in plastic and refrigerate until firm, about 4 hours (or up to 2 days).

3. Heat the oven to 375°F. Line two large baking sheets with parchment. Using a thin, sharp knife, cut the log into ¼-inch slices. Arrange the slices about ½ inch apart on the prepared sheets. Bake until medium golden around the edges and on the bottom, 14 to 17 minutes, rotating the sheets as needed for even baking. If you like, sprinkle the crackers with a little kosher salt just as the baking sheets come out of the oven. Set the sheets on racks to cool. When the coins are completely cool, store them in an airtight container.

PER SERVING: 45 CALORIES | 1g PROTEIN | 4g CARB | 3g TOTAL FAT | 1.5g SAT FAT | 1g MONO FAT | 0.5g POLY FAT | 15mg CHOL | 75mg SODIUM | 0g FIBER

cheddar-cayenne coins

**YIELDS ABOUT 4 DOZEN
1½-INCH COINS**

- **6** oz. (1⅓ cups) all-purpose flour
- **3** oz. (about 1¼ cups) finely shredded sharp Cheddar (or half Cheddar and half Parmigiano-Reggiano)
- **1** tsp. table salt
- **⅛ to ¼** tsp. cayenne
- **¼** lb. (½ cup) unsalted butter, cut into ½-inch pieces, chilled
- **1** large egg yolk
- **2** Tbs. water
- **⅓** cup medium-finely chopped walnuts
- **Kosher salt for sprinkling (optional)**

These are fairly spicy, so use the smaller amount of cayenne if you want a milder kick. Pecans or pine nuts would work in place of the walnuts.

1. Combine the flour, cheese, salt, and cayenne in a food processor. Process until just blended. Add the butter pieces and pulse until the dough resembles coarse crumbs. Stir the yolk and water with a fork and drizzle over the flour mixture. Pulse until the dough begins to form small moist crumbs. Add the chopped nuts and pulse briefly until the crumbs begin to come together.

2. Pile the moist crumbs on an unfloured work surface. With the heel of your hand, push and gently smear the crumbs away from you until they start to come together in a cohesive dough. Using a pastry scraper or a metal spatula, lift up one edge of the dough and fold it into the center (the dough will still be rough, so don't expect a neat, smooth fold). Repeat with the opposite edge, like folding a letter. Turn the dough 45 degrees. Give the dough another smearing and shape it into a 14-inch log that's 1¼ inches in diameter. Wrap in plastic and refrigerate until firm, about 4 hours (or up to 2 days).

3. Heat the oven to 375°F. Line two large baking sheets with parchment. Using a thin, sharp knife, cut the log into scant ¼-inch slices. Arrange the slices about ½ inch apart on the prepared sheets. Bake until medium to deep golden around the edges, 15 to 20 minutes, rotating the sheets as needed for even baking. If you like, sprinkle the crackers with a little kosher salt just as the baking sheets come out of the oven. Set the sheets on racks to cool. When the coins are completely cool, store them in an airtight container.

PER SERVING: 45 CALORIES | 1g PROTEIN | 3g CARB | 3g TOTAL FAT | 1.5g SAT FAT | 1g MONO FAT | 0.5g POLY FAT | 10mg CHOL | 60mg SODIUM | 0g FIBER

shanghai scallion pancakes

YIELDS 8 PANCAKES

- 4 cups (18 oz.) all-purpose flour
- 1½ cups boiling water
- ¼ cup Asian sesame oil
- 2 tsp. kosher salt; more for sprinkling
- ¼ cup minced scallions
- ¼ cup minced fresh cilantro
- 6 Tbs. sesame seeds, toasted in a dry skillet until golden

  About 1¼ cups peanut or grapeseed oil

Make Ahead

You can roll them ahead, stack them separated by parchment, wrap them in plastic, and refrigerate for a day or two or freeze for a month.

Also called Shanghai onion bread, these are rich with the flavor of scallions, cilantro, and sesame. You can serve them whole or cut the pancakes into wedges to offer smaller bites.

1. Put the flour in a large bowl. Add the boiling water and stir until a shaggy dough forms. Gather the dough and scraps together, pressing and kneading to form a dough ball. Knead the dough in the bowl or on a work surface, floured if necessary, until soft but not very sticky, about 8 minutes. The dough should be light and not very resilient; when you stick your finger in, a slight indentation should remain. Cover the dough with a damp towel and let rest for 15 minutes. Knead for another 3 minutes.

2. Put the sesame oil in a small bowl. Shape the dough into an even cylinder. Cut the cylinder into eight equal pieces. Use a rolling pin to roll one piece into a 6-inch round. Brush the top with the sesame oil and then sprinkle on about ¼ tsp. salt, about ½ Tbs. each scallions and cilantro, and about 2 tsp. toasted sesame seeds. Roll up the pancake tightly, stretching to lengthen it slightly. Tie the ends of the cylinder around as if you were forming a knot (see the photo at right). Flatten the knotted ball on a lightly floured surface with your palm and then roll it out again into a 6-inch round. Repeat with the remaining pieces of dough.

3. In a large, heavy skillet, pour enough peanut oil to come to a depth of ¼ inch. Heat the oil to 380°F (a rice noodle will puff into a curlicue within 3 seconds or a cube of bread will turn golden in 15 seconds). Fry one or two pancakes at a time until both sides are golden and slightly crisp, 2½ to 3 minutes per side. Drain on paper towels and sprinkle immediately with kosher salt. Serve hot.

PER PANCAKE: 430 CALORIES | 8g PROTEIN | 50g CARB | 23g TOTAL FAT | 4g SAT FAT | 10g MONO FAT | 8g POLY FAT | 0mg CHOL | 490mg SODIUM | 3g FIBER

Toast the sesame seeds by heating them in a dry, nonstick skillet over medium heat. Shake the pan gently as the seeds toast and transfer them to a cool plate once they turn golden.

how to make scallion pancakes

A liberal brushing of Asian sesame oil gives these pancakes deep flavor.

Roll the pancake as tight as you can around the filling; this will help give the pancake its flaky layers.

Make a stubby knot with the rolled pancake, stopping before one end protrudes through the center hole.

Flatten the knot with your palm and then roll it out again into a 6-inch round. Now the herbs and sesame seeds are pressed between the layers.

Scallion pancakes cook to golden crispness in about 5 minutes.

seared tuna with tropical salsa

YIELDS ABOUT 48 PIECES

- **8** to 9 oz. fresh tuna fillet
- **1** Tbs. vegetable or olive oil

  Kosher salt and freshly ground black pepper

- **¾** cup finely diced fresh pineapple
- **4** scallions (white and light green parts only), thinly sliced
- **2½** Tbs. fresh lime juice
- **1½** Tbs. soy sauce
- **1** tsp. minced fresh ginger
- **1** small, ripe Hass avocado (about 6 oz.), flesh finely diced
- **½** cup coarsely chopped fresh cilantro leaves; plus small whole leaves, for garnish
- **1** 3½-oz. package plain rice crackers

These two-bite hors d'oeuvres look great passed on a tray. Assemble just before serving.

1. Cut the tuna into long, fat, squared-off strips or "logs" 1 to 1½ inches thick. Coat the tuna with the oil and season lightly with salt and pepper. Set a 10-inch, heavy-duty skillet over high heat. When the pan is very hot, after 2 to 3 minutes, sear the tuna logs for 20 to 30 seconds on each side—they should be seared outside and rare inside. Transfer to a clean cutting board and slice ¼ inch thick.

2. In a medium bowl, combine the pineapple, scallions, lime juice, soy sauce, and ginger. Add the avocado and gently stir to combine. Stir in the chopped cilantro.

3. To assemble, set the tuna slices on rice crackers; top each with a small spoonful of the salsa and a whole cilantro leaf. You may have extra crackers or salsa.

PER SERVING: 25 CALORIES | 1g PROTEIN | 3g CARB | 1g TOTAL FAT | 0g SAT FAT | 1g MONO FAT | 0g POLY FAT | <5mg CHOL | 150mg SODIUM | 0g FIBER

asian beef in crisp wonton cups

YIELDS 24; SERVES 6 TO 8

- 24 **square wonton wrappers**
- ½ **lb. beef tenderloin**
- **Kosher salt and freshly ground black pepper**
- ½ **cup finely diced red pepper (about half a medium pepper)**
- ¼ **cup scallions, finely sliced (both green and white parts)**
- 3 **Tbs. fresh lime juice (about 1 lime)**
- 2 **Tbs. fish sauce (nam pla)**
- 2 **Tbs. granulated sugar**
- 1 **tsp. minced garlic**
- 1 **tsp. chile paste with garlic (or chile garlic sauce)**

The wonton cups will keep, unfilled, in an airtight container for up to a week. Fill them right before serving or they'll get soggy. A few of the wonton cups may collapse during baking, so bake a few extras, just in case.

1. Position a rack in the middle of the oven and heat the oven to 375°F. Using mini (2-inch) muffin tins, press the wonton wrappers down into the tin, laying back the corners to make a defined cup. Bake until lightly browned, 8 to 10 minutes. Transfer to a rack and let cool.

2. Meanwhile, season the beef liberally with salt and pepper. Turn on the exhaust fan. Heat an ovenproof sauté pan over high heat until very hot. Add the beef and sear, rolling it onto all sides in the dry pan until it's lightly browned, 3 to 4 minutes total. Transfer the pan to the oven and cook until medium rare (130°F on an instant-read thermometer), 5 to 10 minutes depending on the thickness of the cut. Let the beef rest for 5 minutes and then cut it into julienne (long, thin strips).

3. Combine the beef, red pepper, and scallions in a medium bowl. In a small bowl, combine the lime juice, fish sauce, sugar, garlic, and chile paste and stir until the sugar dissolves. Toss with the beef mixture. Fill the cooled wonton cups with the filling, about 1 Tbs. per cup.

PER SERVING: 140 CALORIES | 9g PROTEIN | 19g CARB | 3g TOTAL FAT | 1g SAT FAT | 1g MONO FAT | 0g POLY FAT | 20mg CHOL | 640mg SODIUM | 1g FIBER

spiced shrimp and avocado toasts

YIELDS 16 CANAPÉS

16 large shrimp (about ½ lb.), peeled, deveined, rinsed, and patted dry

1 tsp. chili powder; more to taste

Kosher salt and freshly ground black pepper

2 Tbs. extra-virgin olive oil

2 small, ripe avocados (about 12 oz. total)

1 Tbs. fresh lime juice; more for sprinkling

3 Tbs. chopped fresh cilantro; plus 16 whole leaves for garnish

Toast Points (recipe p. 64)

If you can't find ripe avocados, buy underripe and put them in a bag with a banana to speed the process.

1. Season the shrimp with 1 tsp. of the chili powder, ¼ tsp. salt, and a few grinds of pepper. Set a heavy 10-inch skillet over medium-high heat for 1 minute. Add the oil and the shrimp and sauté, stirring occasionally, until the shrimp are opaque and firm to the touch, about 2 minutes. Transfer to a cutting board.

2. Pit the avocados and scoop the flesh into a small bowl. Add the lime juice, the chopped cilantro, and a pinch of chili powder. Mash with a fork until relatively smooth and season with a heaping ½ tsp. salt and a few grinds of pepper.

3. To assemble, slice the shrimp in half lengthwise. Spread the mashed avocado over the toasts and slice each toast into four even rectangles. Top each with two halved pieces of shrimp and a cilantro leaf, sprinkle with lime juice and salt, and serve. (The rectangles can be cut into squares for even smaller bites.)

PER SERVING: 100 CALORIES | 3g PROTEIN | 8g CARB | 6g TOTAL FAT | 1g SAT FAT | 4g MONO FAT | 0.5g POLY FAT | 15mg CHOL | 160mg SODIUM | 2g FIBER

party-perfect portabella pizzas

Portabellas, amount as directed below and on facing page

Topping, choose from recipes below and on facing page

Little bites of portabella "pizzas" make fun party fare. The topping recipes here are scaled for two or four large portabella caps, which can then be cut into wedges.

1. To prepare the mushrooms for their toppings, stem them and wipe the caps clean with a moist paper towel. Scrape out the gills with a teaspoon.

2. Rub the caps generously with olive oil on both sides, season with salt and pepper, and either sauté, grill, or broil them until tender, about 5 minutes per side.

white bean & rosemary topping

YIELDS ENOUGH FOR 4 PORTABELLAS

- 1½ **Tbs. olive oil**
- 1 **small sprig fresh rosemary**
- 1 **clove garlic, finely chopped**
- 1 **15-oz. can small white beans, rinsed and drained**
- ¾ **cup diced tomatoes**
- **Kosher salt and freshly ground black pepper**
- 4 **portabellas, prepared as directed above**
- ½ **cup grated Fontina**

Heat the oil in a medium skillet over medium-high heat. Add the rosemary and garlic, and cook, stirring, until fragrant. Add the beans and cook for 5 minutes. Toss in the tomatoes, cook for a minute or so, and season with salt and pepper. Discard the rosemary and portion the mixture evenly onto the four portabella caps. Sprinkle each cap with some grated Fontina and broil briefly to melt the cheese.

PER SERVING: 230 CALORIES | 11g PROTEIN | 24g CARB | 11g TOTAL FAT | 2.5g SAT FAT | 7g MONO FAT | 1.5g POLY FAT | 5mg CHOL | 50mg SODIUM | 6g FIBER

pancetta, onion & sage topping

YIELDS ENOUGH FOR 2 PORTABELLAS

- 1½ **Tbs. olive oil**
- ¼ **lb. finely chopped pancetta**
- 1 **small onion, chopped**
- 1 **Tbs. chopped fresh sage**
- ¼ **cup freshly grated Parmigiano-Reggiano**
- **Freshly ground black pepper**
- 2 **portabellas, prepared as directed above**

Heat the oil in a medium skillet over medium-high heat. Add the pancetta and fry until lightly golden. Add the onion and cook, stirring, until the onion is soft, lowering the heat as needed so the onion doesn't burn. Turn off the heat, add the sage and cheese, and season amply with pepper. Divide between the portabella caps and broil briefly to melt the cheese.

PER SERVING: 420 CALORIES | 16g PROTEIN | 10g CARB | 36g TOTAL FAT | 10g SAT FAT | 20g MONO FAT | 4g POLY FAT | 50mg CHOL | 1,250mg SODIUM | 2g FIBER

sausage & olive topping

YIELDS ENOUGH FOR
2 PORTABELLAS

- ½ Tbs. olive oil

- ⅓ lb. sweet sausage, casing removed

- Pinch of crushed red pepper flakes

- 6 sun-dried tomatoes, chopped

- 8 pitted Kalamata olives, coarsely chopped

- 5 Tbs. heavy cream

- 2 portabellas, prepared as directed on previous page

- ¼ cup grated Parmigiano-Reggiano

- 2 Tbs. chopped fresh flat-leaf parsley

Heat the oil in a medium ovenproof skillet. Crumble the sausage into the pan and cook until cooked through, about 10 minutes. Drain off any excess fat. Stir in the red pepper, tomatoes, and olives. Add 3 Tbs. of the heavy cream and cook, stirring, until the cream is almost gone. Fill the caps and put them back in the skillet. Sprinkle with the cheese. Pour 2 Tbs. cream into the skillet and broil briefly to melt the cheese. Sprinkle with the chopped parsley and serve.

PER SERVING: 390 CALORIES | 18g PROTEIN | 12g CARB | 32g TOTAL FAT | 12g SAT FAT | 16g MONO FAT | 2.5g POLY FAT | 65mg CHOL | 770mg SODIUM | 2g FIBER

roasted potato slices with romesco sauce

1 medium plum tomato (about ¼ lb.), cored and quartered

16 whole almonds, toasted

1 Tbs. coarsely chopped jarred roasted red pepper

2 small cloves garlic

⅛ tsp. cayenne

Kosher salt and freshly ground black pepper

1 Tbs. red-wine vinegar

4 Tbs. extra-virgin olive oil

¾ lb. small red potatoes (1 to 2 inches in diameter), rinsed and dried

Finely grated zest of 2 medium lemons, for garnish

¼ cup fresh flat-leaf parsley leaves, for garnish

The romesco sauce can be made up to three days ahead and refrigerated. Before using, bring it to room temperature and stir well.

1. Position a rack in the top third of the oven; heat the oven to 450°F. Put the tomato, almonds, roasted red pepper, garlic, cayenne, ¼ tsp. salt, and a few grinds of pepper in a food processor. Process, scraping the bowl as needed, until the mixture is somewhat smooth, about 1 minute. Add the vinegar and 1 Tbs. of the olive oil and process until well incorporated. Taste and add more salt if needed.

2. Trim the ends off of each potato and cut the potatoes crosswise into ⅛- to ¼-inch slices. In a bowl, toss the potatoes with the remaining 3 Tbs. olive oil and 1 tsp. salt to coat well. Lay the slices in a single layer on a baking sheet. Roast the potatoes, turning the slices with a spatula and rotating the baking sheet halfway through roasting, until golden brown, 20 to 30 minutes. Let cool slightly.

3. To serve, arrange the potato slices on a serving platter; blot with a paper towel if they look oily. Top each slice with a generous ¼ tsp. of the romesco sauce (you may not use all the sauce). Garnish each with a tiny pinch of lemon zest and a parsley leaf.

PER SERVING: 20 CALORIES | 0g PROTEIN | 1g CARB | 1.5g TOTAL FAT | 0g SAT FAT | 1g MONO FAT | 0g POLY FAT | 0mg CHOL | 65mg SODIUM | 0g FIBER

crunchy chicken drumettes

YIELDS 24 DRUMETTES;
SERVES 8

24 very cold chicken
    drumettes or whole wings

¼ cup soy sauce

2 Tbs. dry sherry

1 Tbs. minced garlic

1 Tbs. minced fresh ginger
   (unpeeled)

1 Tbs. minced scallion

1 Tbs. minced fresh cilantro

½ tsp. freshly ground black
   pepper

   About 2½ qt. canola or
   other vegetable oil

1 large egg

1½ cups cornstarch or water
    chestnut powder

   Hot honey mustard (or
   Dijon mustard flavored
   with honey), for dipping

By pulling the meat down to one end, these wings look more like tiny legs or even popsicles. If you can find water chestnut powder, which is available at Asian markets, use it in place of the cornstarch for extra-crunchy results.

1. Prepare the drumettes: If using whole wings, cut off and discard the wingtips and the middle part of the wing, saving the first section; this is the drumette. Cut around the tip of the smaller end of the drumette to release the skin and meat. With your fingers, pull the meat down toward the larger end, cutting through any tendons with a knife if necessary. The meat should end up in a sack at the end of the bone, with the skin inside and the flesh outside.

2. Make the marinade: In a large bowl, mix the soy sauce, sherry, garlic, ginger, scallion, cilantro, and pepper. Add the drumettes, tossing to coat. Cover and refrigerate for at least 6 hours or overnight.

3. Fry the chicken: Line a plate with paper towels. In a deep, heavy pot, pour in enough oil to come about 2½ inches up the sides and heat until it reaches 380°F (a rice noodle will puff into a curlicue within 3 seconds; a cube of bread will turn golden in 15 seconds). While the oil is heating, drain the marinade from the chicken and discard it. Beat the egg, pour it over the chicken, and toss to coat. Put the cornstarch or water chestnut powder in a deep dish or pie plate. Holding the chicken by the bone, dip the meaty part in the powder so it's well coated. Lightly shake off the excess and place it in the hot oil. Repeat with as many drumettes as will fit without crowding.

4. Cook the drumettes until they're golden, turning so they brown evenly, about 4 minutes. Remove with a slotted spoon or skimmer and set on the lined plate. Repeat the dipping and frying with another batch of drumettes, adjusting the heat to keep the oil temperature constant. Serve hot with the mustard for dipping.

PER SERVING: 200 CALORIES | 10g PROTEIN | 7g CARB | 14g TOTAL FAT | 3g SAT FAT | 7g MONO FAT | 4g POLY FAT | 45mg CHOL | 210 mg SODIUM | 1g FIBER

grilled lamb rib chops
with rosemary and sage crust

SERVES 4

½ cup loosely packed medium-finely chopped fresh flat-leaf parsley

3 Tbs. loosely packed medium-finely chopped fresh rosemary

1½ Tbs. loosely packed medium-finely chopped fresh sage

1 tsp. kosher salt

½ tsp. freshly ground black pepper

12 bone-in lamb rib chops, ½ inch thick

Olive oil for the grill grate

With their natural handles (think popsicles), frenched lamb rib chops make a perfect hors d'oeuvre and can be flavored in myriad ways (see the sidebar below). Grilling suits these chops, but they can also be seared or broiled.

1. Thoroughly mix the parsley, rosemary, sage, salt, and pepper in a shallow baking dish or pie pan. Lightly press the ribs into the herb mixture on both sides. (You can grill the chops right away or cover them tightly with plastic wrap and refrigerate for up to 4 hours.)

2. When you're ready to cook, prepare a charcoal grill or heat a gas grill to medium hot. Oil the grill grate. Use tongs to carefully set the chops on the grill. Cook until the herbs are deep brown but not charred and the meat is medium rare, 3 to 5 minutes per side. If there are flare-ups, move the chops to another part of the grill. To test for doneness, bend or cut into the chops next to the bone and check for medium-rare meat. Transfer to a warm platter and let rest in a warm place for 5 minutes before serving.

PER SERVING: 420 CALORIES | 22g PROTEIN | 1g CARB | 36g TOTAL FAT | 14g SAT FAT | 16g MONO FAT | 3g POLY FAT | 100mg CHOL | 560mg SODIUM | 1g FIBER

"lamb-sicle" flavors

Lamb rib chops make an impressive appetizer, whether broiled, seared, or grilled. Before cooking, coat them with any of the following for a flavor boost:

- Equal amounts kosher salt and brown sugar, with half as much pinemtón (smoked paprika)
- Black olives puréed with olive oil
- A couple of mashed garlic cloves, herbes de Provence, olive oil, salt, and pepper
- Curry powder, kosher salt, grated ginger, orange juice, and fresh mint

mini potato latkes

YIELDS ABOUT 32 LATKES

- **4** medium to large russet or Yukon Gold potatoes (2 lb. total), peeled
- **2** large yellow onions (¾ lb. total)
- **4** large eggs, lightly beaten
- **⅓** cup matzo meal
- **2** tsp. kosher salt; more to taste
- **10** to 15 grinds black pepper; more to taste
- About ¾ cup peanut oil
- Applesauce, sour cream, and chopped chives for serving (optional)

Serve these topped with a little applesauce (recipe below) or a dollop of sour cream and some minced chives. Or go luxe and serve them with smoked salmon or even caviar on top.

1. Using the medium shredding blade of a food processor, grate the potatoes, laying them horizontally in the feed tube to maximize the strand length. Grate the onions (halve or quarter them first if necessary) on top of the potatoes. The onions will turn to mush, and their juices will help keep the potatoes from turning brown. Pick out any ungrated pieces of potato or onion.

2. Lay a clean dishtowel inside a large bowl and transfer the grated mixture into the towel. Roll the towel lengthwise and wring out as much liquid as possible (you can do this over the bowl, discarding the liquid, or right over the sink). Depending on the size of the towel (and your muscles), you may have to do this in batches. Transfer the grated mixture to a bowl. Add the eggs, matzo meal, salt, and pepper; mix well.

3. To form the latkes, scoop up about 2 Tbs. of the mixture with your hands and loosely pat it into a pancake about ½ inch thick, leaving a few straggly strands along the edge. (As you work, liquid will accumulate in the bowl, so lightly squeeze out the excess. The last couple of latkes may need a really firm squeeze.) If you like, you can shape all of the mixture ahead of frying; place the cakes on a baking sheet.

4. When ready to fry, heat a large cast-iron or nonstick skillet with about ⅛ inch of oil and heat over medium high. The oil is hot enough when a piece of potato sizzles when added.

5. In batches, slip the latkes into the hot oil and flatten gently with the back of a spatula. Fry until deep golden brown, about 3 minutes on each side, to be sure the center is fully cooked. If the edges darken very quickly, lower the heat. To prevent excess oil absorption, flip each latke only once. Add oil between batches as needed, making sure the oil heats up again before frying more latkes. Drain the latkes on paper towels or a clean brown paper bag. Serve immediately with applesauce, sour cream, and chopped chives, if you like.

6. Latkes are best served right away, but you can keep them warm in a 250°F oven. Arrange the latkes on a rack set over a baking sheet (to ensure that air circulates around their entire surface, keeping them crisp).

PER SERVING: 65 CALORIES | 2G PROTEIN | 7g CARB | 4g TOTAL FAT | 1g SAT FAT | 2g MONO FAT | 1g POLY FAT | 27mg CHOL | 150mg SODIUM | 0.5g FIBER

applesauce

YIELDS 2¼ CUPS

- **5** or 6 cooking apples, such as McIntosh, peeled, cored, and cut into ½-inch pieces
- **2** Tbs. water
- **¼** tsp. ground cinnamon
- **1** tsp. pure vanilla extract
- **2** Tbs. granulated sugar (optional)
- Juice of ½ lemon

If you like, present the latkes plain with bowls of sour cream and applesauce nearby and let folks garnish the pancakes themselves.

Put all the ingredients in a medium saucepan, cover, and set over low heat. Simmer until the apples are soft, 20 to 25 minutes. Mash with a fork until the mixture is a chunky purée. (Or pass through a food mill for a smoother texture.) Let cool.

mediterranean chicken salad with fennel, raisins, and pine nuts

YIELDS ABOUT 1⅔ CUPS

- ½ small clove garlic, mashed to a paste with a pinch of kosher salt
- 3 Tbs. mayonnaise
- 1 Tbs. olive oil
- 1 Tbs. fresh lemon juice; more to taste
  - Pinch cayenne
- 1 cup chopped or shredded leftover chicken
- ⅓ cup small diced fresh fennel
- 3 Tbs. chopped sweet onion, such as Vidalia
- 2 Tbs. toasted pine nuts
- 2 Tbs. golden raisins
- 2 Tbs. chopped fresh flat-leaf parsley
  - Kosher salt and freshly ground black pepper
  - Toast Points (recipe below), Crostini (recipe facing page), or Pita Chips (recipe p. 87), for serving

The sophisticated ingredients here bring everyday chicken salad to a new level.

In a small bowl, mix the garlic paste, mayonnaise, olive oil, lemon juice, and cayenne. In a medium bowl, combine the chicken, fennel, onion, pine nuts, raisins, and parsley. Stir in the dressing, season to taste with salt and pepper, and refrigerate for at least 1 hour to let the flavors meld. Before serving, taste and add salt, pepper, or lemon juice as needed.

PER ¼ CUP: 170 CALORIES | 8g PROTEIN | 4g CARB | 14g TOTAL FAT | 3g SAT FAT | 5g MONO FAT | 4.5g POLY FAT | 30mg CHOL | 290mg SODIUM | 1g FIBER

toast points

YIELDS 16 TOAST POINTS

- 4 slices (about 4½ x 3½ inches) country white bread (such as Pepperidge Farm)
- 1 Tbs. unsalted butter, melted
  - Kosher salt and freshly ground black pepper

If you plan to serve the toast points already topped, it's easier to spread the topping on the whole piece of bread and then cut it into squares or triangles.

Adjust a rack to 6 inches from the broiler and turn the broiler on to high. Set the bread on a baking sheet, brush one side with the melted butter, and season with salt and pepper. Toast the bread until it's golden brown and crisp on top, 1 to 2 minutes. Flip and cook the other side until golden, about 1 minute. While the bread is still hot, slice off the edges. Let cool slightly and cut into squares or triangles.

PER SERVING: 30 CALORIES | 1g PROTEIN | 5g CARB | 1g TOTAL FAT | 0g SAT FAT | 0g MONO FAT | 0g POLY FAT | 0mg CHOL | 85mg SODIUM | 1g FIBER

crostini

YIELDS 16 CROSTINI

16 baguette slices, between ¼ and ½ inch thick (from about ½ baguette)

2 cloves garlic, cut in half

2 to 3 Tbs. extra-virgin olive oil

Kosher salt

Crostini will keep for a few days in an airtight container.

Adjust a rack to 6 inches from the broiler and turn the broiler on to high. Rub one side of each bread slice with the garlic and set on a baking sheet lined with aluminum foil. Brush the garlic side with the oil and season with salt. Broil until the bread is browned, 1 to 2 minutes. Flip and broil the other side for 1 minute more.

PER SERVING: 30 CALORIES | 1g PROTEIN | 5g CARB | 1g TOTAL FAT | 0g SAT FAT | 0g MONO FAT | 0g POLY FAT | 0mg CHOL | 90mg SODIUM | 1g FIBER

tri-color polenta cups

YIELDS EIGHTY 1-INCH HORS D'OEUVRES

3 cups yellow cornmeal

1 Tbs. kosher salt

1 tsp. freshly ground black pepper

2 oz. grated Parmigiano-Reggiano (about ½ cup)

6 Tbs. unsalted butter

2 bunches fresh basil, blanched, squeezed dry, and finely chopped

1 small roasted red pepper, peeled and puréed (about ¼ cup)

1 cup chopped roasted green chiles

1 cup shredded Monterey Jack

7 oz. goat cheese, crumbled

80 fresh cilantro leaves, for garnish

You can make these with just one flavor of polenta; simply adjust the flavorings accordingly.

1. Bring 8 cups water to a boil in a large saucepan. Stir in the cornmeal, lower the heat to medium, and cook, stirring constantly, until very thick and smooth, about 40 minutes. Season with the salt and pepper. Portion the warm polenta evenly into three bowls. In one, stir in the Parmigiano and 2 Tbs. butter; in the second, the basil and 2 Tbs. butter; in the third, the red pepper and 2 Tbs. butter.

2. Line a jellyroll pan (11 x 17 inches) with plastic wrap. Spread a flavored polenta in an even layer, smoothing with damp fingers if necessary. Let set a few minutes; repeat with the other two layers. Cover with plastic and let the whole thing set up in the refrigerator for at least 3 hours or up to 2 days.

3. With a 1-inch cookie cutter, stamp out about 80 rounds. Scoop out the center with a mini melon baller or spoon and fill each cup with a pinch of the chiles, Monterey Jack, and goat cheese. Cover and refrigerate until ready to serve. Heat in a 300°F oven until warm and cheese is melted, about 10 minutes. Top with a cilantro leaf. Serve immediately.

PER SERVING: 35 CALORIES | 1g PROTEIN | 2g CARB | 2.5g TOTAL FAT | 1.5 SAT FAT | 0.5g MONO FAT | 0g POLY FAT | 5mg CHOL | 125mg SODIUM | 0g FIBER

pan-fried scallops with malt vinegar dipping sauce

SERVES ABOUT 6

- 1 large egg
- ½ cup (2 oz.) plain dry breadcrumbs
- 1¼ lb. "dry" sea scallops (muscle tabs removed if necessary)
- ¼ cup malt vinegar
- 2 tsp. Old Bay® seasoning
- 2 cups neutral oil, such as canola, vegetable, or peanut oil

Crisp outside, tender inside, these taste like tiny bites of the fish in fish-and-chips, especially after a dunk in the malt vinegar sauce.

1. Beat the egg in a shallow dish; put the breadcrumbs in another shallow dish. Working with one scallop at a time, dip it in the beaten egg and then dredge it in the breadcrumbs; set each breaded scallop on a plate or tray as you finish it.

2. In a small bowl, mix the vinegar and Old Bay seasoning.

3. Pour the oil into a 10-inch, straight-sided sauté pan (cast-iron or nonstick works well) over medium-high heat. Heat until the oil begins to shimmer and ripple and it bubbles instantly when the edge of a scallop is dipped into it. Fry the scallops in two batches, turning once with tongs, until golden brown on both sides, about 2 minutes per side. Adjust the heat as necessary to keep the oil hot but not smoking.

4. Transfer the scallops to paper towels to drain. Serve immediately with the sauce.

PER SERVING: 210 CALORIES | 18g PROTEIN | 10g CARB | 11g TOTAL FAT | 1g SAT FAT | 5g MONO FAT | 5g POLY FAT | 65mg CHOL | 450mg SODIUM | 0g FIBER

spiced mediterranean meatballs

- 4 to 6 Tbs. olive oil
- 1 small yellow onion, finely diced
- 1½ tsp. kosher salt; more to taste
- 1 tsp. chili powder
- 1 tsp. ground cumin
- ½ tsp. light brown sugar
- ½ tsp. freshly ground black pepper; more to taste
- ¼ tsp. ground cinnamon
- ¼ tsp. chipotle powder
- ½ lb. ground lamb
- ½ lb. ground beef (preferably 85% lean)
- 2 large eggs, beaten
- ½ cup finely chopped fresh cilantro
- ¼ cup toasted pine nuts, finely chopped
- 2 Tbs. finely chopped currants or raisins
- ⅓ cup plain, dry breadcrumbs; up to 2 Tbs. more if needed (4C® brand works well)
- ¾ cup tomato purée (such as Pomi® brand strained tomatoes)
- ½ cup homemade or low-salt chicken broth
- 1 Tbs. sherry vinegar

This ingredient list looks long, but much of it entails only as much work as opening a spice jar. Serve the meatballs spiked with toothpicks and pass as a jazzy nibble.

1. Heat 2 Tbs. of the olive oil in a 12-inch skillet over medium heat. Add the onion, sprinkle with ½ tsp. of the salt, and cook, stirring, until the onion softens and begins to brown around the edges, 4 to 6 minutes. Add the chili powder, cumin, brown sugar, pepper, cinnamon, and chipotle powder and cook, stirring, for 1 minute. Stir in 1 Tbs. water and scrape the bottom of the pan to pick up the spices. With a heatproof spatula, scrape the mixture into a large bowl and let it cool to room temperature.

2. Add the ground lamb, ground beef, eggs, ¼ cup of the cilantro, the pine nuts, currants, and the remaining 1 tsp. salt to the onion mixture. Gently mix with your hands until the ingredients are well distributed. Mix in the ⅓ cup breadcrumbs to bind the mixture and make it feel less wet, adding more breadcrumbs if needed.

3. With wet hands (to make shaping the balls easier), gently roll the meat into 1-inch meatballs; you should have about 24 small meatballs.

4. Wipe out the skillet and set it over medium heat. Add 2 Tbs. of the oil, and once it's shimmering hot, add about half of the meatballs or as many as will fit without touching. Let them cook undisturbed until they start to brown, about 2 minutes. Continue cooking, moving every minute or so, until they're evenly browned all over, about another 4 minutes; they won't be cooked through but will finish cooking in the sauce. Transfer to a large plate and sprinkle gently with salt. Repeat with the remaining meatballs, adding more oil if needed.

5. Wipe the oil from the skillet and return the skillet to medium heat. Add the tomato purée, chicken broth, and vinegar. Cook, stirring, until the mixture reduces to a thick, saucy consistency, about 3 minutes. Season to taste with salt and pepper. Add the meatballs and the remaining ¼ cup cilantro. Reduce the heat to a gentle simmer, and cook, stirring, until the meatballs are cooked through and hot, about 3 minutes. Keep hot until ready to serve.

PER SERVING: 80 CALORIES | 5g PROTEIN | 3g CARB | 6g TOTAL FAT | 1.5g SAT FAT | 3g MONO FAT | 1g POLY FAT | 30mg CHOL | 130mg SODIUM | 0g FIBER

anchoïade with figs and walnuts

YIELDS ABOUT ¾ CUP

- **3** oz. dried figs (about 8), stems removed, and flesh coarsely chopped
- **1** oz. (¼ cup) shelled walnut halves
- **8** to 10 oil-packed anchovy fillets
- **3** cloves garlic

  Kosher salt
- **¼** cup extra-virgin olive oil
- **2** tsp. Cognac

  Freshly ground black pepper

  Shavings of Parmigiano-Reggiano or aged Manchego, made with a vegetable peeler

  Basic Bruschetta (recipe p. 72) or crostini (recipe p.65), for serving

The sweetness from the figs counters the saltiness of the anchovies in this delicious spread.

1. Put the figs, walnuts, anchovies, garlic, and ¼ tsp. salt in a food processor. Process until finely chopped. Add the olive oil, Cognac, and a few twists of pepper and process again to make a somewhat coarse paste.

2. Taste and adjust the seasonings, if necessary. Spread the anchoïade on bruschetta or crostini and top with a few of the cheese shavings.

PER 1 TBS: 60 CALORIES | 2g PROTEIN | 6g CARB | 3.5g TOTAL FAT | 0.5g SAT FAT | 1.5g MONO FAT | 1.5g POLY FAT | 5mg CHOL | 250mg SODIUM | 1g FIBER

zucchini fritters (kolokithakia keftedes)

**YIELDS 14 TO 18 FRITTERS;
SERVES 8**

- 1 lb. zucchini (about 3 medium)
- 1 cup finely chopped yellow onion
- 2¼ oz. (½ cup) all-purpose flour
- ¼ cup finely chopped fennel stalks and leaves (save the bulb for another recipe)
- 1 Tbs. chopped fresh dill
- 1 tsp. baking powder
- ½ tsp. chopped fresh oregano
- ⅛ tsp. freshly grated nutmeg
- Kosher or sea salt and freshly ground black pepper
- 1 to 1½ cups olive oil for frying
- ¼ cup grated kefalotyri cheese or Parmigiano-Reggiano
- ¼ cup crumbled feta cheese

The fritters can be made and shaped several hours ahead; fry them close to serving. Keep warm in a 200°F oven until ready to serve.

1. Trim the zucchini and coarsely grate them on a box grater. Put the grated zucchini in a colander and squeeze out as much liquid as possible with your hands.

2. In a medium bowl, combine the zucchini, onion, flour, fennel, dill, baking powder, oregano, nutmeg, ½ tsp. salt, and ⅛ tsp. pepper and mix well. The mixture should be just moist enough to form into patties. For each fritter, press 2 generous Tbs. of the mixture into a patty about 3 inches in diameter and ¼ inch thick. Arrange them in a single layer on a cookie sheet.

3. Pour the oil into a 12-inch skillet to a depth of ¼ inch. Heat the oil over medium-high heat until it begins to ripple and bubbles immediately when the edge of one patty is dipped into it. Using 2 slotted metal spatulas (one to lift a patty and the other to push it off the spatula), add as many patties as will fit in the pan without crowding and fry, flipping once, until golden brown and crisp on both sides, 1 to 3 minutes per side. Transfer the fritters to a paper towel–lined plate and repeat with another batch, adding more oil as needed.

4. Arrange the fritters on a platter and sprinkle with both cheeses. Serve warm.

PER SERVING: 80 CALORIES | 3g PROTEIN | 11g CARB | 3.5g TOTAL FAT | 1g SAT FAT | 2g MONO FAT | 0g POLY FAT | 5mg CHOL | 190mg SODIUM | 1g FIBER

pan-fried crisp fennel (finocchi dorati)

SERVES 6 TO 8

- **1 large fennel bulb, trimmed (¾ to 1 lb. after trimming)**
- **2 Tbs. plus ¼ tsp. kosher salt; more as needed**
- **2 large eggs**
- **Freshly ground black pepper**
- **½ cup fine, dry homemade breadcrumbs**
- **2 Tbs. freshly grated pecorino or Parmigiano-Reggiano**
- **2 to 2¼ cups extra-virgin olive oil for frying; more as needed**

These crisp wedges pair nicely with white wine. You can boil and coat the fennel up to 4 hours before frying.

1. Cut the fennel bulb in half lengthwise and then cut each half lengthwise into wedges that are ½ inch wide on the outside. You should get 12 to 16 wedges.

2. Bring about 2½ quarts of water to a boil in a 4-quart saucepan over high heat. Add 2 Tbs. of the salt and the fennel. Boil briskly until the fennel is tender, 5 to 8 minutes. Check for doneness by removing a wedge to taste it. Drain well and set aside to cool.

3. In a shallow bowl, beat the eggs with the remaining ¼ tsp. salt and several grinds of pepper.

4. In another shallow bowl, mix the breadcrumbs with the cheese.

5. Working with one or two wedges at a time, dip in the beaten egg, making sure the exterior is well coated. Lift out with a fork, letting the excess egg drain off. Then dredge in the breadcrumbs, patting the breadcrumbs in place so they adhere (you want to coat them well). Keep the wedges compact; don't let them splay open. Set the wedges on a tray and continue until all are coated.

6. Put ½ inch of oil in a 10-inch straight-sided sauté pan, attach a candy thermometer to the side of the pan, and heat over medium-high heat. When the oil reaches 375°F, add as many wedges as will fit comfortably in a single layer. Don't crowd the pan. Cook until well browned on both sides, turning once with tongs. Total frying time should be about 1 minute. Transfer the wedges to a plate lined with paper towels and sprinkle lightly with salt. Continue frying, adding more oil to the pan as needed, until all the wedges are fried. Serve hot.

PER SERVING: 100 CALORIES I 3g PROTEIN I 8g CARB I 6g TOTAL FAT I 1g SAT FAT I 3.5g MONO FAT I 0.5g POLY FAT I 55mg CHOL I 250mg SODIUM I 2g FIBER

> **If you don't have a thermometer or your thermometer won't reach far enough into the oil to read accurately, you can test the oil temperature by adding a few breadcrumbs. If they sizzle immediately and float to the top, the oil is ready.**

basic bruschetta

SERVES 8 TO 10

Extra-virgin olive oil as needed, about ½ cup

1   **1-lb. loaf rustic country bread or crusty baguette, cut into ½ inch thick slices (cut baguettes on the diagonal)**

1   **to 2 cloves garlic, peeled and halved (optional)**

Toppings (optional; see the ideas below)

At its most basic, bruschetta is slices of rustic bread, drizzled with oil, toasted over a fire, and rubbed with garlic. Toppings only make it better. (Crostini, by the way, is similar to bruschetta, though the slices of the "little toasts" are smaller and thinner.)

1. Coat one or two rimmed baking sheets with olive oil and set the bread slices on top in a single layer. Brush the tops with a little more oil and set aside until you're ready to grill.

2. Prepare a charcoal grill or heat a gas grill to medium high.

3. Grill the bread until one side has dark grill marks or is a deep golden brown all over, and then turn to toast the other side. As soon as the slices are done, rub with the cut side of the garlic, if using, and drizzle with more oil or add a topping of your choice (see the sidebar at left for ideas). Cut into serving-size pieces and serve right away.

PER SERVING: 200 CALORIES | 4g PROTEIN | 23g CARB | 12g TOTAL FAT | 2g SAT FAT | 8g MONO FAT | 1g POLY FAT | 0mg CHOL | 230mg SODIUM | 2g FIBER

topping ideas

- Chopped fresh tomatoes tossed with minced garlic, basil, and olive oil
- Cooked white beans mashed with a little roasted garlic, topped with a bit of sautéed broccoli raab
- Sautéed wild mushrooms, a drizzle of truffle oil, and shaved Parmigiano
- Ricotta topped with fresh fig, prosciutto, fresh mint, and a drizzle of honey

chinese-style spareribs

SERVES 12; YIELDS ½ CUP RUB

FOR THE CHINESE SPICE RUB

- 2 Tbs. ground coriander
- 2 Tbs. hot chili powder
- 2 Tbs. dark brown sugar
- 1 Tbs. five-spice powder
- 1 Tbs. ground fennel seeds
- 1 Tbs. kosher salt
- 1 tsp. crushed red pepper flakes

FOR THE RIBS

- 2 full (13-rib) racks of St. Louis-cut pork spareribs (about 3 lb. each)

  Kosher salt for sprinkling

  Asian Dipping Sauce (recipe below), for serving

For a festive presentation, stack the ribs, drizzle them with dipping sauce, and garnish with sliced scallions.

1. Make the rub: In a small bowl, stir all the ingredients. (The rub can be made days ahead and stored in an airtight container.)

2. Roast the ribs: Position a rack in the center of the oven and heat the oven to 300°F. Sprinkle and press ¼ cup of the rub on both sides of each rib rack. Put the racks, meaty side up, on a broiling pan or a wire roasting rack set over a baking sheet. Lightly season the ribs with salt and put them in the oven. After the first hour, rotate the pan every 30 minutes. (Note: If you use two baking sheets, switch their position in the oven, too.) The ribs will sizzle gently as they cook, and they'll become tender after about 2 hours in the oven.

3. To test for doneness, pick up the center of the ribs with tongs; the ends of the ribs should flop downward (this means the fat and cartilage have broken down), and a skewer inserted between the ribs should meet little resistance. If the meat between the ribs is still tough, keep cooking, checking every 15 minutes and rotating the pan.

4. Remove the rib racks from the oven, put them on a cutting board meaty side down (so they're easier to slice), and slice them into individual ribs. Arrange the ribs on a platter and serve with the sauce on the side.

PER RIB: 210 CALORIES | 15g PROTEIN | 3g CARB | 15g TOTAL FAT | 5g SAT FAT | 7g MONO FAT | 1g POLY FAT | 60mg CHOL | 430mg SODIUM | 0g FIBER

asian dipping sauce

YIELDS ABOUT ⅔ CUP

- ¼ cup soy sauce
- 2 Tbs. granulated sugar
- 2 Tbs. rice vinegar
- 1 Tbs. minced fresh ginger
- 1 tsp. Asian sesame oil

In a medium saucepan over medium heat, bring the soy sauce, sugar, rice vinegar, ginger, and sesame oil to a simmer, stirring occasionally. Remove from the heat and let cool to room temperature. The sauce will keep for about a week in the refrigerator.

california sushi rolls and seared tuna rolls

YIELDS 5 CALIFORNIA ROLLS
(30 PIECES) AND 5 SEARED
TUNA ROLLS (30 PIECES),
WITH A LITTLE LEFTOVER RICE

FOR THE RICE AND WASABI

- 4 **cups raw Japanese sushi rice**
- ½ **cup unseasoned rice vinegar**
- 5 **Tbs. granulated sugar**
- 1 **tsp. kosher salt**
- 6 **Tbs. wasabi powder (yields enough prepared wasabi for assembling and serving 10 rolls)**

FOR THE CALIFORNIA ROLLS

- 3 **sheets toasted nori (dried seaweed)**

  Sesame seeds or flying fish roe, for garnish (optional)

- 1 **medium cucumber, peeled, seeded, and cut into fine julienne**
- 1 **large, ripe avocado, cut into slender wedges**
- 6 **oz. cooked crabmeat or diced cooked shrimp, picked over for shells**

FOR THE TUNA ROLLS

- 3 **sheets toasted nori (dried seaweed)**
- 1 **recipe Seared Tuna (facing page)**
- 14 **oz. package Japanese radish sprouts (Kaiware), or other sprouts, shredded Daikon radish, or julienned cucumber**
- 6 **scallions (green tops only), thinly sliced**

Here are two popular sushi rolls that don't require raw fish.

MAKE THE RICE AND WASABI

1. Measure the rice into a large saucepan and rinse it well until the water runs clear. Drain and measure 4¼ cups water into the pan. Let the rice soak for 20 minutes. Bring the water to a boil, cover, and simmer for 20 minutes. Remove the pan from the heat and let the rice steam, covered, for another 20 minutes.

2. Moisten a shallow wooden bowl and put the cooked rice in it. Mix the vinegar, sugar, and salt in a bowl, stirring to dissolve the sugar. Sprinkle the mixture over the rice and gently stir with a wooden spoon until the rice glistens. Spread the rice over the bottom of the bowl and cool for 20 minutes. Flip the rice over with the wooden spoon and let cool for another 20 minutes.

3. In a small bowl, mix the wasabi powder with cold water (about ¼ cup plus 2 tsp.) to make a paste.

MAKE THE CALIFORNIA ROLLS

1. Stack the sheets of toasted nori and cut in half. Wrap a bamboo mat in plastic wrap (to keep the rice from sticking) and lay a sheet of nori on it.

2. Moisten your hands with a little water to keep the rice from sticking. (Keep a bowl of water handy). Grab a large handful of rice and toss and squeeze it lightly to form a loose oval ball. Starting in an upper corner, spread the rice across the nori until it's about ¼ inch thick. Sprinkle the rice with sesame seeds or flying fish roe and pat evenly.

3. Holding the top corners of the nori, flip it over so the rice is face down. Using your fingers, spread a pinch of wasabi across the middle of the nori. Lay equal amounts (about a small handful) of each filling ingredient down the middle of the nori: start with a row of cucumber, overlap with the avocado slices, and then lay the crab on top.

4. With all eight fingers holding in the ingredients, lift the edge of the mat closest to you with your thumbs. Tucking the ingredients into the middle of the roll, bring the edge of the mat over the ingredients and straight down. Leave ½ inch of the nori exposed at the top edge. Press the roll together with your thumbs and middle fingers, while pressing down on the roll with your index fingers. Lifting just the edge of the mat, pull it forward so that the nori roll rolls another quarter turn. The seam will now be on the bottom. Press again with fingers and thumbs, molding the roll into a squared log.

5. Lift the mat away and transfer the roll to a cutting surface. Dip a sharp knife into a bowl of water and cut the roll in half and then bring one half around and cut both into thirds. Stand the pieces up on a cut side. Serve with the remaining prepared wasabi, the pickled ginger, and soy sauce for dipping.

FOR THE SEARED TUNA

½   lb. fresh tuna fillet

¼   tsp. shichimi (Japanese
     7-spice powder) or a pinch
     of cayenne

⅓   cup soy sauce

FOR SERVING

1   10-oz. jar pickled ginger

     Good-quality soy sauce for
     dipping

MAKE THE SEARED TUNA ROLLS

Follow the recipe on the facing page for making the rice and wasabi. Season the tuna with the shichimi or cayenne and marinate it in the soy sauce for 5 minutes. Sear or grill the tuna in a medium-hot skillet spritzed with nonstick cooking spray for 1½ minutes on each side. Cut into horizontal strips, against the grain. After spreading the rice on the nori, don't flip it over. Instead, arrange a pinch of wasabi, the strips of tuna, radish sprouts, and scallions down the middle. Roll and slice in the same way as on facing page.

CALIFORNIA SUSHI ROLLS PER SERVING: 70 CALORIES | 2g PROTEIN | 13g CARB | 1g TOTAL FAT | 0g SAT FAT | 0.5g MONO FAT | 0g POLY FAT | 5mg CHOL | 60mg SODIUM | 1g FIBER

SEARED TUNA ROLLS PER SERVING: 60 CALORIES | 3g PROTEIN | 12g CARB | 0.5g TOTAL FAT | 0g SAT FAT | 0g MONO FAT | 0g POLY FAT | 5mg CHOL | 115mg SODIUM | 1g FIBER

continued on p. 76 ➤

continued from p. 75

how to make california rolls

Lay the stacked nori on top of a plastic-wrapped bamboo mat.

With damp hands, spread rice across the nori.

Flip the nori so the rice is face down.

Spread the filling ingredients in place on the nori.

Keeping the filling in the middle of the roll, roll the nori into a log.

With the mat removed, cut the log into pieces.

tostones (fried green plantains)

SERVES 6

Vegetable oil for frying

2 **large green plantains (1½ lb. total), peeled and cut into 2-inch-thick slices**

Kosher salt

Tostones, a kind of fried green banana, are a staple food all over the Caribbean. They're great on their own, simply salted and eaten hot as an appetizer.

1. In a heavy, deep-sided skillet (preferably cast iron), heat about 1 inch of oil over medium heat to 350°F.

2. Fry the plantain slices in the oil on one side for 3 to 4 minutes, just until they begin to color very lightly; don't crowd the pan. Turn and cook the other side. Use a slotted spatula or spoon to transfer the plantains to paper towels to drain.

3. When the plantain slices have cooled slightly, lay a piece of brown paper bag or paper towel on top of each slice and, using your fist or the palm of your hand, flatten the slice to about ½ inch. Do this while the plantains are hot; they'll be too hard when they cool.

4. Increase the oil temperature to 375°F and return the plantains to the pan. Fry for 2 to 3 minutes or until golden, turning once. They're done when they rise to the top and make a little pop. Drain on paper towels, sprinkle with salt, and serve hot, or they'll harden.

PER SERVING: 160 CALORIES | 1g PROTEIN | 24g CARB | 8g TOTAL FAT | 1g SAT FAT | 5g MONO FAT | 2g POLY FAT | 0mg CHOL | 180mg SODIUM | 2g FIBER

How to Peel a Green Plantain

Ripe, black plantains can be peeled like a banana, but green ones have very firm, clingy flesh, and there's a trick to peeling them. (The slightly sticky substance under the skin can irritate sensitive skin, so wear gloves if you like.) Start by trimming the ends. To make rounds, as for tostones, cut the plantain in half crosswise. With a sharp paring knife, score the skin along one or more of its ridges, being careful not to cut into the flesh, and then peel off the skin in sections.

artichoke bottoms with shrimp, lemon butter, and herbed breadcrumbs

FOR THE BREADCRUMBS

- 3 Tbs. extra-virgin olive oil
- 3 Tbs. chopped fresh flat-leaf parsley
- 1 Tbs. chopped fresh thyme
- 1 clove garlic, minced
- 1½ cups coarse day-old breadcrumbs

FOR THE ARTICHOKES AND SHRIMP

- Kosher salt
- 6 large artichokes, trimmed down to bottoms
- ¾ lb. medium (51 to 60 per lb.) shrimp, peeled and deveined
- 1½ Tbs. extra-virgin olive oil
- ⅛ tsp. cayenne
- Freshly ground black pepper
- 6 Tbs. unsalted butter
- 3 Tbs. chopped fresh flat-leaf parsley
- 2 Tbs. fresh lemon juice

These stuffed artichoke bottoms are impressive appetizers but also make an elegant main course for two.

MAKE THE BREADCRUMBS

Heat the oil in a 10-inch skillet over medium heat. Add the parsley, thyme, and garlic. Cook, stirring, until fragrant, about 1 minute. Add the breadcrumbs and increase the heat to medium high. Cook, stirring, until the breadcrumbs are golden brown and crisp, about 5 minutes. Immediately transfer to a bowl lined with paper towels. (The crumbs may be made up to 1 day ahead; cool and store in an airtight container at room temperature.)

PREPARE THE ARTICHOKES AND SHRIMP

1. Position a rack in the center of the oven and heat the oven to 400°F.

2. In a 3- to 4-quart saucepan, bring 4 cups of water to a boil over high heat. Add 2 Tbs. salt, drop the artichokes in, and cook until tender, about 10 minutes. Remove from the water with a slotted spoon. Spread out on a clean cloth to cool and dry.

3. Heat a 10- to 11-inch cast-iron skillet over high heat. In a large bowl, toss the shrimp with 1 Tbs. of the olive oil, the cayenne, a pinch of salt, and a few grinds of pepper. Working in two batches, sear the shrimp in the hot pan, turning once, until lightly browned on the edges and opaque throughout, 1 to 2 minutes per side. Transfer each batch of shrimp to a medium bowl.

4. In a small saucepan, gently melt the butter over low heat. When the butter is just starting to foam, add 2 Tbs. of the chopped parsley. Let the parsley sizzle in the butter for 1 or 2 minutes and then whisk in the lemon juice. Add the butter mixture to the bowl with the shrimp and toss.

5. Oil an 8x10-inch baking dish with the remaining ½ Tbs. oil and arrange the artichoke bottoms stem side down in the dish. Season with salt and pepper. Pile 5 to 6 shrimp in the center of each artichoke bottom, including some but not all of the butter. Top with the breadcrumbs and drizzle the remaining butter and the shrimp juices over the top. Sprinkle with the remaining 1 Tbs. parsley and bake until heated through, about 10 minutes. Serve immediately.

PER SERVING: 340 CALORIES | 15g PROTEIN | 24g CARB | 23g TOTAL FAT | 9g SAT FAT | 11g MONO FAT | 2g POLY FAT | 115mg CHOL | 560mg SODIUM | 9g FIBER

artichokes: a guide

Though artichokes are grown in the United States year-round, they peak from March to May (with another small peak in October). Here's what you'll find in your market.

Green Globe artichokes are the most common variety available in the U.S. Round in winter and spring and more conical in summer and fall, they're buttery and meaty, and great for steaming and eating whole or for stuffing. You can also pare them down to hearts and bottoms. Globes are usually too tough to eat raw.

Baby artichokes come from the same plants as the globe artichoke, though they are much smaller. They grow on smaller stems and receive fewer nutrients than their large counterparts (think of them as the runts of the litter). Tighter than globes, they have tenderer leaves and an undeveloped and edible choke that doesn't need to be removed. This makes them ideal for shaving and eating raw.

fresh corn fritters

YIELDS ABOUT 26 BITE-SIZE FRITTERS

4½ oz. (1 cup) all-purpose flour

¼ cup stone-ground yellow cornmeal

2 tsp. baking powder

1 tsp. sugar

½ tsp. table salt; more for sprinkling

½ cup whole milk

¼ cup sour cream

2 large eggs

1 cup fresh corn kernels (from about 1 large or 2 small ears of corn), coarsely chopped

1 1½ cups vegetable oil

1 recipe Charred Tomato Salsa (recipe below)

Instead of an appetizer, try these as a side with grilled chicken or fish or for breakfast with maple syrup.

1. In a medium bowl, stir the flour, cornmeal, baking powder, sugar, and salt. In a small bowl, whisk the milk, sour cream, and eggs. With a rubber spatula, gently stir the egg mixture into the flour mixture until just blended. Stir in the corn. Let sit for 10 to 15 minutes. Meanwhile, position a rack in the center of the oven and heat the oven to 200°F.

2. Pour the oil into a small, heavy frying pan, preferably cast iron, to a depth of ½ inch. Heat over medium heat until it's hot enough that a small dollop of batter sizzles when added. With a spring-lever miniature ice cream scoop or a tablespoon, scoop up a ball of the batter and gently release it into the hot oil. Add three or four more balls of batter to the hot oil, taking care not to crowd the pan. Reduce the heat to medium low so that the fritters cook gently. When golden brown on the bottom and barely cooked around the top edge, after 1 to 2 minutes, use a slotted spatula to turn the fritters and cook until golden on the bottom, 1 to 2 minutes longer.

3. Transfer the fritters to a wire rack set over a baking sheet, sprinkle generously with salt, and keep warm in the oven. Continue to cook the remaining batter in small batches, adding more oil as needed to maintain the ½-inch depth. Serve right away with the salsa.

PER FRITTER: 70 CALORIES | 2g PROTEIN | 7g CARB | 4g TOTAL FAT | 1g SAT FAT | 1.5g MONO FAT | 1g POLY FAT | 20mg CHOL | 120mg SODIUM | 1g FIBER

charred tomato salsa

YIELDS ABOUT ¾ CUP

1 lb. fresh ripe tomatoes (about 3 medium)

1 unpeeled medium clove garlic

½ medium chipotle from a can of chipotle chiles in adobo sauce

Kosher salt

1 Tbs. extra-virgin olive oil

2 Tbs. finely chopped fresh cilantro

1½ tsp. fresh lime juice

This salsa is great on grilled steak or chicken tacos, too. It'll keep in the fridge for up to 1 week.

1. Position an oven rack about 4 inches below the broiler and heat the broiler on high. Arrange the tomatoes and garlic on a rimmed baking sheet and broil until the tomatoes are charred on one side, about 5 minutes. Turn the tomatoes and garlic and char on the second side, about 2 minutes longer. Let cool. Peel the tomatoes and garlic, discarding the skins and saving any juices that are released.

2. In a blender, briefly purée the tomatoes and their juices, the garlic, chipotle chile, and ½ tsp. salt—it needn't be perfectly smooth.

3. In a medium, heavy-based saucepan, heat the oil over medium-high heat. When a drop of the puréed tomato mixture sizzles when added, pour in the remaining purée. Bring to a boil, stirring frequently. Adjust the heat to an active simmer and continue to cook, stirring frequently, until reduced to a scant cup and thickened to a sauce consistency, 8 to 12 minutes. Cool to room temperature. Stir in the cilantro and the lime juice. Season to taste with salt. Serve at room temperature.

corn: a buyer's guide

There are four types of sweet corn: standard sweet, sugar-enhanced, supersweet, and synergistic. You won't see these agricultural terms used at grocery stores or even at farmer's markets, but they help to explain the differences among them in terms of sweetness, tenderness, and how well they store. If you really want to know what type of corn you're buying, ask the farmer. Just be prepared to try something new each time. The corn variety you saw on your last visit is probably not the same one you're going to find on your next. In general, the more sugary varieties of corn take longer to grow and appear later at the market.

STANDARD SWEET Common varieties include Butter and Sugar, with white and yellow kernels, and Silver Queen, with white kernels. This type of corn has a traditional corn flavor and texture, although sweetness varies among varieties. Its sugars are quicker to convert to starch, so it doesn't keep long after harvest.

SUGAR-ENHANCED Delectable, Kandy Korn, and Seneca Dancer are three popular varieties. Known for having a more tender texture than the standard sweet type, sugar-enhanced corn is widely popular. Its degree of sweetness changes with the variety, but the conversion of sugar to starch is slower than that of standard sweet corn, so it holds up better.

SUPERSWEET Varieties include Sun & Stars and Xtra-Sweet. The most sugary of all, this type of corn has less true corn flavor and a firmer, almost crunchy texture, because the skin on the kernels is tougher. It holds its sweetness longer than any other type of corn, which is why you'll often see it in supermarkets, where the corn isn't typically freshly picked.

SYNERGISTIC A popular variety is Serendipity. This type has both the tenderness of sugar-enhanced corn and the more pronounced sweetness of supersweet. It requires more time to mature than sugar-enhanced corn and can be watery if harvested too soon.

spread & scooped

lemony hummus with cumin

YIELDS ABOUT 3 CUPS

⅓ cup plus 1 Tbs. extra-virgin olive oil

4 large cloves garlic, thinly sliced

2 tsp. ground cumin

2 15½-oz. cans chickpeas, drained and rinsed

3 Tbs. tahini

3 Tbs. fresh lemon juice; more to taste

1 Tbs. soy sauce

Kosher salt

Homemade hummus tastes much better than the overpriced stuff sold in the supermarkets. To avoid the most common pitfall— way too much raw garlic—cook the garlic in the olive oil first so it mellows. Soy sauce gives this version a savory edge.

1. In a small saucepan, combine ⅓ cup of the oil with the garlic and cumin. Set over medium-low heat and cook until the garlic softens, about 3 minutes from when you can hear the garlic bubbling quickly. Don't let the garlic brown. Take the pan off the heat and let cool completely.

2. Put the chickpeas, tahini, lemon juice, soy sauce, and ½ tsp. salt in a food processor. Use a fork to fish the softened garlic out of the oil and transfer it to the processor (reserve the oil). Turn the machine on, let it run for about 20 seconds, and then start slowly pouring the garlic-cumin oil through the machine's feed tube. Be sure to scrape the pan with a rubber spatula to get all of the cumin and oil. Pour ¼ cup cool water down the tube. Stop the machine, scrape the sides of the bowl, and continue processing until the hummus is creamy and almost smooth. Season to taste with more salt and lemon juice, if you like.

3. For best results, let the hummus sit at room temperature for an hour or two before serving so the flavors can meld. Or better yet, make it a day ahead, refrigerate it, return it to room temperature, and adjust the seasonings before serving. To serve, spread the hummus in a shallow dish and drizzle with the remaining 1 Tbs. oil. It will keep for about a week in the refrigerator.

PER ¼ CUP: 180 CALORIES | 4g PROTEIN | 18g CARB | 10g TOTAL FAT | 1g SAT FAT | 6g MONO FAT | 2g POLY FAT | 0mg CHOL | 270mg SODIUM | 3g FIBER

tomatillo and avocado salsa

YIELDS ABOUT 1 CUP

- **1 medium tomatillo, husked, washed, and coarsely chopped**
- **1 Tbs. thinly sliced scallion**
- **½ tsp. chopped garlic**
- **½ tsp. seeded and minced serrano chile; more to taste**
- **1 large, ripe avocado, pitted, peeled, and coarsely chopped**
- **Kosher salt and freshly ground black pepper**

This salsa can be refrigerated in an airtight container for up to 2 days. It's also tasty on pork tacos or with quesadillas.

In a food processor, combine the tomatillo, scallion, garlic, and chile and process until finely chopped, about 15 seconds. Add the avocado and pulse until just combined. The salsa should be chunky. Season with salt, pepper, and more chile to taste.

PER 1 TBS.: 20 CALORIES | 0g PROTEIN | 1g CARB | 2g TOTAL FAT | 0g SAT FAT | 1g MONO FAT | 0g POLY FAT | 0mg CHOL | 35mg SODIUM | 1g FIBER

What Are Tomatillos?

Tomatillos are a perfect match for chile peppers, onions, and cilantro—all key ingredients in salsa verde, a popular Mexican sauce for grilled meats and fish. Tomatillos are also good with avocados, corn, lime, and scallions.

How to buy and store them

Look for firm fruits without blemishes and with their papery husks firmly attached. When fresh, tomatillos are a vibrant green color. Don't buy ones that have turned a yellowish green, as they're past their prime. Store tomatillos in their husks in a paper bag and refrigerate for up to a week.

How to cook with them

To prep tomatillos, peel the husk and rinse off the sticky residue it leaves behind. You don't need to remove the seeds. If eaten raw, tomatillos can be a little acidic and sharp-tasting (sometimes a good thing). When cooked, their flavor tends to mellow, letting their sweeter side shine. Toss raw chopped tomatillos in salads, or roast or grill them whole and add them to salsas and dips. You can also cut them into wedges before stirring into stews and braises, or sauté them in small chunks and add them to omelets or scrambled eggs.

sweet and sour eggplant relish (caponata)

YIELDS ABOUT 4 CUPS

1 medium eggplant (about 1½ lb.) unpeeled, top and bottom trimmed

Kosher salt

½ cup extra-virgin olive oil; more as needed

3 large inner ribs celery, sliced crosswise ½ inch thick

½ yellow bell pepper, cut into ½-inch dice

½ red bell pepper, cut into ½-inch dice

1 small yellow onion, chopped

1 14-oz. can diced tomatoes (with their juices)

2 Tbs. red-wine vinegar

4 tsp. granulated sugar

2 anchovy fillets, minced (optional)

¼ cup green olives, pitted and slivered

3 Tbs. drained and rinsed capers (coarsely chopped if large)

Serve at room temperature with pita chips (recipe on facing page) or other crisps.

1. Cut the eggplant into 1-inch cubes. Spread the cubes on a baking sheet lined with paper towels, sprinkle with 1 Tbs. salt, and let sit for 1 hour. Pat dry with more paper towels.

2. Heat the oil in a large saucepan over medium-high heat until hot. Working in batches, fry the eggplant, stirring occasionally, until deep golden brown on several sides, 5 to 6 minutes per batch. Adjust the heat as needed to keep the oil hot but not smoking. Transfer each batch with a slotted spoon to dry paper towels to drain.

3. Reduce the heat to medium and if the pan is dry, add 1 Tbs. oil. Add the celery, sprinkle with salt, and cook, stirring frequently, until softened with just a hint of crunch, about 5 minutes. Transfer the celery to a bowl. If the pan is dry, add 1 Tbs. oil. Add the peppers, sprinkle with salt, and cook, stirring frequently, until softened, 5 to 6 minutes. Transfer to the bowl with the celery.

4. If the pan is dry, add another 1 Tbs. oil. Add the onion, sprinkle with salt, and cook, stirring frequently, until softened and starting to brown around the edges, 3 to 5 minutes. Increase the heat to medium high and pour in the tomatoes and their juices. Add the vinegar, sugar, and anchovies, if using. Bring to a vigorous simmer and cook until the juices have thickened slightly to the consistency of tomato soup, 3 to 5 minutes. Add all the cooked vegetables as well as the olives and capers. Reduce the heat to medium and simmer for another 5 minutes. Let cool completely and then cover and refrigerate overnight. Before serving, bring to room temperature and add salt to taste.

PER 1 TBS.: 23 CALORIES | 0g PROTEIN | 1g CARB | 2g TOTAL FAT | 0g SAT FAT | 1g MONO FAT | 0g POLY FAT | 0mg CHOL | 150mg SODIUM | 0g FIBER

golden onion and thyme dip

YIELDS ABOUT 2¼ CUPS

- **2 Tbs. extra-virgin olive oil**
- **1 large Spanish or 2 large yellow onions (about 1 lb. total), finely diced**
- **Kosher salt**
- **8 oz. cream cheese**
- **6 Tbs. sour cream**
- **1 scant Tbs. fresh thyme leaves, chopped**
- **Pinch of cayenne**
- **Freshly ground black pepper**
- **Pita Chips (recipe below)**

Forget that packet of dried soup mix: This is the real deal, with sautéed onions and a hit of cayenne. It's delicious served with pita chips or sweet bell pepper sticks.

Heat the oil in a large skillet over medium-high heat. Add the onion, season with ½ tsp. salt, and sauté, stirring often, until the onion softens completely and starts to brown, about 9 minutes. Transfer to a food processor and add the cream cheese, sour cream, thyme, and cayenne. Pulse until the mixture is well combined. Season with salt and pepper to taste. Refrigerate until ready to serve. Serve with pita chips.

PER SERVING: 75 CALORIES | 1g PROTEIN | 2g CARB | 7g TOTAL FAT | 4g SAT FAT | 2g MONO FAT | 0.3g POLY FAT | 17mg CHOL | 331mg SODIUM | 0.3g FIBER

pita chips

YIELDS 32 CHIPS

- **2 pita breads (preferably plain and 8 inches wide)**
- **3 Tbs. extra-virgin olive oil**
- **Kosher salt and freshly ground black pepper**

Go beyond chips and crackers with these simple toasted pita chips, which are sturdy enough to stand up to even chunky dips and salsas.

Heat the oven to 450°F. Slice each pita into 8 even triangular pieces and then tear each piece apart at the seam to get a total of 32 pieces. Toss the pieces in a large bowl with the oil, ¼ tsp. salt, and some pepper. Spread in a single layer on a large baking sheet. Bake, flipping after 5 minutes, until the chips are crisped and slightly browned, about 7 minutes total.

PER CHIP: 20 CALORIES | 0g PROTEIN | 2g CARB | 1g TOTAL FAT | 0g SAT FAT | 0.5g MONO FAT | 0.5g POLY FAT | 0mg CHOL | 40mg SODIUM | 0g FIBER

spinach and artichoke dip

spinach and artichoke dip

SERVES 8

- **1** **10-oz. package frozen leaf spinach, thawed, squeezed dry, and chopped**
- **1** **16-oz. can artichoke hearts, drained, thinly sliced, and patted dry**
- **1** **cup freshly grated Parmigiano-Reggiano**
- **¾** **cup mayonnaise**
- **¾** **cup sour cream**
- **Kosher salt and freshly ground black pepper**

This warm and cheesy classic tastes great with toasted pita chips (recipe p. 87).

1. Position a rack in the center of the oven and heat the oven to 425°F.

2. In a large bowl, mix the spinach, artichokes, ¾ cup of the Parmigiano, the mayonnaise, sour cream, ½ tsp. salt, and ¾ tsp. pepper. Transfer to a 1-quart (or slightly smaller) baking dish and sprinkle with the remaining ¼ cup Parmigiano. (You can refrigerate the dip at this point for up to a day; let sit at room temperature while the oven heats.)

3. Bake until the top of the dip browns and the inside warms through, about 25 minutes. Let cool slightly and serve.

PER SERVING: 230 CALORIES | 4g PROTEIN | 5g CARB | 22g TOTAL FAT | 6g SAT FAT | 5g MONO FAT | 9g POLY FAT | 20mg CHOL | 280mg SODIUM | 1g FIBER

greek feta and olive oil dip

YIELDS ABOUT ¾ CUP

- **½** **lb. feta, roughly crumbled**
- **¼** **cup milk**
- **¼** **cup extra-virgin olive oil**
- **Minced fresh jalapeño to taste**
- **2** **to 3 Tbs. cream cheese (optional)**

Instead of the expected cheese dip, go Greek with chtipiti (pronounced shti-pity). It can be served as a dip for crudités (cucumbers are especially good) or spread on bread and topped with roasted red peppers.

In a blender, mix the feta with the milk until grainy. With the blender running, slowly pour in the oil and blend to a thick glossy cream. Stir in the jalapeño. To mellow the tang of the dip or to get a creamier texture, mix in the cream cheese.

PER SERVING: 200 CALORIES | 6g PROTEIN | 2g CARB | 19g TOTAL FAT | 8g SAT FAT | 9g MONO FAT | 1.5g POLY FAT | 40mg CHOL | 440mg SODIUM | 0g FIBER

creamy white bean and herb dip

SERVES 6 TO 8

- 2 15½-oz. cans cannellini beans, rinsed and drained
- 4 oz. cream cheese (½ cup)
- ⅓ cup chopped yellow onion
- 2 Tbs. fresh lemon juice
- 1 anchovy fillet, rinsed and patted dry (optional)
   Kosher salt and freshly ground black pepper
- 2 Tbs. extra-virgin olive oil
- 3 Tbs. thinly sliced fresh chives
- 1 Tbs. chopped fresh marjoram or oregano
   Crudités, crusty sourdough bread, or crackers, for serving

This new take on bean dip is equally good served cold or at room temperature.

1. In a food processor, combine the beans, cream cheese, onion, lemon juice, anchovy (if using), 1 tsp. salt, and ½ tsp. pepper and process until smooth. With the motor running, drizzle in the oil. Transfer the spread to a large bowl and fold in 2 Tbs. of the chives and the marjoram. Season to taste with salt and pepper.

2. Transfer the spread to a serving bowl, garnish with the remaining 1 Tbs. chives, and serve with crudités, bread, or crackers.

PER SERVING: 170 CALORIES | 5g PROTEIN | 16g CARB | 9g TOTAL FAT | 3.5g SAT FAT | 4g MONO FAT | 1g POLY FAT | 15mg CHOL | 300mg SODIUM | 4g FIBER

shrimp with spicy asian peanut dipping sauce

SERVES 6 TO 8

- 2 medium limes
- ½ cup creamy peanut butter (preferably natural)
- 2 tsp. Asian garlic chile paste (like Huy Fong Foods'® Tuong Ot Toi Viet Nam®); more to taste
- 3 Tbs. chopped fresh mint; more for sprinkling
- 1 lb. poached, grilled, or steamed shrimp (16 to 20 per lb.), peeled, with tails left on

The mint is a cool complement to the chile and peanut butter.

Grate ½ tsp. zest from one of the limes and then juice both limes. In a food processor, blend the lime zest and ¼ cup lime juice with the peanut butter, chile paste, and ¼ cup cold water. Add more lime juice and chile paste to taste, plus another 1 or 2 Tbs. water as needed to loosen the mixture to a thin dipping sauce consistency. Transfer the sauce to a medium bowl and stir in the mint. (You can make the sauce up to 1 hour ahead.) Sprinkle the sauce with additional mint and serve with the shrimp.

PER SERVING: 160 CALORIES | 15g PROTEIN | 5g CARB | 9g TOTAL FAT | 1g SAT FAT | 0g MONO FAT | 0g POLY FAT | 110mg CHOL | 135mg SODIUM | 1g FIBER

creamy pine nut and tahini sauce (tarator sauce)

YIELDS 1½ CUPS

1 cup pine nuts

2 small cloves garlic, minced

6 Tbs. tahini, well stirred

¼ cup fresh lemon juice; more to taste

1 Tbs. olive oil; more to taste

Kosher salt and freshly ground black pepper

Cayenne (optional)

Chopped fresh flat-leaf parsley or cilantro, for garnish

This all-purpose Middle Eastern sauce works well as a spread for toasted pita bread and vegetables.

Purée the pine nuts and garlic in a food processor until they form a paste. Add the tahini and the lemon juice and purée again. With the machine running, mix in cold water 1 Tbs. at a time until the sauce is thinned to the consistency of sour cream (you'll need ⅓ to ½ cup water). Add 1 Tbs. olive oil (or more) for a slightly more spreadable consistency. Season with salt and pepper and another 1 to 2 Tbs. lemon juice if you like. If you'd like some heat, add cayenne to taste. This sauce thickens as it sits; add cold water as needed to thin it. Garnish with parsley or cilantro and serve at room temperature.

PER 1 TBS.: 60 CALORIES | 2g PROTEIN | 2g CARB | 6g TOTAL FAT | 1g SAT FAT | 2g MONO FAT | 2g POLY FAT | 0mg CHOL | 50mg SODIUM | 1mg FIBER

What Is Tahini?

Have you ever wondered what gives Middle Eastern dips like baba ghanouj (eggplant dip) and hummus (chickpea dip) their wonderfully rich and creamy qualities? The answer is tahini, a paste made of ground sesame seeds. It has a rich, nutty taste that helps to amplify the flavors of other foods. Full of B vitamins, calcium, phosphorus, and iron, it's also good for you.

Where to buy it

Imported and domestic tahini is sold in cans and jars at natural-foods stores and some supermarkets (look in the international or natural-foods section or next to the peanut butter). A good domestic brand to look for is Joyva®, made in Brooklyn, New York.

How to store it

Tahini keeps almost indefinitely when stored in a cool, dark cupboard. It doesn't require refrigeration, although you can keep it in the fridge if you like (just let it return to room temperature before using). Because it contains no emulsifiers, the sesame oil tends to separate from the solids over time, but it will remix on its own if you turn the can or jar upside down about 30 minutes before you plan to use it.

How to use it

Use a little tahini to thicken a vinaigrette that's flavored with Asian sesame oil. Or combine some tahini with vinegar, soy sauce, and chile paste (or hot sauce) for a great dipping sauce.

warm herbed goat cheese

YIELDS ABOUT 1 CUP

½ lb. fresh goat cheese, softened at room temperature

2½ tsp. finely chopped fresh thyme leaves; plus 1 or 2 sprigs, for garnish

2 Tbs. extra-virgin olive oil; more for drizzling

Freshly cracked black pepper

Grilled bread or Basic Bruschetta (recipe p. 72), for serving

Serve this topping family-style in a little gratin dish, and let guests spread the warm cheese on the grilled bread themselves.

1. Heat the oven to 350°F. In a small bowl, stir the goat cheese, chopped thyme, and oil until blended. Spread the cheese mixture in an ovenproof ceramic crock or small gratin dish. Drizzle with a bit more olive oil and top with a few grinds of pepper. Lay the thyme sprigs on top.

2. Bake until the cheese is warm and creamy, about 10 minutes. Serve in the crock, surrounded with grilled bread.

PER 1 TBS: 70 CALORIES | 3g PROTEIN | 0g CARB | 6g TOTAL FAT | 3g SAT FAT | 2g MONO FAT | 0g POLY FAT | 10mg CHOL | 75mg SODIUM | 0g FIBER

fresh tuna pâté scented with rosemary

SERVES 8

6 large sprigs fresh rosemary

2 tsp. olive oil

½ lb. very fresh tuna

6 oz. (¾ cup) unsalted butter, at room temperature

2 Tbs. fresh lemon juice

Kosher salt and freshly ground black pepper

This supple, buttery spread comes together quickly and looks great packed into a pretty little bowl or ramekin and surrounded by toasts and crackers. Be very careful not to overcook the tuna, as it will make a dry pâté.

1. Arrange the rosemary in an even layer in a nonstick skillet, add the oil, and heat over medium until the herbs are fragrant. Place the tuna on the rosemary branches and cook until the cooked white of the flesh has traveled about one-third of the way up the side of the tuna steak, about 5 minutes. Turn the tuna over and cook until cooked but still quite pink inside, another 5 minutes. (The tuna will continue to cook as it cools.) Remove the tuna from the pan and allow it to cool. Pull off any clinging herbs.

2. In a food processor, combine the cooled tuna, the butter, and lemon juice. Season with a couple of pinches of salt and a few grinds of pepper and then process until smooth. Put the spread into a ramekin or small bowl, lightly cover the top with plastic wrap, and refrigerate until set. Grind more pepper over the top before serving with crackers or toasts.

PER SERVING: 190 CALORIES | 6g PROTEIN | 0g CARB | 19g TOTAL FAT | 11g SAT FAT | 6g MONO FAT | 1g POLY FAT | 60mg CHOL | 85mg SODIUM | 0g FIBER

bagna cauda

1 small head fresh garlic (about 2 oz.)

1 600g-can salt-packed anchovies, well rinsed and filleted (see sidebar below) or a similar amount of oil-packed anchovy fillets

1½ cups extra-virgin olive oil

Boldly flavored with garlic and anchovies, warm bagna cauda provides a delicious contrast to an assortment of crisp, seasonal vegetables, such as sliced fennel bulb, broccoli, or cauliflower. This recipe is easily halved.

1. Peel the garlic, cut the cloves in half lengthwise, and slice each one as thin as possible.

2. In a heavy-based saucepan, combine the garlic slices, anchovies, and olive oil and cook over low heat, stirring often, until the anchovies have fallen apart and the garlic has softened in texture and pungency, 12 to 15 minutes. Serve warm. (Bagna cauda will keep, refrigerated, for up to 5 days; reheat it gently before serving.)

PER 1 TBS.: 110 CALORIES | 4g PROTEIN | 0g CARB | 10g TOTAL FAT | 2g SAT FAT | 7g MONO FAT | 1g POLY FAT | 15mg CHOL | 550mg SODIUM | 0g FIBER

how to fillet salt-packed anchovies

Salt-packed anchovies have the truest flavor of all cured anchovies and make the best bagna cauda; but they need a little more preparation than do jarred or canned oil-packed anchovies.

As soon as you open a can of salt-packed anchovies, remove all the fish and rinse them with cold water to dislodge the salt. Then, working under a slow running faucet over a colander, turn the rinsed anchovy belly side up and run your finger from the head end through the tail; this separates the fillets and exposes the backbone. Lift the backbone and lateral pin bones away from the fillet and discard them.

Soak the fillets in cold water for about 20 minutes and then lay them on an absorbent towel to dry.

If you're not using the entire can of anchovies, put the leftover fillets in a jar, cover with an inch of olive oil, cover the jar, and store in a cool, dry place.

white bean and artichoke dip

YIELDS ABOUT 2 CUPS

1   15½-oz. can cannellini beans, drained and rinsed

1   14½-oz. can artichoke hearts, drained and rinsed

1   small clove garlic, chopped

2   Tbs. fresh lemon juice

2   Tbs. olive oil; more for drizzling

3   Tbs. freshly grated Parmigiano-Reggiano

1   tsp. chopped fresh rosemary

Kosher salt and freshly ground black pepper

Cayenne

This dip couldn't be easier to make; all the ingredients come together in a food processor.

In a food processor, blend the beans, artichoke hearts, garlic, and lemon juice to a smooth paste. With the machine running, add the oil. If needed, add 1 to 2 Tbs. water to get a smooth consistency. Blend in the cheese and rosemary; season with salt and pepper. Transfer to a medium bowl, sprinkle with 2 generous pinches cayenne, and drizzle with oil.

PER SERVING WITH PITA CHIPS: 230 CALORIES | 7g PROTEIN | 30g CARB | 10g TOTAL FAT | 2g SAT FAT | 6g MONO FAT | 1g POLY FAT | 0mg CHOL | 480mg SODIUM | 6g FIBER

crudités with creamy buttermilk herb dip

SERVES 12; YIELDS 3 CUPS DIP

1   cup plain whole-milk yogurt

1   cup sour cream

1   cup freshly grated Parmigiano-Reggiano

½   cup buttermilk

1   cup thinly sliced fresh chives

2   Tbs. chopped fresh dill

2   Tbs. chopped fresh thyme

1   small clove garlic, minced and mashed to a paste with a pinch of salt

1   Tbs. cider vinegar

¼   tsp. Tabasco; more to taste

Kosher salt and coarsely ground black pepper

Assorted vegetables, washed and trimmed

When choosing your crudités, go with whatever looks good at the market.

1. In a large bowl, whisk the yogurt, sour cream, Parmigiano, buttermilk, herbs, garlic paste, vinegar, Tabasco, and 1½ tsp. each salt and pepper. Season with more Tabasco, salt, and pepper to taste. Let sit for 15 minutes.

2. Arrange the vegetables on a large platter, with the dip in the center, or put each vegetable in its own bowl and arrange with the dip on a tray.

Make Ahead

The dip can be made up to 1 day ahead.

PER SERVING: 110 CALORIES | 5g PROTEIN | 13g CARB | 5g TOTAL FAT | 3.5g SAT FAT | 0g MONO FAT | 0g POLY FAT | 20mg CHOL | 250mg SODIUM | 3g FIBER

crudités with creamy
buttermilk herb dip

beer and cheddar fondue

YIELDS ABOUT 5 CUPS;
SERVES 6 TO 8

- 1 Tbs. unsalted butter
- ½ small yellow onion, minced
  (about ⅓ cup)
- 1 large clove garlic, minced
- 12 oz. Emmentaler cheese,
  coarsely grated (about
  3 lightly packed cups)
- 8 oz. extra-sharp white
  Cheddar, coarsely grated
  (about 2 lightly packed cups)
- 4 oz. Gruyère, coarsely grated
  (about 1 lightly packed cup)
- 2 Tbs. cornstarch
- 1 tsp. dry mustard (such as
  Coleman's®)
  Freshly ground black pepper
- 1 tsp. caraway seeds, coarsely
  ground in a spice grinder or
  with a mortar and pestle
- 1 12-oz. can lager-style beer,
  preferably Budweiser®
- 3 Tbs. Amontillado sherry
  Kosher salt
  Dipping ingredients
  (sidebar below)

Amontillado, a medium-dry sherry, provides a nice contrast to the bitter beer and the sharp Cheddar.

1. Melt the butter in a 1½- to 2-quart flameproof fondue pot over medium-low heat. (If your fondue pot isn't flameproof, use a heavy, narrow saucepan.) Add the onion and garlic and cook, stirring occasionally, until completely soft and beginning to caramelize, 15 to 20 minutes.

2. Meanwhile, in a large bowl, toss the Emmentaler, Cheddar, and Gruyère with the cornstarch, mustard, and ½ tsp. pepper.

3. Add the caraway seeds to the pot and stir to toast them slightly, about 2 minutes. Add the beer, increase the heat to high, and bring to a boil. Reduce the heat to medium low and simmer to mellow the flavor of the beer, about 3 minutes.

4. Sprinkle the cheese mixture into the pot a large handful at a time, stirring each batch in a back and forth pattern so that the cheese doesn't ball up as it melts. Continue adding and stirring until all of the cheese is melted, smooth, and thick, adjusting the heat as necessary to maintain barely a simmer. Stir in the sherry and season to taste with salt. (If using a saucepan, transfer the fondue to a fondue pot.) Set the fondue pot over a low flame at the table to keep it warm. Serve with the dipping ingredients.

PER SERVING: 380 CALORIES | 23g PROTEIN | 6g CARB | 27g TOTAL FAT | 17g SAT FAT | 8g MONO FAT | 1g POLY FAT | 90mg CHOL | 450mg SODIUM | 0g FIBER

fondue dipping options

Serve some or all of the following as dipping options for your fondue:

- Sourdough or ciabatta cubes
- Pear and apple slices
- Steamed carrots and cauliflower
- Boiled baby or fingerling potatoes
- Cornichons or baby pickles
- Grilled or broiled sliced sausage

warm black bean and chipotle dip

SERVES 12

2   Tbs. extra-virgin olive oil; more for the baking dish

2   medium tomatoes, cored and cut into medium dice

2   tsp. kosher salt; more as needed

1   large yellow onion, finely diced

3   large cloves garlic, minced

1   Tbs. chili powder

2   15 ½-oz. cans black beans, rinsed and drained well

2   canned chipotles en adobo, minced (about 1 Tbs.), plus 3 Tbs. adobo sauce from the can

3   Tbs. cider vinegar

1½ cups fresh (or thawed frozen) corn kernels

1½ cups (6 oz.) grated sharp Cheddar

1½ cups (6 oz.) grated Monterey Jack

¾   cup chopped fresh cilantro

Freshly ground black pepper

Tortilla chips, for serving

This is a great party dip that can be fully assembled up to 2 days ahead. Keep covered and refrigerated until ready to bake.

1. Heat the oven to 425°F. Grease a 1½-qt. baking dish with oil and line a baking sheet with foil. Set the tomatoes in a colander over the sink and sprinkle with 1 tsp. of the salt.

2. Heat the oil in a large (12-inch) skillet over medium-high heat until shimmering hot. Reduce the heat to medium, add the onion, sprinkle with 1 tsp. salt, and cook, stirring, until softened and translucent, 4 to 6 minutes. Add the garlic and chili powder and cook, stirring, for 1 minute. Add half of the black beans, the chipotles and adobo sauce, and ¾ cup water and bring to a boil. Cook until the liquid reduces by about half, 2 to 3 minutes.

3. Transfer the bean mixture to a food processor, add the vinegar, and process until smooth. Let cool for a couple of minutes and then transfer to a large bowl. Add the rest of the beans, the tomatoes, corn, half of each of the cheeses, and ½ cup of the cilantro. Mix well and season to taste with salt and pepper.

4. Transfer to the baking dish and sprinkle with the remaining cheeses. Bake on the foil-lined baking sheet (to catch drips) until the cheese melts and browns around the edges, about 15 minutes (longer if refrigerated). Sprinkle with the remaining cilantro and serve with the tortilla chips for dipping.

PER SERVING: 230 CALORIES | 12g PROTEIN | 19g CARB | 12g TOTAL FAT | 6g SAT FAT | 4.5g MONO FAT | 0.5g POLY FAT | 30mg CHOL | 510mg SODIUM | 4g FIBER

garlic roasted shrimp cocktail

1½ lb. jumbo shrimp (16 to
   20 per lb.), shells peeled,
   tails left on

2 cloves garlic, finely chopped
   (about 1 Tbs.)

2 Tbs. extra-virgin olive oil

½ tsp. kosher salt

¼ tsp. cracked black pepper

   Cocktail Sauce with Red
   Onion and Jalapeño (recipe
   below)

Roasting the shrimp with garlic gives them a punch that's great with the spicy cocktail sauce below.

Heat the oven to 450°F. Devein the shrimp, if necessary. In a large bowl, toss the shrimp with the garlic, olive oil, salt, and pepper. Spread the shrimp on a heavy-duty rimmed baking sheet in a single layer. Roast for 3 minutes, turn the shrimp over with tongs, and continue roasting until the shrimp are opaque and firm, another 2 to 4 minutes. Transfer the shrimp to a shallow dish, cover loosely, and refrigerate. When the shrimp are thoroughly chilled (after about 2 hours), serve them with the cocktail sauce.

PER SERVING: 130 CALORIES | 18g PROTEIN | 0g CARB | 6g TOTAL FAT | 1g SAT FAT | 4g MONO FAT | 1g POLY FAT | 170mg CHOL | 390mg SODIUM | 0g FIBER

cocktail sauce with red onion and jalapeño

½ cup tomato ketchup

½ cup chili sauce

¼ cup grated red onion (from
   about ¼ medium onion,
   using the large holes on a
   box grater)

½ tsp. finely chopped fresh
   jalapeño

3 Tbs. prepared horseradish

1 Tbs. fresh lemon juice; more
   to taste

⅛ tsp. kosher salt; more to taste

This sauce is best made a day in advance and keeps well for up to a week.

Put all the ingredients in a bowl and stir to combine. Chill, covered, until ready to use. Just before serving, taste and add more lemon juice and salt as needed.

PER ¼ CUP: 60 CALORIES | 1g PROTEIN | 16g CARB | 0g TOTAL FAT | 0g SAT FAT | 0g MONO FAT | 0g POLY FAT | 0mg CHOL | 1,140mg SODIUM | 1g FIBER

crispy potatoes with tangy tomato sauce (patatas bravas)

SERVES 8

FOR THE SAUCE

- 1½ Tbs. extra-virgin olive oil
- ⅓ cup chopped onion (½ small)
- ⅓ cup chopped carrot (1 small)
- 2 medium cloves garlic, smashed and peeled
- 1 Tbs. dry white wine
- ¼ tsp. sweet pimentón or regular paprika
- ¼ tsp. ground cumin
- 1½ cups canned tomatoes (with their juices), coarsely chopped
- 3 large sprigs fresh thyme
- 1 tsp. granulated sugar
- ¼ tsp. Tabasco sauce; more to taste

  Kosher salt and freshly ground black pepper
- ¼ tsp. sherry vinegar

FOR THE POTATOES

- 2½ lb. (about 8 medium) Yukon Gold, white, or red potatoes, scrubbed and cut into 1-inch pieces (no need to peel)
- ½ cup extra-virgin olive oil
- 1 tsp. kosher salt
- 1 tsp. chopped fresh rosemary (optional)

Roasting the potatoes in a good amount of olive oil gives them a crisp fried flavor without the hassle of deep-frying. The sauce can be made up to 3 days ahead.

1. Make the sauce: In a small (1- or 2-qt.) saucepan, heat the 1½ Tbs. olive oil over medium heat. Add the onion, carrot, and garlic and cook, stirring frequently, until softened but not browned, about 5 minutes. Add the wine and let it reduce until almost evaporated, about 1 minute. Add the pimentón and cumin and stir for about 15 seconds. Add the tomatoes and their juices, the thyme sprigs, sugar, Tabasco, ¼ tsp. salt, and a few grinds of pepper.

2. Reduce the heat to a gentle simmer and cook, uncovered, stirring occasionally, to reduce the sauce somewhat and intensify its flavor. This should take about 1 hour; depending on how much juice you started with, you may need to add up to ½ cup water during simmering to keep the consistency saucy rather than dry.

3. Fish out the spent thyme sprigs. Purée the sauce with an immersion blender or a regular blender (vent the top and hold a folded dishtowel over the lid) until it's smooth and creamy; you can thin it with a little water if needed. Stir in the sherry vinegar. Taste and add salt and pepper, if needed. The sauce should be slightly spicy, and you should have about 1½ cups.

4. Roast the potatoes: Heat the oven to 425°F. Toss the potatoes with the olive oil, 1 tsp. salt, and the rosemary (if using) on a large rimmed baking sheet. Roast, turning the potatoes with a metal spatula every 15 minutes, until they're browned and crisp outside and tender inside, about 45 minutes.

5. Put the potatoes in a serving dish and put the sauce in a small dish next to the potatoes, along with a spoon.

PER SERVING: 260 CALORIES | 3g PROTEIN | 27g CARB | 16g TOTAL FAT | 2.5g SAT FAT | 12g MONO FAT | 2g POLY FAT | 0mg CHOL | 310mg SODIUM | 3g FIBER

goat cheese, pesto, and sun-dried tomato terrine

YIELDS ABOUT 1½ CUPS

10   oz. goat cheese

¼   to ½ cup heavy cream

     Kosher salt and freshly ground black pepper

3   Tbs. basil pesto (homemade or store-bought)

5   oil-packed sun-dried tomatoes, drained and finely chopped

¼   cup pine nuts, toasted and coarsely chopped

     Extra-virgin olive oil for drizzling

     Pita chips (recipe p. 87), for serving

As pretty to look at as it is delicious to eat, this will become a favorite party staple.

1. Line the inside of a 2-cup, sharply sloping bowl (about 4 inches across the top) with plastic; let the ends extend over the sides a few inches. In a mixing bowl, mash the goat cheese and ¼ cup of the cream with a fork and season with ¼ tsp. salt and a few grinds of pepper; add more cream if the cheese hasn't softened. Spoon about one-third of the cheese into the lined bowl and pack it into an even layer. Spread the pesto almost completely to the sides of the first layer of cheese. Top with another third of the cheese, the sun-dried tomatoes, and all but ½ Tbs. of the pine nuts. Top with the remaining cheese. Pack down, fold the plastic over, and refrigerate for at least 30 minutes.

2. Half an hour before serving, take the bowl out of the refrigerator. Pull on the edges of the plastic to loosen the terrine from the bowl. Invert the terrine onto a plate, drizzle with a little olive oil, and let sit for ½ hour to warm up. Sprinkle with the remaining pine nuts, season liberally with pepper, and serve with the pita chips.

PER 1 TBS. WITHOUT PITA CHIPS: 70 CALORIES | 3g PROTEIN | 1g CARB | 6g TOTAL FAT | 3g SAT FAT | 2.5g MONO FAT | 1g POLY FAT | 10mg CHOL | 75mg SODIUM | 0g FIBER

guacamole with roasted chile, cumin, and feta

YIELDS ABOUT 2 CUPS

- **1** small fresh green New Mexico or poblano chile
- **1** medium lime
- **3** medium, firm-ripe avocados (6 to 7 oz. each), pitted and peeled
- **3** medium scallions, white and light green parts only, chopped
- **5** Tbs. chopped fresh cilantro
- **¼** tsp. ground cumin, preferably freshly ground

  Kosher salt
- **½** cup medium-diced fresh tomato
- **2** radishes, slivered (about 2 Tbs.), for garnish
- **1** Tbs. crumbled feta, for garnish

  Store-bought or homemade corn tortilla chips, for serving

Rather than the expected jalapeño, this recipe uses roasted poblano or New Mexico chile for a more rounded flavor. A pinch of cumin, crumbled feta, and crisp slivered radishes flatter the avocado as well.

1. On a gas stove, turn a burner to high and set the chile directly over the flame, turning it with tongs, until completely charred, 5 to 8 minutes. Alternatively, on an electric stove, heat the broiler on high and char the chile on a baking sheet placed directly under the broiler. Put the chile in a bowl, cover, and set aside to steam and loosen the skin. When cool enough to handle, peel, seed, and finely chop.

2. Finely grate the zest from the lime and then squeeze the juice. Put the avocado in a bowl and coarsely mash with a potato masher. Stir in the lime zest and 2 Tbs. of the lime juice along with the scallions, cilantro, cumin, and ½ tsp. salt. Season to taste with salt and lime juice, and then fold in the chile and tomato.

3. Heap the guacamole into a bowl and garnish it with the radishes and feta. Serve with tortilla chips.

PER 2 TBS.: 70 CALORIES | 1g PROTEIN | 4g CARB | 6g TOTAL FAT | 1g SAT FAT | 3.5g MONO FAT | 0.5g POLY FAT | 0mg CHOL | 45mg SODIUM | 3g FIBER

Avocados: A Buyer's Guide

Here's a roundup of the most common avocado varieties. Any type can be used in these recipes.

• **Hass.** These are the avocados you're most likely to find at the grocery store. Their advantage—and the reason retailers like them—is that their pebbly skins are tough and protective, which makes the fruits easier to handle, store, and ship. Plus, you can tell when they're ripe because the skin turns black as the flesh softens.

• **Fuerte.** Another common grocery store variety, Fuerte avocados are large and distinctively pear-shaped with thin, smooth, light-green skin.

• **Bacon.** Large and oval, this variety has smooth, thin, dark-green skin and a pleasantly nutty aftertaste. It's named after James Bacon, who developed it in 1954.

• **Pinkerton.** This variety is distinguished by thick, darkish-green skin, an elongated pear shape, and a very small seed.

• **Zutano.** An early-fall to early-winter variety, the medium to large pear-shaped Zutano has shiny yellow-green skin and light-textured flesh.

• **Reed.** Large, round, and plump with a thick skin that's slightly pebbly, Reed is the only avocado variety grown in the summer.

how to remove the pit from an avocado

To neatly remove the pit from a halved avocado, carefully but firmly chop the blade of a chef's knife into the pit. Give a twist and lift the pit out. To safely remove the pit from the knife, either push it off with your fingers coming over the back (dull) side of the knife or scrape it off against the inside edge of the sink.

fiery green tomato salsa

- **2** green tomatoes (about ½ lb. each), sliced ½ inch thick
- **1** medium jalapeño
- **2** ripe red tomatoes (about 6 oz. each)
- **½** small onion, chopped
- **1** Tbs. olive oil
- **1** Tbs. fresh lemon juice
- **1** Tbs. minced fresh oregano or mint leaves

   Pinch of granulated sugar

   Kosher salt and freshly ground black pepper

Green tomatoes, with their firm texture and tart, almost lemony flavor, make a terrific ingredient for herb- and chile-spiked salsas like this one.

1. Heat a broiler to high or prepare a hot charcoal fire. Broil or grill the green tomatoes (about 4 minutes per side) until seared but not soft; chop them coarsely. Broil or grill the jalapeño until blackened, seal it in a paper bag for 5 minutes, and let steam. Peel and seed it; mince the flesh. Halve the red tomatoes, squeeze out the juice, and coarsely chop the flesh.

2. In a medium bowl, combine the green and red tomatoes, the jalapeño, onion, olive oil, lemon juice, oregano or mint, and sugar; add salt and pepper to taste. Mix well, taste, and adjust the seasonings.

PER ¼ CUP: 45 CALORIES | 1g PROTEIN | 6g CARB | 2g TOTAL FAT | 0.5g SAT FAT | 1g MONO FAT | 0.5g POLY FAT | 0mg CHOL | 130mg SODIUM | 1g FIBER

Make Ahead

This dip can be made 1 day ahead and refrigerated.

Why Green Tomatoes?

Green tomatoes, with their light flavor and juicy but firm texture, are incredibly versatile vegetables that respond well to any number of cooking techniques. You can begin to enjoy green tomatoes before the red ones ripen, plus they'll store for weeks in the refrigerator, so you'll have green tomatoes long after the ripe ones are gone. In choosing green tomatoes, you often find some with traces of pink. Go ahead and add them to the cart—it just means that you won't need to cook them quite as long and that their flavor will be slightly sweeter.

smoky eggplant and white bean dip with pita crisps

YIELDS 1½ CUPS DIP; SERVES 6

- **5 Tbs. extra-virgin olive oil; more for the pan**
- **1½ lb. small eggplant (2 to 3 small), trimmed and cut in half lengthwise**
- **Kosher salt and freshly ground black pepper**
- **2 anchovy fillets (optional)**
- **1 small clove garlic**
- **1 cup canned cannellini beans, drained and rinsed**
- **3 pitas (preferably pocketless), each cut into 8 wedges**
- **2 Tbs. fresh lemon juice; more to taste**
- **1 Tbs. chopped fresh mint, plus 1 Tbs. small leaves for garnish**
- **2 tsp. chopped fresh oregano**
- **2 Tbs. pine nuts, toasted**

This dip is also delicious with crudités, especially crisp bell peppers and fennel. Salt-packed anchovies must be rinsed and filleted before they can be used, but the big, meaty fillets and their superior flavor make them well worth the effort.

1. Position a rack 4 inches from the broiler and heat the broiler to high. Line a rimmed baking sheet with foil and grease lightly with oil. Rub the eggplant all over with 2 Tbs. of the oil and sprinkle the flesh side with ½ tsp. salt and ¼ tsp. pepper. Lay the eggplant, flesh side down, on the baking sheet. Broil until the skin is charred and the eggplant flesh is very tender, 20 to 30 minutes.

2. Meanwhile, if using anchovies, mash them into a paste with the side of a chef's knife. Roughly chop the garlic, sprinkle it with a generous pinch of kosher salt, and mash it into a paste with the side of a chef's knife. Transfer the anchovy and garlic pastes to a food processor and add the beans, 2 Tbs. of the oil, and 1 Tbs. water. Purée until smooth.

3. When the eggplant is done, set it aside to cool briefly. Meanwhile, in a medium bowl, toss the pita wedges with the remaining 1 Tbs. oil and ¼ tsp. salt. Arrange in a single layer on a baking sheet. Lower the rack so it's 6 inches from the broiler. Broil the pita wedges until golden brown on both sides, 1 to 2 minutes per side.

4. Scrape the eggplant flesh from the skin and add the flesh to the puréed beans in the food processor, along with the lemon juice, chopped mint, and oregano. Pulse briefly to create a chunky dip. Adjust the seasoning with more salt, pepper, or lemon juice to taste. Serve sprinkled with the pine nuts and mint leaves, with the pita crisps on the side for dipping.

PER SERVING: 270 CALORIES | 7g PROTEIN | 31g CARB | 15g TOTAL FAT | 2g SAT FAT | 9g MONO FAT | 3g POLY FAT | 0mg CHOL | 430mg SODIUM | 8g FIBER

fava bean purée

YIELDS ABOUT 1½ CUPS

½ cup extra-virgin olive oil; more for drizzling

2 large cloves garlic, chopped

1 tsp. finely chopped fresh rosemary or thyme

Kosher salt and freshly ground black pepper

3 lb. fava beans, shelled and peeled, to yield 2 cups

2 Tbs. fresh lemon juice; more to taste

Parmigiano-Reggiano, for garnish

This simple purée showcases the wonderful nutty flavor of favas.

1. Put a 10-inch skillet over medium-high heat. Add ¼ cup of the oil, the garlic, rosemary or thyme, ½ tsp. salt, and ⅛ tsp. pepper and cook until you begin to hear a sizzling sound and the aromatics are fragrant, 1 to 2 minutes. Add the fava beans. Stir until the beans are well coated with the oil and aromatics and then add 1 cup of water. Bring to a boil, reduce the heat to medium, and cook until the water has nearly evaporated and the fava beans are tender, about 12 minutes. Add more water if the pan looks dry before the favas are done. Remove from the heat.

2. Transfer the fava mixture to a food processor. Add the remaining ¼ cup olive oil and the lemon juice and purée until smooth, stopping to scrape the bowl as needed. Season to taste with more salt and lemon juice. Drizzle with a little olive oil before serving.

3. Serve on crostini (page 65) and top with freshly grated Parmigiano-Reggiano.

PER SERVING: 90 CALORIES | 4g PROTEIN | 10g CARB | 5g TOTAL FAT | 0.5g SAT FAT | 3.5g MONO FAT | 0.5g POLY FAT | 0mg CHOL | 35mg SODIUM | 2g FIBER

> **Use the purée as a dip for vegetables, pita chips, or bread. Thin it a little by adding water, lemon juice, or olive oil (or a little of each).**

crudités with creamy roquefort dip

SERVES 16

Kosher salt

1 lb. broccoli

1 lb. small or medium carrots, preferably with green tops

1 bunch celery (about 1¼ lb.)

1 medium head radicchio

1 medium fennel bulb, fronds trimmed

8 radishes, preferably with green tops

Creamy Roquefort Dip (recipe on facing page)

Make Ahead

Prep the vegetables a day ahead. Store them separately in sealed containers or zip-top bags and refrigerate them to keep them crisp.

What follows is mostly a guide to trimming and storing crudité vegetables so that they look and taste their best. You can substitute other vegetables, like bell pepper strips and cucumber slices.

1. Combine 4 qt. water and ¼ cup kosher salt in a large pot and bring to a boil over high heat. Meanwhile, trim most of the stem off the broccoli to separate the florets. Using a small, sharp knife, trim the stem of each floret so it's 1½ to 2 inches long. Starting at the top of the stem (just beneath the tiny buds), cut through the stem lengthwise and divide the floret in half—preferably without using the knife to cut through the flowery buds. Repeat the process, dividing each floret into two to four pieces, until the top of each floret is about the size of a quarter. Have ready a bowl of ice water. Boil the florets until they turn bright green, about 1 minute. Drain the florets in a colander and then plunge them into the ice water to stop the cooking and set the broccoli's color. Drain again.

2. Trim the carrot tops, but leave about 1½ inches of the green tops intact. Peel the carrots and cut them lengthwise into halves, quarters, or sixths, depending on the size.

3. Remove the tough outer celery ribs; reserve for another use. Trim the tops of the ribs and about 1½ inches from the root end. Starting with the large ribs, cut each lengthwise into long, thin sticks about ¼ inch wide. Trim the large leaves from the celery heart and cut each rib in the same manner, preserving as many of the tender leaves as possible.

4. Discard the outer leaves of the radicchio. Trim the root end and cut the radicchio in half through the core. Cut each half into wedges ¼ inch thick; the core should hold each wedge intact.

5. Trim any stalks from the top of the fennel bulb and cut it in the same manner as the radicchio, but don't discard the outer layers unless they're discolored.

6. Trim the tops of the radishes, leaving about 1 inch of the green tops. (If the leaves are especially nice, leave a few intact for garnish.) Quarter each radish lengthwise.

7. Store the vegetables. When ready to serve, arrange the vegetables on a large platter or in a shallow basket. Mist the crudités lightly with water to keep them looking fresh. Serve with the dip on the side.

PER SERVING WITHOUT DIP: 30 CALORIES | 2g PROTEIN | 7g CARB | 0g TOTAL FAT | 0g SAT FAT | 0g MONO FAT | 0g POLY FAT | 0mg CHOL | 110mg SODIUM | 3g FIBER

creamy roquefort dip

YIELDS ABOUT 2½ CUPS

- **1** medium clove garlic

  Kosher salt

- **½ lb. Roquefort**

- **1½ cups crème fraîche or sour cream**

  Freshly ground black pepper

- **½ cup heavy cream**

Roquefort is an intensely flavored blue cheese made from sheep's milk. Store any leftover well wrapped in the refrigerator

In a mortar or with the flat side of a chef's knife, mash the garlic to a paste with a pinch of salt. Transfer to a medium bowl and add the Roquefort. Roughly mash the cheese with the back of a spoon. Stir in the crème fraîche or sour cream and several grinds of pepper, and then add the heavy cream until the consistency is slightly thinner than sour cream. (It should cling to the vegetables nicely but not be thick and goopy.) Taste and add more salt and pepper if needed. Refrigerate until shortly before serving. (The dip will thicken in the refrigerator but will return to its original consistency as it comes to room temperature.)

PER 1 TBS.: 25 CALORIES | 1g PROTEIN | 0g CARB | 2g TOTAL FAT | 1.5g SAT FAT | 0.5g MONO FAT | 0g POLY FAT | 5mg CHOL | 50mg SODIUM | 0g FIBER

how to cut bell pepper sticks

Squarely cut off the top and bottom. Reserve the trimmed ends. The pepper will now be shaped like a cylinder.

Slice the cylinder open and work the knife along the inside of the pepper (with the blade parallel to the work surface), removing the ribs and seeds while unrolling the pepper so that it lies flat.

You now have a neat rectangle of bell pepper that you can cut into sticks. You can trim and chop the reserved ends as well.

pear-ginger chutney

- ½ cup packed light brown sugar
- ½ cup cider vinegar
- 2 Tbs. seeded and minced jalapeño
- 1 12-inch cinnamon stick
- 1 whole clove
- 2 lb. firm-ripe pears, peeled, cored, and cut into ½-inch cubes (about 5 cups)
- 1 cup finely diced yellow onion
- ¼ cup dried cranberries
- ¼ cup chopped crystallized ginger
- 1 tsp. mustard seeds
- 1 tsp. grated fresh ginger
- Kosher salt

Serve this fresh-tasting, lightly spiced pear and ginger chutney on a cracker or with ham or turkey.

1. Combine the sugar, vinegar, jalapeño, cinnamon stick, and clove in a large, heavy-duty saucepan. Cook over medium-high heat until the sugar is completely dissolved, 3 to 4 minutes.

2. Stir in the pears, onion, cranberries, crystallized ginger, mustard seeds, fresh ginger, and ¼ tsp. salt. Reduce the heat to medium low, cover, and simmer, stirring occasionally, until the mixture is soft and the liquid has reduced somewhat, about 45 minutes. Uncover and continue to simmer until the liquid has almost evaporated, about another 10 minutes. Remove the cinnamon stick and clove. If you're not canning the chutney, let cool, portion into 3 clean 8-oz. jars, and refrigerate for up to 1 week.

PER 2 TBS.: 50 CALORIES | 0g PROTEIN | 14g CARB | 0g TOTAL FAT | 0g SAT FAT | 0g MONO FAT | 0g POLY FAT | 0mg CHOL | 15mg SODIUM | 1g FIBER

canning the chutney

Put 3 empty 8-oz. glass canning jars in a large pot of water fitted with a rack insert. The water should completely cover the jars. Cover, bring to a boil, and then turn off the heat. Put the lids in a bowl and cover with very hot water (boiling water can ruin the seal).

Remove the jars from the water and drain them. Divide the chutney among the 3 hot jars. Fill to within ½ inch of the top and wipe the edges clean with a paper towel. Screw the lids on tightly.

Return the jars to the pot of water and make sure the water covers them by at least 2 inches. Boil, covered, for 10 minutes. Use tongs to remove the jars; let them cool undisturbed on the counter. You should hear a popping sound as the jars cool, indicating that the vacuum seals have worked. Store in a cool place for up to 6 weeks.

country pâté with pistachios

FOR THE SPICE MIX

- 2 tsp. kosher salt
- 1 tsp. freshly ground black pepper
- ½ tsp. freshly ground allspice
- ½ tsp. freshly ground coriander
- ½ tsp. dried ground ginger
- ¼ tsp. freshly ground nutmeg

FOR THE PÂTÉ

- 3 Tbs. unsalted butter
- 1 cup finely chopped onion
- ½ cup dry white wine
- ¼ lb. chicken livers, trimmed
- Kosher salt and freshly ground black pepper
- ½ lb. fat back, chopped
- ½ lb. ground pork
- ½ lb. ground veal
- 1 large egg
- 2 Tbs. all-purpose flour
- 3 Tbs. Cognac or brandy
- ½ cup diced ham
- ¼ cup skinned pistachio nuts

FOR MOLDING AND SERVING

- ¾ lb. thinly sliced pancetta
- Slices of good crusty bread
- Dijon mustard
- Cornichons (optional)

Served with slices of crusty bread and a good Dijon mustard, pâté is the kind of appetizer you can put out on the table and let people feast on. Pâté needs to be made at least a day ahead; a few days is better.

MAKE THE SPICE MIX

In a small bowl, mix the salt, pepper, allspice, coriander, ginger, and nutmeg.

MAKE THE PÂTÉ

1. Heat 2 Tbs. of the butter in a small skillet over medium heat. Add the onion and cook, stirring, until very tender, about 10 minutes. Add the wine and cook until reduced by about two-thirds. Transfer to a large bowl.

2. Clean the skillet and heat the remaining 1 Tbs. butter in it over medium heat. Season the livers with salt and pepper and sauté until medium rare, about 3 minutes per side. Let cool and then chop into ½-inch pieces.

3. Whip the fat back in a food processor until creamy (or mince it fine with a sharp knife) and add it to the onion.

4. Add the pork, veal, egg, and flour to the onion and mix with a wooden spoon until thoroughly combined. Stir in the Cognac, ham, pistachios, the spice mix, and the chopped chicken livers.

MOLD, BAKE, AND SERVE

Heat the oven to 350°F. Follow the steps on the facing page to shape, bake, cool, and slice the pâté. Serve in slices with the bread, mustard, and cornichons, if using.

PER 1 OZ.: 80 CALORIES | 4g PROTEIN | 1g CARB | 6g TOTAL FAT | 2g SAT FAT | 3g MONO FAT | 1g POLY FAT | 25mg CHOL | 190mg SODIUM | 0g FIBER

Choosing a Pâté Mold

You don't need a special lidded terrine to make pâté. Any pan that conducts heat slowly will do. (It doesn't even have to be a loaf shape.) Just check that the volume is similar.

how to shape, bake, cool, and slice pâté

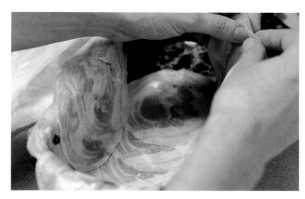

Line an 8-inch loaf pan, terrine, or similar dish with overlapping slices of pancetta, allowing the excess to hang over the sides. Spoon the pâté mixture into the mold, pressing on it gently. Fold the pancetta over the top and add more slices, if needed, to cover the entire loaf.

Seal with foil or a lid and set the dish in a roasting pan. Fill the pan with enough hot water to come halfway up the sides. Bake in the oven until the internal temperature reaches 160°F, about 1 hour and 50 minutes. Remove from the oven and let the pâté cool to room temperature in the water bath.

Partially remove the foil or lid and pour off any excess juices. Fit a clean loaf pan on top of the pâté and fill it with 1 to 2 lb. of cans (or set up a similar weight). Secure the weight with rubber bands and refrigerate for at least 24 hours or up to 3 days.

To serve, invert the pâté on a cutting board; it should slide out easily. If not, run a knife around the edge to loosen it. Remove the pancetta slices or leave them on and rinse the whole pâté quickly under running water to remove any congealed juices. Dry it with paper towels.

Cut the cold pâté into ½-inch slices and let them sit for about 30 minutes to let the full flavor develop. (Pâté tastes best when served at room temperature, but it's easier to slice when it's cold.)

baked brie with dried cherries and thyme

1 ½-lb. wheel of Brie (about 4 inches in diameter), at room temperature

1 sheet frozen puff pastry, thawed

⅓ cup dried cherries, coarsely chopped

2 tsp. chopped fresh thyme

1 Tbs. unsalted butter, melted

So easy, yet so impressive, this baked Brie gets an added flavor twist with dried cherries and thyme.

1. Position a rack in the center of the oven and heat the oven to 425°F.

2. Slice off the top rind of the Brie and discard. On a sheet of waxed paper or parchment, roll the pastry out to a 12-inch square and cut two 6-inch rounds from it. Put one of the rounds on a small rimmed baking sheet, sprinkle with half of the dried cherries and thyme, leaving a ½-inch border around the edge, and gently press so they adhere.

3. Set the Brie, rind side down, on top of the pastry, sprinkle with the remaining cherries and thyme, and cover with the other pastry. Crimp the edges together to seal in the cheese. Brush the top of the dough with the butter. Bake until the pastry browns, about 20 minutes. Let cool for 15 to 20 minutes and then serve.

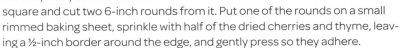

PER SERVING: 150 CALORIES | 6g PROTEIN | 6g CARB | 11g TOTAL FAT | 6g SAT FAT | 3.5g MONO FAT | 0g POLY FAT | 30mg CHOL | 200mg SODIUM | 0g FIBER

rosemary flatbread

YIELDS ABOUT TWENTY
8-INCH FLATBREADS

18 oz. (3 cups) semolina flour

13½ oz. (3 cups) unbleached
     all-purpose flour

2 tsp. kosher salt; more for the
   finished breads

3 Tbs. chopped fresh rosemary

1⅔ cups water

½ cup extra-virgin olive oil;
   more for the finished breads

People go crazy for these crackerlike breads.

1. In a large bowl, whisk the semolina and all-purpose flours with the salt and rosemary. Make a well in the center and pour in the water and the olive oil. With a fork, pull the dry ingredients into the wet ones until a mass forms. Knead the dough just until smooth, 2 to 3 minutes; be careful not to overwork it. Cover with plastic wrap and chill for at least 1 hour.

2. Put a pizza stone in the oven and heat the oven to 450°F. Work with one 2½-oz. piece of dough (about the size of a large egg) at a time; keep the rest of the dough covered. On a very lightly floured surface, flatten a piece of dough with the palm of your hands and roll it out as thin as possible; the shape should be free-form. Transfer the rolled dough directly to the stone in the hot oven; a pizza peel works well, but you can also pick up the dough with two hands and drape it onto the stone. (If the dough folds onto itself, let it bake for a few minutes and then try unfolding it.) You'll need to bake the dough in batches. Bake until crisp and light golden brown, 8 to 10 minutes. Let cool slightly and then brush with olive oil and sprinkle with salt.

PER SERVING: 260 CALORIES | 5g PROTEIN | 33g CARB | 11g TOTAL FAT | 2g SAT FAT | 8g MONO FAT | 1g POLY FAT | 0mg CHOL | 430mg SODIUM | 1g FIBER

sliced & served

chicken quesadillas with chipotle crema and pico de gallo

FOR THE CHIPOTLE CREMA

- 1   **7-oz. can chipotles en adobo**
- ¾   **cup Mexican crema or sour cream**
-   **Kosher salt**

FOR THE FILLING

- 4   **cups shredded cooked chicken**
- 1   **cup grated Monterey Jack**
- 1   **cup grated Mexican melting cheese, such as queso quesadilla, Chihuahua, or Oaxaca**
- ½   **cup crumbled Cotija cheese or queso anejo**
-   **Pico de Gallo (recipe below)**

FOR ASSEMBLING THE QUESADILLAS

- 12   **8-inch flour tortillas**
- 2⅔   **cups thinly sliced romaine lettuce (from 1 small head, quartered lengthwise)**

It's worth seeking out a variety of Mexican cheeses for a more complex flavor. It's also perfectly fine to use an equal amount of Monterey Jack.

MAKE THE CHIPOTLE CREMA

1. Pour the contents of the chipotles can into a blender. Rinse out the can with 2 Tbs. water and add it to the blender. Purée until smooth.

2. In a small bowl, whisk the crema, 2 tsp. of the chipotle purée, and ¼ tsp. salt. Add more chipotle purée if you want more heat. Set aside ¼ cup of the chipotle purée for the filling and save the rest for another use.

MAKE THE FILLING AND ASSEMBLE THE QUESADILLAS

1. Heat the oven to 200°F. Heat a cast-iron griddle or a large cast-iron pan over medium heat. Meanwhile, in a medium bowl, mix the chicken, cheeses, 1½ cups pico de gallo, and the reserved ¼ cup chipotle purée. Spread about ½ cup of the filling evenly over half of one of the tortillas and fold it in half. Repeat with the remaining tortillas and filling.

2. Put as many quesadillas as you can fit in one layer on the hot griddle. Cook, flipping once, until golden brown on both sides, 2 to 4 minutes per side. Repeat until all the quesadillas are cooked, keeping the finished ones warm on a baking sheet in the oven.

3. Cut each quesadilla into 3 wedges. Fan the wedges on small plates and mound a small pile of lettuce to the side of each serving. Garnish each with 2 Tbs. of the pico de gallo and 1 or 2 Tbs. of the chipotle crema.

PER SERVING: 560 CALORIES | 40g PROTEIN | 49g CARB | 22g TOTAL FAT | 11g SAT FAT | 8g MONO FAT | 2g POLY FAT | 105mg CHOL | 1,290mg SODIUM | 4g FIBER

pico de gallo

- 4   **cups seeded and diced fresh tomatoes (3 large)**
- 1   **cup small-diced white or sweet onion (1 medium)**
- ⅓   **cup fresh lime juice**
- 2   **to 3 serrano chiles, stemmed and finely chopped**
- ¼   **cup chopped fresh cilantro**
-   **Kosher salt**

Pico de gallo is a zesty Mexican salsa made with fresh tomatoes, onions, and chiles.

In a large bowl, combine the tomatoes, onion, lime juice, serranos, cilantro, and 2 tsp. salt. Mix well, cover, and let sit at room temperature for 1 hour. Season to taste with more salt if necessary. If not using right away, refrigerate for up to 3 days. Strain before using.

PER 1 TBS.: 5 CALORIES | 0g PROTEIN | 1g CARB | 0g TOTAL FAT | 0g SAT FAT | 0g MONO FAT | 0g POLY FAT | 0mg CHOL | 45mg SODIUM | 0g FIBER

cabbage, leek, and bacon tart

SERVES 6 TO 8

1 small head Savoy cabbage

   Kosher salt

2 medium leeks, all but
   2 inches of the light green
   part removed

2 Tbs. unsalted butter

½ lb. slab bacon, cut into
   ¼-inch cubes, blanched
   and thoroughly dried

   Freshly ground black pepper

3 extra-large eggs

1 cup heavy cream

3 oz. (¾ cup) coarsely grated
   Gruyère

1 partially baked tart shell in a
   12-inch porcelain quiche pan
   or a 12 ½-inch metal tart pan
   (recipe on facing page)

¼ cup freshly grated
   Parmigiano-Reggiano

This is a great cool-weather tart. The flavors of the leeks, Savoy cabbage, and bacon go especially well together.

1. Remove and discard the outer leaves of the cabbage and cut the cabbage into quarters. Bring a large pot of salted water to a boil; add the cabbage and cook just until tender, 10 to 12 minutes. Drain well. When cool enough to handle, put the cabbage in a cotton kitchen towel and wring out all the excess moisture. Cut out and discard the pieces of core. Slice the cabbage crosswise into very fine strips and measure out 2 tightly packed cups (save the remainder to add to a soup or sauté).

2. Cut the leeks in half lengthwise and then crosswise into ¼-inch slices. Put the slices in a colander and rinse thoroughly under warm water. Drain well and set aside.

3. In a large, heavy skillet, melt the butter over medium heat, add the bacon, and sauté until browned. Remove with a slotted spoon and set aside. Discard all but 2 Tbs. of the fat in the skillet; add the leeks and 2 Tbs. water, and simmer over low heat until tender, 5 to 7 minutes. Add the shredded cabbage and the bacon, season with salt and pepper, and sauté over medium heat for 5 minutes, stirring often. Let cool completely.

4. Heat the oven to 350°F. If using a tart pan with a removable bottom, put it on a baking sheet. In a large bowl, combine the eggs and cream and whisk until well blended. Stir in the cabbage mixture and Gruyère. Pour into the prepared tart shell, spread evenly, and sprinkle with the Parmigiano.

5. Bake until the custard has set and the top is lightly browned, 35 to 40 minutes. Let cool for 15 to 20 minutes before serving.

PER SERVING: 660 CALORIES | 15g PROTEIN | 29g CARB | 54g TOTAL FAT | 29g SAT FAT | 19g MONO FAT | 4g POLY FAT | 220mg CHOL | 860mg SODIUM | 2g FIBER

basic tart dough

- **9 oz. (2 cups) all-purpose unbleached flour**
- **½ tsp. table salt**
- **6 oz. (12 Tbs.) unsalted butter, cut into small pieces and chilled**
- **6 Tbs. ice water**

This is a great go-to recipe for tarts of all types.

MAKE THE DOUGH

In a food processor, combine the flour, salt, and butter. Using short pulses, process until the mixture resembles oatmeal. Add the ice water and pulse quickly until the mixture begins to come together—don't let it actually form a ball. Transfer the mixture to a lightly floured surface and gather it into a ball with your hands. Gently flatten the ball into a smooth disk about 1½ inches thick and wrap it in plastic or foil. Refrigerate until firm enough to roll, at least 1 hour.

ROLL AND SHAPE THE SHELL

Roll the dough on a lightly floured surface into a round about ⅛ inch thick. Roll the dough over your rolling pin and lift it over a 12-inch porcelain quiche pan or a 12½-inch metal tart pan. Unroll it loosely over the tart pan and gently press the dough into the pan without stretching it. Fold a bit of the excess dough inward to form a lip. Roll the rolling pin back and forth over the pan. Remove the severed dough from the outside of the pan. Unfold the lip of dough and press it down into the sides of the pan to form a double thickness. Prick the bottom of the shell all over with a fork, cover with aluminum foil, and freeze for at least 30 minutes or as long as overnight. At this point, the shell can also be wrapped and kept frozen for up to 2 weeks.

PARTIALLY BAKE THE SHELL

Arrange a rack in the center of the oven and heat the oven to 425°F. Remove the foil, line the frozen shell with parchment or fresh foil, fill it with dried beans or pie weights, and put it on a baking sheet. Bake until the sides are set, about 12 minutes. Remove the parchment and weights and continue to bake until the dough is just beginning to brown lightly, another 6 to 8 minutes. Let cool on a wire rack until needed.

leek tart with bacon and gruyère

SERVES 12

FOR THE TART SHELL

- **9 oz. (2 cups) unbleached all-purpose flour**
- **1 Tbs. chopped fresh thyme**
- **¼ tsp. table salt**
- **¼ tsp. freshly ground black pepper**
- **5½ oz. (11 Tbs.) cold unsalted butter, cut into ½-inch cubes**
- **5 to 6 Tbs. ice-cold water**

FOR THE FILLING

- **3 thick slices bacon, cut into small dice**
- **1 oz. (2 Tbs.) unsalted butter**
- **3 large leeks (white and light green parts only), cleaned and sliced crosswise ¼ inch thick to yield about 4 cups**
- **1 Tbs. unbleached all-purpose flour**
- **2 large eggs**
- **⅓ cup heavy cream**
- **⅓ cup whole milk**
- **¾ tsp. kosher salt**
- **⅛ tsp. freshly grated nutmeg**
- **Freshly ground black pepper**
- **⅔ cup grated Gruyère (or Emmentaler)**

Cut into thin wedges and serve along with aperitifs. It's delicious warm or at room temperature.

1. Make the tart shell: In a food processor, pulse the flour, thyme, salt, and pepper to blend thoroughly. Add the butter and pulse until the butter pieces are about the size of rice grains (about eight 1-second pulses). Add the ice water 1 Tbs. at a time through the feed tube while pulsing in short bursts until the dough starts coming together. It may still look crumbly, but if you press it with your fingers, it should become compact. (Don't add more water than absolutely necessary to get the dough to cling together.) Turn the dough out onto a clean work surface and, using your hands, gather and press the dough into a rough ball, blotting up the stray crumbs. Transfer the dough to a piece of waxed paper, shape it gently into a disk, and wrap it tightly to keep it from drying out. Refrigerate for at least 45 minutes. (The dough can be made up to 2 days ahead.)

2. Position a rack in the center of the oven and heat the oven to 450°F.

3. Unwrap the dough, set it on a lightly floured surface, and if necessary, let sit until pliable. Roll the dough out to a 14-inch circle about ⅛ inch thick.

4. Transfer the dough to an 11-inch fluted tart pan with a removable bottom and press it carefully into the corners and up the sides of the pan. Let the edges of the dough hang over the rim of the pan and then roll the rolling pin over the top of the pan to cut away the excess dough. Prick the surface of the dough all over with a fork, line it with parchment, and fill it with pie weights or dried beans. Put the pan on a rimmed baking sheet and bake until the edges of the tart shell are dry and flaky (but not browned), about 10 minutes. Remove the weights and parchment; the center should still be moist and raw. Prick the bottom again and return the shell to the oven. Bake until the bottom surface is completely dry, 5 to 7 minutes more. Remove from the oven and let cool. Lower the oven temperature to 375°F.

5. Make the filling: In a 12-inch skillet, cook the bacon over medium heat until it's crisp and golden brown, about 5 minutes. With a slotted spoon, transfer the bacon to a dish and set aside. Discard all but about 2 tsp. of the bacon fat. Set the skillet over medium-low heat, add the butter, let it melt, and then add the leeks. Stir to coat them with the fat, cover, and cook, stirring occasionally, until soft, 8 to 10 minutes. Stir the flour into the leeks and cook uncovered, stirring, for about 2 minutes to cook off the raw-flour flavor. Set aside and let cool slightly.

6. In a medium bowl, lightly whisk the eggs. Add the cream, milk, salt, nutmeg, and several grinds of pepper and whisk until blended. Add the bacon and leeks to the mixture and stir to combine.

7. To assemble the tart, scatter ⅓ cup cheese over the cooled tart shell and pour in the egg mixture. Spread the leeks evenly. Scatter the remaining ⅓ cup cheese evenly over the top. Bake until the custard is set and the top is light golden brown, about 35 minutes. Let cool on a rack for at least 30 minutes before serving.

8. Store leftovers in the refrigerator, covered. Reheat for 10 to 15 minutes at 350°F.

PER SERVING: 270 CALORIES | 7g PROTEIN | 20g CARB | 19g TOTAL FAT | 11g SAT FAT | 5g MONO FAT | 1g POLY FAT | 85mg CHOL | 200mg SODIUM | 1g FIBER

savory mushroom and goat cheese tart

FOR THE CRUST

- 6¾ oz. (1½ cups) unbleached all-purpose flour
- ¼ tsp. table salt
- ¼ lb. (½ cup) cold unsalted butter, cut into ½-inch pieces
- 4 to 5 Tbs. ice water

FOR THE FILLING

- ½ lb. fresh goat cheese, softened at room temperature
- ¼ cup mascarpone cheese or sour cream
- 1 small clove garlic, minced
- 1 Tbs. minced fresh chives
- Kosher salt and freshly ground black pepper

FOR THE TOPPING

- 2 Tbs. unsalted butter
- 2 Tbs. olive oil
- 1 lb. fresh mushrooms (preferably a mix), wiped clean, trimmed, and sliced about ¼ inch thick
- 2 Tbs. finely chopped shallots
- 1 Tbs. whole fresh thyme leaves
- Kosher salt and freshly ground black pepper

This tart pairs nicely with a crisp white wine.

1. Make the crust: Put the flour and salt in a food processor and pulse a few times to blend. Add the butter and pulse until the mixture resembles coarse cornmeal. Add the ice water, 1 Tbs. at a time, pulsing until the dough comes together in a rough ball. Remove the dough, shape it into a disk, wrap it in plastic, and chill for 1 hour.

2. Make the filling: In a small bowl, combine the goat cheese, mascarpone, garlic, chives, salt, and pepper, mixing with a fork until well blended. Set aside.

3. Make the topping: In a 12-inch skillet, heat the butter and oil over medium-high heat until the butter is foaming. Add the mushrooms and shallots and cook, stirring occasionally, until the mushrooms are just lightly browned, about 5 minutes. Add the thyme, season well with salt and pepper, and cook another minute.

4. Assemble and bake: Position a rack in the middle of the oven and heat the oven to 450°F. Line a baking sheet with parchment. On a lightly floured surface, roll the chilled dough into a 13-inch round. Transfer the dough to the parchment-lined sheet. Dollop the cheese mixture all over the dough and carefully spread it to within 1 inch of the edge. Top with the mushrooms. Fold the edge of the dough over the filling, pleating it as you go. Bake until golden brown, about 30 minutes. Serve warm.

PER SERVING: 400 CALORIES | 10g PROTEIN | 22g CARB | 30.5 TOTAL FAT | 18g SAT FAT | 9g MONO FAT | 2g POLY FAT | 70mg CHOL | 505mg SODIUM | 1.5g FIBER

grilled prosciutto, fontina, and sun-dried tomato sandwiches

- **1** Tbs. extra-virgin olive oil
- **2** medium cloves garlic, smashed
- **5** oz. baby spinach (about 5 lightly packed cups)

  Kosher salt and freshly ground black pepper
- **1¼** cups grated Fontina
- **¼** cup freshly grated Parmigiano-Reggiano
- **6** oil-packed sun-dried tomatoes, drained and chopped
- **3** 7- to 8-inch pitas, each split into two rounds
- **6** very thin slices prosciutto, preferably imported (about 3½ oz.)

These gooey, salty wedges are perfect cocktail companions. You can cook these sandwiches on a panini press instead of in a skillet if you prefer.

1. Heat the oven to 250°F. Heat the oil and garlic in a 10-inch heavy-duty skillet (preferably cast iron) over medium-high heat until the garlic starts to sizzle steadily and browns in places, about 2 minutes. Add the spinach, sprinkle with ¼ tsp. each salt and pepper, and cook, tossing, until just wilted, about 2 minutes. Transfer the spinach to a colander. Let cool for a couple of minutes, discard the garlic, and gently squeeze out the excess liquid from the spinach.

2. In a medium bowl, toss the spinach with the Fontina, Parmigiano, sun-dried tomatoes, and ¼ tsp. pepper. Set 3 of the pita halves on a workspace and top each with 2 slices of the prosciutto. Top each evenly with the spinach mixture and set the remaining 3 pita halves on top.

3. Wipe the skillet clean with a paper towel and heat the pan over medium heat. When the pan is hot, add one of the pita sandwiches and set another medium heavy skillet on top of the sandwich. Put 2 lb. of weights (cans work well) in the empty skillet and cook the sandwich until the bottom starts to brown, about 2 minutes. Flip and cook the other side until it browns and the cheese starts to melt out the sides, about 2 minutes. Transfer to a baking sheet and keep warm in the oven. Cook the remaining sandwiches in the same manner. Cut the sandwiches in wedges and serve.

PER SERVING: 150 CALORIES | 8g PROTEIN | 13g CARB | 7g TOTAL FAT | 3.5g SAT FAT | 2.5g MONO FAT | 0.5g POLY FAT | 25mg CHOL | 490mg SODIUM | 1g FIBER

oven-roasted pepper tart
with prosciutto and goat cheese

SERVES 6 TO 8

FOR THE TART SHELL

- 7 oz. (1½ cups) all-purpose flour
- ½ tsp. kosher salt
- 4 oz. (8 Tbs.) cold unsalted butter, cut into ½-inch pieces
- 1 large egg yolk

FOR THE FILLING

- 2 medium red or orange bell peppers
- 2 Tbs. extra-virgin olive oil
- 1 medium yellow onion, thinly sliced
- 1 Tbs. coarsely chopped fresh thyme
  Kosher salt and freshly ground black pepper
- 1 cup heavy cream
- 2 eggs
- 2 thin slices prosciutto, cut into thin strips
- 6 large fresh basil leaves, chopped
- 1 Tbs. finely grated Parmigiano-Reggiano
- ⅓ cup crumbled goat cheese

Before they're added to the tart filling, the bell peppers are oven-roasted, so they develop a soft, silky texture and intensified sweetness.

1. Make the tart shell: In a large bowl mix the flour and salt. With a pastry blender, cut in the butter until the mixture resembles coarse, fresh breadcrumbs. In a small dish, lightly beat the egg yolk with 2 Tbs. cold water. Drizzle it over the flour mixture and stir with a fork until the egg is evenly distributed. With the fork, stir in 2 to 4 Tbs. cold water, 1 Tbs. at a time, until the dough starts gathering into clumps. If you press some of the dough between your fingers, it should hold together. Dump the dough onto a counter. Gently press and gather the dough together, shaping it into a disk. Wrap in plastic wrap and chill for at least 1 hour.

2. Roll the chilled dough on a lightly floured surface into a circle ³⁄₁₆ inch thick and 12 to 13 inches in diameter. Drape the dough over your rolling pin and lift it over a 9½-inch fluted tart pan with a removable bottom. Unroll the dough and gently press it into the pan without stretching it. Then pass the rolling pin over the rim to cut off the excess dough. Wrap and freeze for at least 30 minutes.

3. Position a rack in the center of the oven and heat the oven to 375°F. Line the chilled tart shell with foil and fill it with dried beans or pie weights. Let the excess foil stand straight up, rather than folding it over the edges of the pan. Bake until the pastry edges are light golden, about 30 minutes. Carefully remove the foil and weights. Bake until the base of the pastry is beginning to turn golden, about 10 minutes more. If the pastry puffed at all, gently press down the bubbles before cooling completely on a rack.

4. Make the filling: Position a rack in the center of the oven and heat the oven to 400°F. Put the peppers on a rimmed baking sheet and roast in the oven, turning every 15 minutes until browned and wrinkled all over, 45 to 60 minutes. Remove the peppers from the oven, cover with a dishtowel, and set aside to cool. Turn the oven down to 375°F.

5. Seed, peel, and cut the peppers into wide strips or bite-size pieces. Set aside.

6. Heat the olive oil in a 10-inch skillet over medium heat. Add the onion, half the thyme, ½ tsp. salt, and ¼ tsp. pepper and cook, stirring frequently, until the onion is very soft and golden brown, 15 to 20 minutes. Reduce the heat to medium low or low if it looks like the onion is burning. Set aside at room temperature to cool.

7. In a small bowl, whisk the cream, eggs, and ¼ tsp. each salt and pepper. In a medium bowl, mix the peppers, onions, prosciutto, basil, Parmigiano, and the remaining thyme.

8. Put the tart shell on a baking sheet. Distribute the pepper mixture in the tart shell and scatter the goat cheese over it. Slowly drizzle the egg mixture over the filling until it reaches the rim of the pastry (you may not need it all). Bake the tart until the custard is set, 30 to 35 minutes. Cool on a rack and serve warm or at room temperature.

PER SERVING: 350 CALORIES | 7g PROTEIN | 20g CARB | 27g TOTAL FAT | 15g SAT FAT | 9g MONO FAT | 1.5g POLY FAT | 145mg CHOL | 300mg SODIUM | 1g FIBER

sun-dried tomato tart with fontina and prosciutto

- 1 large egg yolk

  All-purpose flour, for dusting

- 1 sheet frozen puff pastry (about 8 oz.), thawed according to package directions

- ¼ cup finely chopped oil-packed sun-dried tomatoes

- ½ cup grated Fontina (about 2 oz.)

- 4 thin slices prosciutto (preferably imported, about 2 oz.), cut crosswise into thin strips

- 2 to 3 Tbs. freshly grated Parmigiano-Reggiano

Frozen puff pastry makes this tart simple yet impressive.

1. Position a rack in the center of the oven and heat the oven to 400°F. Line a rimmed baking sheet with parchment. Whisk the egg yolk with ½ tsp. water.

2. Lightly dust a work surface with flour and gently unfold the pastry sheet. Roll out the pastry, eliminating the creases, to a 10 x 14-inch rectangle. Cut the rectangle in half lengthwise to make two 5 x 14-inch rectangles, and if the edges are uneven or ragged, trim them. Transfer both pastries to the baking sheet. With the tines of a fork, press a ¼-inch border around the edge of the pastry. Brush the egg mixture along the border (you won't need all of it). Poke the rest of the pastry all over with the fork to keep the pastry from puffing too much. Bake both pastry rectangles until firm and golden, about 12 minutes. Remove the pastry from the oven and increase the temperature to 475°F.

3. Let the pastry rectangles cool slightly and press them gently to flatten any large air pockets. Scatter a thin layer of the sun-dried tomatoes on both rectangles. Scatter the Fontina over the top. Arrange the prosciutto strips on top of the Fontina, either draping them in a random pattern or arranging them evenly. Sprinkle the top with the Parmigiano. Bake until the cheese has melted, about 5 minutes. Let cool for a few minutes, then cut into strips or small squares to serve.

PER SERVING: 170 CALORIES | 6g PROTEIN | 11g CARB | 11g TOTAL FAT | 4g SAT FAT | 5g MONO FAT | 1g POLY FAT | 25mg CHOL | 390mg SODIUM | 1g FIBER

broccoli and herb frittata

SERVES 8

1 **lb. broccoli**

Kosher salt

5 **large eggs, beaten
with a fork to blend**

½ **cup freshly grated
Parmigiano-Reggiano**

2 **Tbs. chopped
fresh basil**

**Freshly ground
black pepper**

1 **Tbs. unsalted butter**

1 **Tbs. olive oil**

A frittata makes a nice hors d'oeuvre when served in thin wedges. Be sure to cook the broccoli until completely tender. Substitute fresh mint or dill for the basil, if you like.

1. Separate the broccoli florets from the stems and then pare the stems with a knife. Leave the floret clusters whole unless they're especially large; if so, cut them in half. Bring a large pot of salted water to a boil over high heat. Add the stems and cook for 4 minutes; add the florets and cook both for another 6 minutes. (Alternatively, put them all in at the same time and remove the florets first.)

2. With a sharp paring knife, check to see if the broccoli is tender all the way through. With tongs or a slotted spoon, transfer the pieces to ice water as they're done. When cool, drain the broccoli well and chop it finely.

3. Position a rack 8 inches from the broiler element and heat the broiler on high. In a large bowl, combine the eggs, broccoli, cheese, basil, 1 tsp. salt, and ¼ tsp. pepper. Heat the butter and oil in an ovenproof 10-inch, nonstick skillet over medium heat. When the butter and oil are hot, add the egg mixture, spreading it evenly. Turn the heat to very low and cook until the mixture is mostly set, 15 to 18 minutes. The surface will still be undercooked, but the edges will be firm and visibly lighter in color. Move the skillet to the oven and broil until the frittata feels just firm throughout, about 5 minutes.

4. Set a cutting board or a large platter over the skillet and invert both. Let the frittata cool to room temperature before cutting into wedges to serve.

PER SERVING: 240 CALORIES | 16g PROTEIN | 7g CARB | 17g TOTAL FAT | 7g SAT FAT |
7g MONO FAT | 2g POLY FAT | 285mg CHOL | 580mg SODIUM | 3g FIBER

how to make the perfect frittata

Cook the filling in a hot skillet and pour in the eggs.

Check to see if the eggs are set underneath.

Finish cooking under the broiler.

stilton, apple, and leek tart
with a spiced whole-wheat crust

YIELDS ONE 10- OR 11-INCH
TART; SERVES 8 TO 10

FOR THE TART SHELL

- 6 oz. (1½ cups) sifted unbleached all-purpose flour
- 2 oz. (½ cup) sifted whole-wheat flour
- 1 tsp. ground coriander
- ¼ tsp. ground mace
  Pinch cayenne
- 1 tsp. kosher salt
- ¼ lb. (½ cup) cold unsalted butter, cut into bits
- 4 to 6 Tbs. ice water

FOR THE FILLING

- 1 medium leek (about ¼ lb.; white and light green parts only), trimmed
- 1 Tbs. unsalted butter
- 1 medium apple (Fuji or other sweet-tart variety), unpeeled, cored, and cut into ¼-inch cubes
- 3 large eggs
- 1 cup half-and-half or light cream
- ½ tsp. kosher salt
- ¼ tsp. freshly ground black pepper
- ¼ tsp. grated nutmeg
- ½ lb. Stilton, trimmed of rind and crumbled

Serve hard cider with this tart; its flavor will underscore the apples.

1. Make the tart shell: In a medium bowl, stir the two flours, coriander, mace, cayenne, and salt. By hand or using a food processor, cut the butter into the flour mixture until the butter bits resemble oatmeal. Mix in just enough ice water to form a ball of dough (be sparing). Gently flatten the dough into a smooth disk about 1½ inches thick. Roll the dough on a lightly floured surface into a round about ⅛ inch thick. Drape the dough over the rolling pin and lift it over a 10- or 11-inch fluted tart pan with a removable bottom. Unroll it loosely over the pan and gently press the dough into the pan without stretching it. Trim any excess dough from the rim of the pan. Cover with plastic and chill for at least 1 hour.

2. Heat the oven to 400°F. Fit a piece of heavy-duty aluminum foil over the dough and fill it with dried beans or pie weights. Bake until the dough is cooked through but not yet browned, 20 to 25 minutes. Remove the foil and weights and bake until the dough is evenly and lightly browned, about another 10 minutes. Remove from the oven and let cool.

3. Make the filling: Split the leek lengthwise into quarters and then cut crosswise into squares. Soak in cold water, swishing to loosen the dirt. Scoop the leeks from the water using a skimmer or slotted spoon and drain.

4. Heat the butter in a medium skillet; add the leeks and apples. Cook over medium heat, stirring, until the leeks are brightly colored and the apples are softened, about 5 minutes. Remove from the heat and let cool.

5. Lightly beat the eggs, half-and-half, salt, pepper, and nutmeg.

6. Fill and bake the tart: Heat the oven to 300°F. Cover the underside and edges of the tart pan with heavy-duty foil to prevent leaks and put the pan on a baking sheet. Distribute the leeks and apples evenly over the tart shell. Sprinkle the crumbled Stilton between the apples and leeks. Pour the custard over the top. Bake until the custard has just set in the middle, about 45 minutes. Let cool to room temperature before serving.

PER SERVING: 320 CALORIES | 10g PROTEIN | 22g CARB | 22g TOTAL FAT | 13g SAT FAT | 6g MONO FAT | 1g POLY FAT | 120mg CHOL | 730mg SODIUM | 2g FIBER

What Is Stilton?

Made from cow's milk, Stilton is an English blue cheese with extremely fine veins of mold in a characteristic radial pattern that can look like shattered porcelain. This trait gives the cheese its overall blueing and allows for even flavoring. Good Stilton has a dry, rough, brown rind and a creamy, ivory interior.

black bean and goat cheese quesadillas with guacamole

- 3 Tbs. olive oil
- 1 small yellow onion, finely chopped
- 1 15-oz. can black beans, rinsed and drained
- 1 tsp. ground cumin
- 1 tsp. chili powder
- ½ cup chopped fresh cilantro
- Kosher salt and freshly ground black pepper
- 1 large or 2 small, ripe avocados, pitted and peeled
- 2 tsp. fresh lime juice; more to taste
- 3 to 4 oz. fresh goat cheese, crumbled
- 6 8-inch flour tortillas

Make Ahead

These quesadillas can be assembled up to a day ahead and cooked just before serving.

Homemade guacamole gives these quesadillas a burst of fresh flavor.

1. In a medium skillet, heat 2 Tbs. of the oil over medium heat. Add the onion and cook, stirring, until soft, about 5 minutes. Add the beans, cumin, chili powder, and ½ cup water and cook, stirring occasionally, until almost all the water has evaporated, 5 to 7 minutes. Take the pan off the heat. With the back of a fork, break up the beans to make a chunky mash. Stir in half of the cilantro and season with salt and pepper.

2. In a small bowl, combine the avocado, lime juice, and remaining cilantro and mash into a chunky paste. Season to taste with salt, pepper, and more lime juice.

3. Spread the black bean mixture evenly over three of the tortillas. Scatter the goat cheese over the beans and cover with the remaining tortillas.

4. Lightly coat a large heavy skillet with oil and heat over medium heat. Set one of the quesadillas in the skillet and cook until lightly browned, about 2 minutes. Flip the quesadilla over and brown on the other side for 1½ minutes. Remove from the pan, cook the remaining quesadillas (add more oil to the pan each time), and cut each into eight wedges. Serve each wedge with a dollop of the guacamole.

PER SERVING: 250 CALORIES | 8g PROTEIN | 24g CARB | 14g TOTAL FAT | 4g SAT FAT | 8g MONO FAT | 2g POLY FAT | 10mg CHOL | 460mg SODIUM | 5g FIBER

gravlax

SERVES 6 OR MORE

- **2** **1-lb. fresh fillets of salmon, skin on**
- **1** **bunch fresh dill, with stems**
- **¼** **cup granulated sugar**
- **2** **Tbs. coarse sea salt**
- **1** **tsp. black peppercorns, cracked**
- **½** **tsp. whole allspice, cracked**

Serve gravlax at a party and devour morning-after leftovers with cream cheese and bagels.

1. Gently run your fingertips over the cut side of the fish to locate the prick of pin bones. When you feel a bone, grasp its tip with heavy-duty tweezers or needle-nose pliers and tug it toward the fillet's head end. Wash and shake dry the bunch of dill. Trim the dill to the same length as the fillets. Combine the sugar, salt, pepper, and allspice and rub this mixture on both sides of the salmon fillets.

2. Put one fillet, skin side down, in a nonaluminum baking dish that's just large enough to hold the salmon. Cover the fillet with the dill; the herb should be thick and well distributed. Lay the other fillet on top, skin side up. Cover the dish tightly with plastic wrap and refrigerate it. After 24 hours, unwrap the dish, flip the "sandwich" upside down. Rewrap the dish and return it to the refrigerator for another 24 to 30 hours. At the end of the curing period, liquid released by the gravlax will cover the bottom of the dish. Unwrap the dish, separate the fillets, and scrape away the herbs and spices. Reserve some of the curing liquid.

3. To slice the gravlax, use a thin, sharp knife with a scalloped (but not serrated) edge. Hold the knife at a 10-degree angle and, starting from the tail end, begin slicing the gravlax into pieces no thicker than 1/16 inch. The slices should be so thin that you can see through the flesh and watch the knife's movement. After you've sliced all the gravlax, remove the bloodline. To do this, fold each slice in half; the bloodline will form a triangle. Use a small, sharp, straight-edged knife to remove the triangle with one slice.

4. Arrange the gravlax slices on a platter and lightly brush with the reserved curing liquid. Serve with thin slices of toasted bread.

PER SERVING: 80 CALORIES | 8g PROTEIN | 2g CARB | 4g TOTAL FAT | 1g SAT FAT | 1.5g MONO FAT | 1.5g POLY FAT | 20mg CHOL | 1,230mg SODIUM | 0g FIBER

caramelized onion and thyme tarts

YIELDS 4 TARTS; SERVES 16

FOR THE DOUGH

- **9 oz. (2 cups) unbleached all-purpose flour**
- **1 Tbs. granulated sugar**
- **1¼ tsp. kosher salt**
- **6 oz. (12 Tbs.) cold unsalted butter, cut into ½-inch pieces**
- **Ice water**

FOR THE TOPPING

- **1 Tbs. extra-virgin olive oil**
- **1 Tbs. unsalted butter**
- **3 medium yellow onions, very thinly sliced (about 4 cups)**
- **2 tsp. chopped fresh thyme**
- **Kosher salt**
- **1 egg, lightly beaten**

You can make the tart dough a few days in advance and the filling up to a day ahead; but plan to assemble and bake the tarts just before serving.

1. Make the dough: Combine the flour, sugar, and salt in a large bowl. Add half of the butter and gently toss with your hands to coat each piece with flour. Using a pastry cutter or two table knives, cut the butter into the flour until it's the texture of coarse meal. Add the remaining butter, gently toss again to coat each piece, and quickly cut again until the larger pieces are about the size of large peas. In two or three additions, sprinkle about ⅓ cup ice water into the bowl, lightly tossing the mixture between your fingers to moisten it evenly. Stop adding water when the dough looks ragged and rough but holds together when you gently squeeze a small clump in your palm. Shape the dough into a brick (be careful not to knead it, just squeeze it gently into a solid mass). Cut the dough in half crosswise. Press each half into a flat rectangle about ½ inch thick and wrap tightly in plastic. Refrigerate the dough for at least 2 hours. (The dough can also be refrigerated for up to 2 days or frozen for up to a month. Thaw it overnight in the refrigerator before using.)

2. Make the topping: Heat a 12-inch skillet over medium-high heat for 1 minute and then add the olive oil and butter. When the butter has melted, add the onion, thyme, and ½ tsp. salt and sauté until the onion is tender and lightly browned, 6 to 8 minutes. Taste the onion and add more salt if necessary—it should be well seasoned. Transfer the onion to a medium bowl and set aside to cool. (This may be done up to a day ahead; keep covered and refrigerate.)

3. Roll the dough: Remove one rectangle of dough from the fridge. Cut it in half crosswise. Working with one half at a time, roll it on a lightly floured surface into a ⅛-inch-thick narrow rectangle, about 14 inches long and 5 inches wide. (If the dough is too cold to roll easily, let it warm at room temperature for 10 to 20 minutes until pliable.) Put the dough on a baking sheet lined with parchment (two narrow rectangles should fit side by side), top with a second sheet of parchment, and refrigerate. Repeat with the remaining dough and refrigerate until you're ready to prepare the tarts. (This may be done up to 4 hours ahead; keep covered. To conserve space, stack all four rectangles on one baking sheet between layers of parchment.)

4. Assemble the tarts: About 1 hour before serving, position oven racks in the upper and lower thirds of the oven and heat the oven to 375°F. About 40 minutes before serving, divide the onion into four equal portions and spread in a thin, even layer on the dough rectangles, leaving a 1-inch border. (You may not need to use it all; a thick layer will weigh down the tart slices and they'll flop when your guests pick them up.) Fold the exposed border over the onion—if the dough is too thick in the corners, trim as necessary. Brush the folded edges with the egg. Bake the tarts until the crust is well browned, about 30 minutes, switching the positions of the baking sheets halfway through. Remove the tarts from the oven and let cool briefly on the baking sheet. Cut each tart into slices and serve.

PER SERVING: 160 CALORIES | 2g PROTEIN | 14g CARB | 11g TOTAL FAT | 6g SAT FAT | 3g MONO FAT | 0g POLY FAT | 40mg CHOL | 130mg SODIUM | 1g FIBER

greek spinach and feta pie (spanakopita)

**YIELDS ONE 9 X13 X 2-INCH PIE;
SERVES 8**

FOR THE FILLING

- 2 lb. fresh spinach, washed, dried, trimmed, and coarsely chopped
- 3 Tbs. extra-virgin olive oil
- 1 bunch scallions (about 3 oz. or 10 small), white and light green parts only, trimmed and finely chopped
- 2 cups (10 oz.) crumbled feta cheese
- ½ cup finely grated Greek Kefalotyri cheese or Parmigiano-Reggiano
- 2 large eggs, lightly beaten
- ½ cup finely chopped fresh dill
- ⅓ cup finely chopped fresh flat-leaf parsley
- ¼ tsp. freshly grated nutmeg
- Kosher or fine sea salt

FOR THE ASSEMBLY

- ⅓ cup extra-virgin olive oil for brushing; more as needed
- 18 9 x 14-inch sheets frozen phyllo dough, thawed and at room temperature
- 2 tsp. whole milk

Spanakopita can also be made with other greens, such as dandelion or chard, in place of spinach. You can use 1 lb. of frozen chopped spinach instead of fresh. Thaw the spinach overnight or in a colander under warm running water. Squeeze out the liquid and skip the pan-wilting step.

1. Position a rack in the center of the oven and heat the oven to 375°F.

2. Make the filling: Heat a 10-inch straight-sided sauté pan over medium-high heat. Add a few large handfuls of the spinach and cook, tossing gently with tongs. As the spinach starts to wilt, add the rest a few handfuls at a time. Cook until all the spinach is wilted and bright green, about 4 minutes. With a slotted spoon, transfer the spinach to a colander set in a sink. Let cool slightly and squeeze with your hands to extract as much of the remaining liquid as you can.

3. Wipe the pan dry with a paper towel. Heat the oil in the pan over medium heat. Add the scallions and cook until soft and fragrant, about 4 minutes. Stir in the spinach, turn off the heat, and let cool for 5 minutes. Then stir in the cheeses, eggs, dill, parsley, nutmeg, and ½ tsp. salt and mix thoroughly.

4. Assemble the pie: With a pastry brush, lightly coat the bottom and sides of a 9 x 13 x 2-inch baking pan with some of the oil. Working quickly, lightly oil one side of a phyllo sheet and lay it in the pan oiled side up and off center so that it partially covers the bottom and reaches halfway up one long side of the pan (the edge on the bottom of the pan will be about 1 inch from the side). Lightly oil the top of another phyllo sheet and lay it oiled side up and off center so it reaches halfway up the other long side of the pan. (If your pan has sloped sides, the sheets may be slightly longer than the bottom of the pan; if so, let the excess go up one short side of the pan and then alternate with subsequent sheets.) Repeat this pattern with 4 more phyllo sheets.

Make Ahead

You can make this pie up to 4 hours ahead. Keep warm, if desired, or serve at room temperature.

Working with Phyllo

Phyllo dries out very fast and becomes brittle when exposed to the air. Experienced cooks who work quickly can likely oil each phyllo sheet directly on the stack without ever covering it. However, cooks who aren't as familiar with phyllo may want to oil one sheet at a time on a countertop, keeping the phyllo stack covered with plastic wrap topped with a slightly damp towel (the towel keeps the plastic weighted down). This will prevent the stacked phyllo sheets from drying out. Just fold back the towel and plastic each time you need a new sheet.

5. Next, lightly oil the tops of 3 phyllo sheets and layer them oiled side up and centered in the pan. Spread the filling evenly over the last layer.

6. Repeat the oiling and layering of the remaining 9 phyllo sheets over the filling in the same way you layered the previous 9. With the oiled bristles of the pastry brush, push the edges of the phyllo down around the sides of the pan to enclose the filling completely.

7. With a sharp knife, score the top phyllo layer into 24 rectangles, being careful not to cut all the way through to the filling. Using the same pastry brush, brush the milk along all the score marks (this will keep the phyllo from flaking up along the edges of the squares). Bake the spanakopita until the top crust is golden brown, 35 to 45 minutes. Let cool until just warm. Cut out the rectangles carefully along the score marks and serve.

PER SERVING: 400 CALORIES | 13g PROTEIN | 28g CARB | 27g TOTAL FAT | 9g SAT FAT | 14g MONO FAT | 2.5g POLY FAT | 90mg CHOL | 790mg SODIUM | 3g FIBER

What Is Feta?

Originally from Greece, feta is a rindless, white cheese aged in brine. It can range widely in texture and flavor; some are soft and moist, others hard and dry. Some are crumbly, others more creamy. Some are salty, others more tangy. The differences come from how the cheese was made, whether it contains sheep's, goat's, or cow's milk, and how long it was cured. Traditional Greek feta usually consists entirely of sheep's milk, although it may contain up to 30% goat's milk. But feta is made in dozens of other countries, too, including France, Spain, Israel, Australia, and the United States, where it's mostly made with cow's milk.

Whether it's crumbly, hard, and dry, or soft, moist, and creamy, good feta should taste and smell fresh. Compared to most cheeses, feta has a pronounced but pleasing acidic tang. If it smells or tastes overly sour, or if it has developed a peppery aftertaste, it's probably over the hill.

Buying feta in whole blocks, bricks, or wedges makes sense for the same reasons that you buy Parmesan in big chunks: it stays fresher for longer, it doesn't dry out, and its flavor packs more punch. Also, it gives you more options. Sometimes you want to slice a thick slab of feta and other times you need large crumbles. Finally, feta sold in whole pieces is often—though not always—a sign of a better-quality feta.

spanish potato tortilla

SERVES 12

1¾ cups olive oil or vegetable oil for frying

1¾ lb. (about 5 medium) low- to medium-starch potatoes, such as Yukon Gold, peeled

Kosher salt

12 to 14 oz. onions (2 to 3 medium), diced

5 medium cloves garlic, very coarsely chopped (optional)

6 large eggs

Freshly ground black pepper (optional)

If you have a mandoline, it will make short work of slicing the potatoes.

1. In a 10½-inch nonstick skillet that's at least 1½ inches deep, heat the oil on medium high. While the oil is heating, slice the potatoes thinly, about ⅛ inch. Transfer to a bowl and sprinkle on 2 tsp. salt, tossing to distribute it well.

2. When the oil is very hot (a potato slice will sizzle vigorously around the edges without browning), gently slip the potatoes into the oil with a skimmer or slotted spoon. Fry the potatoes, turning occasionally (trying not to break them) and adjusting the heat so they sizzle but don't crisp or brown. Set a sieve over a bowl or line a plate with paper towels. When the potatoes are tender, after 10 to 12 minutes, transfer them with the skimmer to the sieve or lined plate.

3. Add the onions and garlic (if using) to the pan. Fry, stirring occasionally, until the onion is very soft and translucent but not browned (you might need to lower the heat), 7 to 9 minutes. Remove the pan from the heat and, using the skimmer, transfer the onion and garlic to the sieve or plate with the potatoes. Drain the oil from the skillet, reserving at least 1 Tbs. (strain the rest and reserve to use again, if you like), and wipe out the pan with a paper towel so it's clean. Scrape out any stuck-on bits, if necessary.

4. In a large bowl, beat the eggs, ¼ tsp. salt, and ⅛ tsp. pepper (if using) with a fork until blended. Add the drained potatoes, onions, and garlic and mix gently to combine with the egg, trying not to break the potatoes (some will anyway).

5. Heat the skillet on medium high. Add the 1 Tbs. reserved oil. Let the pan and oil get very hot (important so the eggs don't stick), and then pour in the potato and egg mixture, spreading it evenly. Cook for 1 minute and then lower the heat to medium low, cooking until the eggs are completely set at the edges, halfway set in the center, and the tortilla easily slips around in the pan when you give it a shake, 8 to 10 minutes. You may need to nudge the tortilla loose with a knife or spatula.

6. Set a flat, rimless plate that's at least as wide as the skillet upside down over the pan. Lift the skillet off the burner and, with one hand against the plate and the other holding the skillet's handle, invert the skillet so the tortilla lands on the plate (it should fall right out). Set the pan back on the heat and slide the tortilla into it, using the skimmer to push any stray potatoes back in under the eggs as the tortilla slides off the plate. Once the tortilla is back in the pan, tuck the edges in and under itself (to neaten the sides). Cook until a skewer inserted into the center comes out clean, hot, and with no uncooked egg on it, another 5 to 6 minutes.

7. Transfer the tortilla to a serving platter and let cool for at least 10 minutes. Serve warm, at room temperature, or slightly cool. Cut into small squares or wedges, sticking a toothpick in each square if you like.

PER SERVING: 170 CALORIES | 5g PROTEIN | 15g CARB | 10g TOTAL FAT | 2g SAT FAT | 7g MONO FAT | 1g POLY FAT | 105mg CHOL | 400mg SODIUM | 2g FIBER

how to build a potato tortilla

Fry the potato slices, but don't let them brown or crisp.

When the eggs are mostly cooked, set a flat, rimless plate over the pan. Don't forget to give the pan a good shake to confirm that the tortilla is loose.

Holding the plate firmly in place, invert the pan so the tortilla falls onto the plate.

three-cheese quesadillas with garlic butter

SERVES 8 TO 12

- **2** small cloves garlic, unpeeled
- **2** Tbs. salted butter, at room temperature
- **8** oz. Monterey Jack, coarsely grated (2 cups)
- **1¼** oz. (½ cup) finely grated Parmigiano-Reggiano
- **4** oz. fresh goat cheese, crumbled (¾ cup)
- **4** 9- or 10-inch flour tortillas (burrito size)

You can assemble any quesadilla up to 2 hours ahead if its filling isn't very wet; wet fillings, like tomatoes, should not be assembled more than 30 minutes ahead. Keep them covered and refrigerated until ready to cook.

1. Position a rack in the center of the oven; heat the oven to 200°F. In a small pot, bring 2 cups water to a boil over high heat. Add the garlic cloves and cook until soft, about 5 minutes. Drain the garlic, let it cool slightly, peel, and put it in a small bowl. With a fork, mash the garlic to a coarse paste and then add the butter and mix well.

2. In a medium bowl, combine the Monterey Jack, Parmigiano, and goat cheese. Spread the garlic butter on one side of each tortilla and set the tortillas on a work surface, buttered side down. Distribute the cheese mixture among the tortillas, covering only half of each and leaving a 1-inch margin at the edge. Fold the tortillas in half to enclose the filling, creating a half-moon.

3. In a 10- or 12-inch nonstick skillet over medium heat, cook two of the quesadillas, covered, until golden brown, about 4 minutes. Uncover and flip the quesadillas. Cook until the second side is golden brown and the cheese has melted completely, about 2 minutes. Transfer the quesadillas to the oven to keep warm and repeat with the remaining two quesadillas. (You can hold the cooked quesadillas in the warm oven for up to 30 minutes.) Cut the quesadillas into small wedges and serve.

PER SERVING: 190 CALORIES | 9g PROTEIN | 13g CARB | 12g TOTAL FAT | 7g SAT FAT | 3.5g MONO FAT | 0.5g POLY FAT | 25mg CHOL | 310mg SODIUM | 1g FIBER

- Spread butter on the outside of the tortillas to add flavor.
- Use a nonstick skillet to cook the quesadillas.
- Cover the quesadillas briefly while they cook for good melting.

creating your own quesadillas

The best base cheeses for quesadillas are good melters—those that are relatively high in moisture, rather than drier, aged ones. Fresh cheeses like ricotta and goat cheese also work well in combination with melting cheeses. Once you've chosen your cheeses, try adding some of the other ingredients here. For how to make quesadillas, follow the directions in the recipe on the facing page; use plain salted butter in place of the garlic butter, if you like.

filling ideas

FROM THE PRODUCE AISLE
- Baby arugula
- Baby spinach
- Eggplant, diced and cooked
- Fresh corn, cooked
- Mushrooms, sliced and cooked
- Tomatoes, diced

FROM A JAR OR CAN
- Black beans, drained
- Chiles (canned, or fresh and roasted), chopped
- Oil-packed sun-dried tomatoes, drained and thinly sliced
- Olives, pitted and slivered
- Roasted red peppers, thinly sliced

COOKED MEATS (cut into ½-inch-wide pieces or shredded)
- Chicken
- Pork tenderloin
- Steak (flank or skirt)
- Cured meats
- Bacon or pancetta, cooked and crumbled or diced
- Prosciutto, thinly sliced

COOKED SEAFOOD
- Crabmeat, in pieces
- Shrimp, chopped
- Squid, sliced

AROMATICS, HERBS & SPICES
- Fresh herbs, chopped
- Garlic, chopped and sautéed
- Leeks, chopped and sautéed
- Onions or shallots, chopped and sautéed
- Red pepper flakes
- Scallions, chopped

choice cheeses

GOOD MELTING CHEESES
- Asiago (not aged)
- Blue
- Brie
- Colby
- Cheddar
- Fontina
- Gouda (not aged)
- Gruyère
- Manchego
- Monterey Jack
- Mozzarella
- Pecorino (not aged)
- Provolone
- Queso Oaxaca
- Teleme

FRESH CHEESES TO USE IN COMBINATION WITH MELTING CHEESES
- Goat cheese
- Feta
- Fromage blanc
- Ricotta

classic margherita pizza

YIELDS ONE 12-INCH PIZZA

- 1 **ball of Basic Pizza Dough (recipe p. 144), refrigerated for at least 8 hours**

  Olive oil for the work surface

  Unbleached bread flour or semolina for dusting

- 1 **cup No-Cook Pizza Sauce (recipe on facing page)**

- 12 **oz. sliced fresh mozzarella or 1 cup grated low-moisture mozzarella (or a combination)**

- 16 **to 24 large fresh basil leaves, thinly sliced (a chiffonade, see p. 22)**

The key to this pizza is to use only a small amount of sauce and cheese. Too much sauce will make the dough soggy, and too much cheese will make it greasy.

1. Take the dough out of the refrigerator, set it on a lightly oiled work surface, and divide into 4 equal pieces of about 7 oz. each. Roll each piece into a tight ball. Line a baking sheet with parchment and lightly oil it with olive oil or cooking spray. Set each ball at least an inch apart on the parchment. Lightly spray or brush the balls with olive oil and cover loosely with plastic wrap. Let the dough warm up and relax at room temperature for 1½ to 2 hours.

2. If you have a baking stone, put it on the middle rack of the oven. If not, set a rimmed baking sheet upside down on the middle rack to serve as a baking platform. Heat the oven to its highest setting. Fill a small bowl with bread flour or semolina and dust a 12-inch-square area of a clean work surface with a generous amount. Prepare a peel for transferring the pizzas to the oven by dusting the peel with bread flour or semolina. (Or use a rimless cookie sheet or the back of a rimmed baking sheet, also dusted with flour.)

3. With floured hands, transfer one of the dough balls to the floured work surface. Sprinkle the dough lightly with flour and gently press it with your fingertips into a round disk—you're trying to merely spread the dough, not squeeze all the gas from it. With floured hands, carefully lift the disk of dough and rest it on the back of your hands and knuckles. Using the tips of your thumbs, stretch the outer edge as you slowly rotate the dough until it is 10 to 12 inches in diameter (see the left photo on p. 145). The edge should be the only place where you exert any pressure. If necessary, let the dough hang off one of your hands so that gravity provides some of the stretch. Despite the pressure on the edge, it will remain thicker than the inner section of the dough, which should be nearly paper thin. Don't pull the dough forcefully into a circular shape or it will stretch from the center and possibly rip. If the dough begins to resist and keeps shrinking back into a smaller circle, lay it on the floured work surface and let it rest for about 2 minutes.

4. Lay the shaped dough on the floured peel and top it with sauce, leaving ½ inch of the outer rim sauce free. Layer on the mozzarella and sprinkle with the basil.

5. Carefully slide the pizza onto the baking stone using a jerking motion to get it to slide. (If it sticks to the peel, carefully lift the stuck section and toss a little flour under it.) Bake until the edge is puffy and brown with a slight char and the underside is brown and fairly crisp, 5 to 7 minutes (the hotter the oven, the faster and better it will cook). Rotate it after 3 minutes for even browning. Remove the pizza from the oven with either the peel or a long metal spatula and put it on a cutting board. Let it rest for 1 to 2 minutes before slicing and serving.

PER SERVING: 670 CALORIES | 28g PROTEIN | 94g CARB | 20g TOTAL FAT | 8g SAT FAT | 8g MONO FAT | 2g POLY FAT | 45mg CHOL | 1,400mg SODIUM | 4g FIBER

no-cook pizza sauce

YIELDS 3¼ CUPS

1 28-oz. can crushed or ground tomatoes

2 Tbs. red-wine vinegar or lemon juice

Kosher salt or table salt and freshly ground black pepper

OPTIONAL INGREDIENTS

1 tsp. dried (or 1 Tbs. finely chopped fresh) oregano, basil, marjoram, thyme, or parsley

3 to 5 cloves garlic, minced or pressed

This sauce can be refrigerated for a week or frozen for up to 6 months.

In a large bowl, whisk the tomatoes, vinegar or lemon juice, and any optional ingredients. Add just enough water to thin the sauce so that it's easy to spread. Season with salt and pepper.

PER SERVING: 20 CALORIES | 1g PROTEIN | 5g CARB | 0g TOTAL FAT | 0g SAT FAT | 0g MONO FAT | 0g POLY FAT | 0mg CHOL | 170mg SODIUM | 1g FIBER

continued on p. 144 ➤

continued from p. 143

basic pizza dough

YIELDS 4 INDIVIDUAL PIZZAS

- **1 lb. (3½ cups) unbleached bread flour; more as needed**
- **2 tsp. granulated sugar or honey**
- **1½ tsp. table salt (or 2½ tsp. kosher salt)**
- **1¼ tsp. instant yeast**
- **1½ Tbs. extra-virgin olive oil; more as needed**
- **Semolina flour (optional)**

It's best to mix the dough at least a day before you plan to bake. The dough keeps for up to 3 days in the refrigerator or for 3 months in the freezer.

Combine the flour, sugar or honey, salt, yeast, and olive oil in a large bowl or in the bowl of an electric stand mixer. Add 11 fl. oz. (1¼ cups plus 2 Tbs.) cool (60°F to 65°F) water. With a large spoon or the paddle attachment of the electric mixer, mix on low speed until the dough comes together in a coarse ball, 2 to 3 minutes by hand or 1 to 2 minutes in the mixer. Let the dough rest, uncovered, for 5 minutes.

KNEAD THE DOUGH

If using an electric mixer, switch to the dough hook. Knead the dough for 2 to 3 minutes, either by hand on a lightly floured work surface or with the mixer's dough hook on medium-low speed. As you knead, add more flour or water as needed to produce a ball of dough that is smooth, supple, and fairly tacky but not sticky. When poked with a clean finger, the dough should peel off like a Post-it® note, leaving only a slight residue. It may stick slightly to the bottom of the mixing bowl but not to the sides.

CHILL THE DOUGH

Lightly oil a bowl that's twice the size of the dough. Roll the dough in the bowl to coat it with the oil, cover the bowl tightly with plastic wrap, and refrigerate for at least 8 hours or up to 3 days. It will rise slowly in the refrigerator but will stop growing once completely chilled. If the plastic bulges, release the carbon dioxide buildup by lifting one edge of the plastic wrap and then reseal. Use the dough at this point, or follow the directions below to freeze for up to 3 months.

TO FREEZE THE DOUGH

After kneading the dough, divide it into 4 pieces. Freeze each ball in its own zip-top freezer bag. The balls will ferment somewhat in the freezer, and this counts as the rise. Before using, thaw completely in their bags overnight in the fridge or at room temperature for 2 to 3 hours. Then treat the dough exactly as you would regular overnighted dough, continuing with the directions for making pizza (see p. 142).

Pizza Variations

Smoked Cheese Pizza (Pizza Pugliese)
Make as you would a Classic Margherita Pizza but substitute smoked mozzarella or smoked Gouda for half of the fresh or low-moisture mozzarella. (Don't use the smoked cheese exclusively, as it will overpower the other toppings.)

Better Than Pepperoni Pizza
You can certainly use pepperoni, which is really just an Americanized version of a spicy Italian Calabrese-style salume. But there are a number of excellent Italian cured salami products, including the always popular Genoa salami and various types of garlic and cayenne versions. For these quick-cooking pizzas, use about the same amount of tomato sauce and cheese as in the Margherita but add about ¼ cup meat. Crisp the meat in a dry sauté pan or in the oven first, and then put it under the cheese to keep it from burning.

White Pizza (Pizza Bianca)
Instead of using tomato sauce, make a topping for each pizza by combining ⅓ cup whole-milk ricotta, ⅓ cup grated low-moisture mozzarella or provolone, 1 Tbs. olive oil, ¼ tsp. dried or 2 tsp. chopped fresh oregano, ¼ tsp. dried or 1 tsp. chopped fresh thyme, and salt and pepper to taste.

how to make pizza

Carefully stretch the pizza dough into a circle with your hands and knuckles. If the dough is resistant to stretch, let it rest for a few minutes.

Spread on the pizza sauce with a light hand to avoid a soggy crust.

fresh spinach and gruyère pizza

FOR THE DOUGH

1	tsp. active dry yeast
¼	tsp. granulated sugar
½	cup warm water (100°F to 120°F)
1½	cups all-purpose flour
½	tsp. kosher salt
	Olive oil for the mixing bowl

FOR THE PIZZA

¼	lb. sliced smoked bacon or pancetta (about five ½-inch-thick slices), cut into ½-inch pieces
	Olive oil for brushing the dough
¼	cup thinly sliced scallions (white and light green parts)
4	oz. coarsely grated Gruyère cheese

FOR THE SALAD TOPPING

2	tsp. red-wine vinegar
½	tsp. Dijon mustard
2	Tbs. olive oil
	Kosher salt and freshly ground black pepper
4	oz. loose baby spinach or ½ bunch tender young spinach, washed and spun dry
1	hard-cooked egg, chopped

If you want to omit the bacon in this recipe, increase the cheese just a bit.

MAKE THE DOUGH

In a bowl, dissolve the yeast and sugar in the water. Let rest until foamy, about 5 minutes. Add the flour and salt; mix until blended. Knead the dough on a very lightly floured surface for 10 minutes or until smooth and elastic. Put it in a lightly oiled bowl, cover loosely, and set in a warm place (70°F to 80°F) until doubled in bulk, about 2 hours.

MAKE THE PIZZA

Put a baking stone on the upper middle rack of the oven and heat the oven to 475°F. In a small skillet over medium heat, brown the bacon. Drain on paper towels and set aside. On a heavily floured surface, flatten the dough ball. Roll the dough into a 12-inch round, lifting and stretching from underneath with the back of your hands. (If the dough resists, let it rest for a few minutes and then resume rolling.) The edges should be about ¼ inch thick, and the center a bit thinner. Transfer the dough to a floured pizza paddle or the floured back of a baking sheet. Brush the dough with the oil and sprinkle the scallions evenly to within ½ inch of the edge. Sprinkle on the cheese and bacon. Transfer the pizza onto the baking stone in the oven with a quick jerk of the paddle. Check the pizza after 2 or 3 minutes and deflate any giant bubbles.

MAKE THE TOPPING

While the pizza bakes, whisk the vinegar, mustard, and oil; season with salt and pepper. When the edges of the crust are lightly browned and the cheese is bubbling, 10 to 12 minutes, transfer the pizza to a cutting board. Toss the spinach with the vinaigrette and pile it on the pizza. Sprinkle with the chopped egg, slice with a chef's knife, and serve immediately.

PER SERVING: 430 CALORIES, 18g PROTEIN | 38g CARB | 23g TOTAL FAT | 8g SAT FAT | 11g MONO FAT | 2g POLY FAT | 90mg CHOL | 830mg SODIUM | 2g FIBER

how to prep spinach

With one quick pass of the knife, bunched spinach is easy to trim.

Unless the leaves are very young, spinach should be stemmed. Be sure to remove the especially tough stems of savoyed spinach.

Give spinach a good dunk. Particularly gritty leaves may need a couple of changes of water to be thoroughly cleaned.

rustic rosemary tarts

3 oz. Bûcheron goat cheese
   (or fresh goat cheese)

3 Tbs. heavy cream

   All-purpose flour, for dusting

1 sheet frozen puff pastry
   (about 8 oz.), thawed
   according to package
   directions

1 lemon

3 Tbs. fresh rosemary leaves

   Freshly ground black pepper

The whole rosemary leaves crisp up as this rich tart bakes.

1. Position a rack in the center of the oven and heat the oven to 450°F.

2. Thinly slice the cheese and then crumble and tear it into a small bowl. If the cheese has a rind, make sure it's torn into small pieces. Add the cream and mash together with a fork until combined.

3. Lightly dust a work surface with flour and gently unfold the pastry sheet. Roll out the pastry, eliminating the creases, to a 12 x 17-inch rectangle. Use a pizza cutter or a sharp knife to cut the pastry in half lengthwise and then cut a ¾-inch strip off all 4 edges of each piece of pastry. Transfer the two large pieces of pastry to a 13 x 18-inch rimmed baking sheet. Dip a pastry brush in water and brush a ¾-inch border around each large piece of pastry. Stack the trimmed strips of pastry onto the damp dough, creating a border all the way around.

4. Dollop and spread the cheese mixture inside the borders of each pastry. Evenly grate the zest of the lemon over the cheese. Scatter the rosemary leaves and grind a little pepper evenly over the top. Bake the tarts until puffed and deep golden brown on the top and golden on the bottom, about 17 minutes, rotating the pan halfway through baking. Cut each tart into 3 or 4 pieces and serve hot.

PER SERVING: 220 CALORIES | 4g PROTEIN | 15g CARB | 16g TOTAL FAT | 4.5g SAT FAT | 3.5g MONO FAT | 7g POLY FAT | 15mg CHOL | 130mg SODIUM | 1g FIBER

stuffed & skewered

lamb skewers with
green olive and mint sauce

lamb skewers with green olive and mint sauce

YIELDS 4 SKEWERS

¾ lb. boneless lamb shoulder chops or lamb leg steaks, trimmed of extra fat and cut into 1-inch cubes

3 Tbs. extra-virgin olive oil

1 tsp. minced garlic

1 tsp. ground cumin

Pinch of crushed red pepper flakes

Kosher salt

2 tsp. red-wine vinegar

1 tsp. honey

2 Tbs. chopped pitted green olives

2 Tbs. chopped fresh mint leaves

These meaty skewers cook quickly and are a hearty addition to any appetizer platter.

1. In a medium bowl, combine the lamb with 1 Tbs. of the olive oil, ½ tsp. of the garlic, ½ tsp. of the cumin, the red pepper flakes, and ½ tsp. salt. Toss to coat.

2. Prepare a hot grill fire or heat the broiler on high with the top oven rack set so the broiler pan will be 2 to 3 inches away from the element.

3. In a small bowl, combine the vinegar, honey, olives, and the remaining garlic, cumin, and olive oil. Stir in the mint.

4. Thread the lamb onto 4 small skewers. (If using wooden skewers, soak them in water for 20 minutes before using so they don't burn.) Broil or grill the lamb, flipping once, until browned and sizzling, 3 to 4 minutes per side. Transfer the skewers to plates, spoon over the sauce, and serve immediately.

PER SERVING: 470 CALORIES | 35g PROTEIN | 4g CARB | 35g TOTAL FAT | 9g SAT FAT | 22g MONO FAT | 3g POLY FAT | 120mg CHOL | 800mg SODIUM | 0g FIBER

spicy grilled pork and grape kebabs

SERVES 4

1½ tsp. curry powder

¼ tsp. ground cumin

¼ tsp. ground paprika

¼ tsp. ground coriander

⅛ tsp. ground cinnamon

2 Tbs. olive oil

3 Tbs. orange juice

1 clove garlic, finely chopped

1 lb. pork tenderloin, trimmed and cut into 1-inch cubes

¼ lb. large, firm, seedless grapes, such as the Flame variety

1 to 2 Tbs. coarsely chopped fresh flat-leaf parsley

Kosher salt

This recipe is based on traditional tapas from Spain; the sweet grape is an unexpected but lovely counter to the spicy meat. The spice rub that's used in this recipe can also be used to flavor grilled vegetables and other meats, especially chicken, which means you may want to make more than the recipe calls for.

1. Combine the curry powder, cumin, paprika, coriander, and cinnamon; store the spice rub in an airtight container until ready to use.

2. In a small bowl, mix the olive oil, orange juice, and garlic.

3. Thread the pork onto skewers alternately with the grapes. Sprinkle the spice rub all over the kebabs and then pour the marinade over all. Marinate, refrigerated, for at least an hour and up to a day, turning occasionally. Grill the kebabs over a hot fire until the pork is cooked through but still moist, 8 to 10 minutes. Stack the kebabs on a serving platter; sprinkle with the parsley, and season with a little salt.

PER SERVING: 240 CALORIES | 24g PROTEIN | 6g CARB | 13g TOTAL FAT | 3g SAT FAT | 8g MONO FAT | 1g POLY FAT | 75mg CHOL | 200mg SODIUM | 1g FIBER

marinated feta and olive skewers

YIELDS 24 SKEWERS

- **2 tsp.** fennel seeds
- **2 tsp.** finely grated orange zest
- **3 Tbs.** fresh orange juice
- **1 tsp.** cracked black peppercorns
- **4 oz.** feta, cut into twenty-four ½-inch cubes
- **24** 6-inch skewers
- **24** fresh mint leaves
- **¼** large English cucumber (seeded, if desired), cut into ½-inch chunks
- **12** pitted green olives, cut in half

Each skewer has it all: salty cheese and olives balanced with the tang of orange and fennel seed, a kick from cracked pepper, and a cooling effect from cucumber and mint.

1. In a medium bowl, combine the fennel seeds, orange zest and juice, and pepper. Gently stir in the feta and marinate for 1 hour at room temperature or up to 3 hours in the refrigerator.

2. To assemble the skewers, push a mint leaf about ¾ inch up the skewer, then add a chunk of cucumber, and an olive half. Gently place a cube of the marinated feta on the end.

PER SERVING: 15 CALORIES | 1g PROTEIN | 1g CARB | 1g TOTAL FAT | 0.5g SAT FAT | 0g MONO FAT | 0g POLY FAT | 5mg CHOL | 75mg SODIUM | 0g FIBER

Make Ahead

These skewers can be made several hours ahead and stored in the refrigerator until ready to serve. Allow to come to room temperature before serving.

hoisin-glazed
flank steak spirals

SERVES 8 TO 10

- **1 lb. flank steak**
- **Kosher salt**
- **½ cup hoisin sauce**
- **2 tsp. Asian chile sauce (like Thai Sriracha) or Tabasco sauce**
- **2 medium carrots, shredded and squeezed dry in a paper towel**
- **1 red bell pepper, cored, seeded, and cut into thin, 2-inch-long strips**
- **1 bunch scallions (dark green parts only), halved lengthwise if thick and cut into 2-inch lengths**

Pass these colorful little spirals as an hors d'oeuvre, or serve them over greens lightly coated in a sesame-ginger dressing as a first course salad.

1. Position a rack about 6 inches away from the broiler element and heat the broiler to high.

2. Cut the flank steak crosswise (against the grain) at a very sharp angle (about 30 degrees) to form thin slices of beef between ⅛ and ¼ inch thick and about 2½ inches wide; you should have about 12 long slices of beef. Season the beef with ½ tsp. salt. Mix the hoisin sauce with the chile sauce and then brush on both sides of the beef (you may not need all the sauce). Sprinkle the carrots, red bell pepper, and scallions with ¼ tsp. salt. Arrange the scallions and peppers in an alternating pattern down the length of each strip of beef. Sprinkle the carrots over the scallions and peppers. Roll the pieces of beef lengthwise into tight spirals and set them, seam side down, on a heavy baking sheet lined with aluminum foil. Brush the tops with some of the remaining hoisin sauce.

3. Broil the beef until it starts to brown (but doesn't burn) and is firm to the touch, 4 to 6 minutes. Turn off the broiler but let the beef sit in the oven for another 3 minutes so the inside cooks through but is still slightly pink; you can check by slicing into one of the thicker rolls. To serve, insert 2 or 3 toothpicks evenly down the length of each roll. Slice between the toothpicks to get bite-size pieces.

PER SERVING: 120 CALORIES | 9g PROTEIN | 9g CARB | 5g TOTAL FAT | 2g SAT FAT | 2g MONO FAT | 0g POLY FAT | 20mg CHOL | 440mg SODIUM | 1g FIBER

scallop and mushroom rosemary kebabs

YIELDS 8 SMALL OR 4 LARGER
APPETIZERS

- **8** 7-inch fresh rosemary sprigs
- **8** large "dry" sea scallops (about 16 oz.), side muscle removed
- **8** large cremini mushrooms (about 8 oz.), stemmed and cleaned
- Kosher salt and freshly ground black pepper
- **1** cup fresh breadcrumbs
- **3** Tbs. extra-virgin olive oil
- **½** small clove garlic, peeled
- **½** cup crème fraîche
- **2** tsp. Dijon mustard
- **2** tsp. fresh lemon juice
- **½** tsp. finely grated lemon zest

Make Ahead

The skewers can be threaded, seasoned, and refrigerated for up to 2 hours before broiling.

Firm, woody rosemary sprigs make the best skewers.

1. Strip the leaves from the bottom 4 inches of each rosemary sprig—the sprigs will be your skewers. Finely chop 2½ tsp. of the rosemary leaves and set aside (save the remaining leaves for another use).

2. Use a sharp wooden or metal skewer to poke holes through the sides of the scallops and the mushrooms. Carefully push the rosemary skewers through the holes, using 1 scallop and 1 mushroom per skewer. Don't worry if the mushrooms crack a little; they'll stay on the skewer. Season all over with ¼ tsp. salt and a few grinds of pepper. Put the kebabs on a baking sheet, mushroom caps stem side down. Cover the leafy ends of the sprigs with foil to prevent charring.

3. Mix the breadcrumbs with 1 Tbs. of the olive oil, 1½ tsp. of the chopped rosemary, ½ tsp. salt, and a pinch of pepper.

4. Chop the half garlic clove, sprinkle it with ¼ tsp. salt, and mash it to a paste with the side of a chef's knife. In a small bowl, whisk the garlic paste, crème fraîche, mustard, lemon juice, lemon zest, and the remaining 1 tsp. chopped rosemary. Season to taste with salt and pepper.

5. Position a rack 4 inches from the broiler and heat the broiler on high. Brush the mushroom caps (they should still be stem side down) and scallops with the remaining 2 Tbs. olive oil. Broil until beginning to brown and the scallops are almost cooked through, 3 to 5 minutes. Remove the pan from the oven and carefully flip the skewers. Fill the mushroom caps with 1 tsp. of the breadcrumbs. Spoon 1 Tbs. of the crème fraîche mixture per skewer into the mushrooms and over the scallops—it's fine if some slides off the scallops. Evenly mound the remaining breadcrumbs onto the mushrooms and scallops and pat gently to adhere. Broil until the breadcrumbs are nicely browned, another 1 to 2 minutes. Remove the foil and transfer to serving plates with a spatula.

PER SERVING: 170 CALORIES | 11g PROTEIN | 6g CARB | 11g TOTAL FAT | 4.5g SAT FAT | 5g MONO FAT | 1g POLY FAT | 30mg CHOL | 310mg SODIUM | 0g FIBER

tiny twice-baked potatoes

YIELDS 24 PIECES

- 24 baby Yukon Gold or red potatoes, each about 2 inches across (2 to 2¼ lb.)
- 2 Tbs. olive oil
- 2 tsp. chopped fresh thyme

  Kosher salt and freshly ground black pepper
- 3 oz. bacon (about 3 thick slices), cooked until crispy and crumbled
- 6 Tbs. thinly sliced fresh chives
- ½ cup crème fraîche or sour cream
- ½ cup coarsely grated Parmigiano-Reggiano

Make Ahead

You can stuff the potatoes up to 2 days ahead; refrigerate wrapped in plastic. Bring to room temperature before the second baking.

The round shape of Yukon Golds makes those potatoes easy to hollow out but you can also twice-bake little fingerling potatoes, and they'll look just like miniature baked potatoes.

1. Heat the oven to 425°F. Put the potatoes on a large baking sheet and toss with the olive oil. Sprinkle with 1 tsp. of the thyme, 1 tsp. salt, and ½ tsp. pepper and toss again. Bake the potatoes until they feel perfectly tender when pierced with a skewer, 20 to 25 minutes. Remove from the oven and let rest until cool enough to handle, about 10 minutes. If not working ahead, increase the oven temperature to 450°F.

2. Carefully hollow out each potato: Begin by slicing off the top; use a small spoon or a melon baller to scoop out most of the flesh inside, transferring it to a large bowl. Discard the tops. Mash the potato flesh with a masher or a fork, then combine it with the bacon, ¼ cup of the chives, the crème fraîche, the remaining 1 tsp. thyme, ½ tsp. salt, and ¼ tsp. pepper. Season to taste with more salt and pepper.

3. Using a small spoon and your fingers, fill the hollowed potatoes with this mixture; it should mound a bit. Sprinkle on the Parmigiano.

4. Return the potatoes to the 450°F oven and bake until the filling heats through, 8 to 10 minutes. Sprinkle with the remaining chives and serve warm.

PER SERVING: 70 CALORIES | 2g PROTEIN | 7g CARB | 3.5g TOTAL FAT | 1.5g SAT FAT | 1.5 MONO FAT | 0g POLY FAT | 5mg CHOL | 105mg SODIUM | 1g FIBER

ham, gruyère, and honey-mustard palmiers

YIELDS ABOUT 44 PALMIERS

- **1** sheet (about 9 oz.) frozen puff pastry, thawed
- **2** Tbs. honey Dijon mustard
- **3** oz. (about 1 cup) shredded Gruyère
- **¼** cup (about 1 oz.) finely grated Parmigiano-Reggiano
- **4** oz. very thinly sliced baked ham

When thawing frozen puff pastry, you'll need 30 to 45 minutes depending on the temperature of your kitchen (the sheet should be very pliable, like a thick sheet of modeling clay). You can also thaw the pastry in the refrigerator overnight, and it will be pliable more quickly.

1. Heat the oven to 425°F. On a lightly floured work surface, roll the pastry to a 10 x 14-inch rectangle. Using the back of a spoon, spread the pastry evenly with the mustard. Sprinkle on the Gruyère and Parmigiano in an even layer.

2. Arrange the ham in a single, even layer, tearing or cutting pieces to fit. Lay a piece of parchment or waxed paper on top and gently roll and press with the rolling pin to compress the layers. Gently peel off the paper without disturbing the ham.

3. Cut the rectangle in half widthwise to make two 10 x 7-inch bands. Gently roll 1 long edge of a band into the center and then roll the opposite edge in so the 2 rolls meet in the middle and resemble a double scroll. Press lightly to stick the 2 rolls together. Repeat with the second band. (The rolls can be assembled to this point and held in the refrigerator for several hours.)

4. With a very sharp knife, slice each band into about 22 pieces, just under ½ inch each. Arrange the palmiers on 2 parchment-lined or nonstick baking sheets and bake until deep golden brown and no longer doughy in the center (break one open to be sure), 10 to 12 minutes. Be careful not to let the bottoms burn. Let cool on a rack and serve just slightly warm or within an hour if possible.

PER SERVING: 45 CALORIES | 2g PROTEIN | 3g CARB | 3g TOTAL FAT | 0.5g SAT FAT | 0.5g MONO FAT | 1.5g POLY FAT | 5mg CHOL | 55mg SODIUM | 0g FIBER

mushroom and sun-dried tomato pockets

ham, gruyère, and honey-mustard palmiers

mushroom and sun-dried tomato pockets

YIELDS 24 POCKETS

1 small shallot or ¼ medium onion (about 1 oz. total)

10 oz. cremini or white mushrooms, rinsed and dried; stems trimmed off

1 Tbs. vegetable oil

Kosher salt

Hot sauce (like Tabasco)

1 Tbs. finely chopped oil-packed sun-dried tomatoes, drained

¼ cup (about 1 oz.) finely grated Parmigiano-Reggiano

1 sheet (about 9 oz.) frozen puff pastry, thawed

1 egg, beaten

These pockets make a wonderful vegetarian addition to any party spread.

1. Heat the oven to 425°F. In a food processor, pulse the shallot or onion until finely chopped. Add half of the mushrooms and pulse until very finely chopped (don't over process or the mushrooms will become a purée). Empty the bowl, pulse the remaining mushrooms, and combine with the other mushrooms. (You can also do this by chopping everything finely with a knife.)

2. Heat the oil in a large skillet over medium high, add the mushroom mixture and 1 tsp. salt, and sauté until all of the mushrooms' liquid has been released and evaporated completely, 8 to 10 minutes; the mixture should start to brown and stick around the edges. Season with a few shakes of the hot sauce. Remove from the heat and stir in the sun-dried tomatoes and Parmigiano. Taste and adjust the seasonings.

3. Spread the filling on a plate and chill in the freezer while you prepare the pastry.

4. On a lightly floured work surface, roll the pastry sheet to a 10 x 15-inch rectangle. Prick the dough all over and then cut it into 4 long strips, each 2½ inches wide. Cut each of these strips into 6 equal pieces, to yield a total of twenty-four 2½-inch squares.

5. Put a heaping teaspoon of the filling in the center of each square. Dab each corner with a little of the beaten egg and then bring all 4 corners up to the center and pinch well to fuse them together. You should have little square pouches, with some of the mushroom filling showing. If there's any egg left, brush it on the exteriors of the pockets.

6. Arrange the pockets on a parchment-lined or nonstick baking sheet and bake until they're puffed and deep golden on the sides and bottom and the pastry is no longer doughy, 15 to 16 minutes. Let them cool on a rack for a few minutes and serve warm.

PER SERVING: 70 CALORIES | 1g PROTEIN | 5g CARB | 5g TOTAL FAT | 1g SAT FAT | 1.5g MONO FAT | 2.5g POLY FAT | 10mg CHOL | 80mg SODIUM | 0g FIBER

grilled figs with goat cheese and mint

SERVES 4

½ cup (3½ to 4 oz.) soft fresh goat cheese

2 Tbs. fresh breadcrumbs

About 6 mint leaves, stacked, rolled into a cylinder, and sliced into thin strips

1 Tbs. finely chopped flat-leaf parsley

Kosher salt and freshly ground black pepper

12 fresh Mission figs

12 very thin slices pancetta

1 Tbs. honey

½ tsp. very finely chopped fresh thyme

Very thinly sliced pancetta crisps nicely on the grill; its salty, meaty—but not smoky—flavor goes really well with the sweetness of the fig and the creaminess of the cheese. Serve with some good crusty bread.

1. In a small bowl, combine the goat cheese, breadcrumbs, mint, and parsley; season with salt and pepper. Cut the figs nearly in half lengthwise, keeping them attached at the broad end. Hollow the center slightly with your thumb. Stuff each fig with about 1 tsp. of the goat cheese mixture and squeeze very gently to close.

2. Wrap a slice of pancetta around each fig, overlapping with each revolution. Don't wrap the pancetta too tightly or you'll force the filling out or cause the figs to split. Cover the figs with plastic wrap and refrigerate (for up to a day) until ready to grill.

3. Grill the figs over a moderately hot fire to crisp the pancetta and to warm the figs and cheese, 8 to 10 minutes. Transfer the figs to a serving dish. Combine the honey and thyme, and drizzle over the figs.

PER SERVING: 260 CALORIES | 13g PROTEIN | 35g CARB | 9g TOTAL FAT | 5g SAT FAT | 3g MONO FAT | 1g POLY FAT | 30mg CHOL | 700mg SODIUM | 5g FIBER

mini savory clafoutis

YIELDS 48

Butter or oil for the muffin tins

¼ **cup cornstarch**

1¼ **cups whole milk**

2 **large eggs**

2 **large egg yolks**

1 **cup heavy cream**

½ **tsp. kosher salt**

Pinch cayenne

Grated or crumbled cheese (about ½ cup total); see the list below for ideas

Tidbit of choice; see the list below for ideas

1 **to 2 Tbs. finely chopped fresh herb, such as basil, chives, dill, or flat-leaf parsley**

The batter for these tiny, crust-less quiches comes together so quickly that you can whisk it by hand at the last moment, though it will also keep, covered and refrigerated, for a day. The cornstarch and pepper settle to the bottom after 10 minutes, so if you do work ahead, you'll need to rewhisk. The clafoutis can also be baked ahead and reheated in a 400°F oven for 5 minutes.

1. Position a rack in the top third of the oven and heat the oven to 450°F. Butter or oil mini muffin tins.

2. Put the cornstarch in a medium bowl. Whisking steadily, slowly pour in ½ cup of the milk, mixing until quite smooth. Whisk in the whole eggs and egg yolks, mixing again until smooth, and then gradually whisk in the rest of the milk, the cream, salt, and cayenne.

3. Put ½ tsp. of the grated or crumbled cheese and one of the tidbits from the list below plus a pinch of fresh herb into each muffin cup. Add 2 Tbs. of the batter and bake until the clafoutis puff and start to turn golden, 15 to 18 minutes. Let cool in the pan on a rack for 20 minutes and then carefully run a paring knife or offset spatula around the rim of each muffin cup. Carefully lift each clafoutis out of its cup and serve.

PER SERVING: 30 CALORIES | 1g PROTEIN | 1g CARB | 2.5g TOTAL FAT | 1.5g SAT FAT | 1g MONO FAT | 0g POLY FAT | 25mg CHOL | 20mg SODIUM | 0g FIBER

tiny but tasty fillings

When making such teeny tarts, the key is to add just enough filling so as not to overwhelm the scant amount of batter. Start with ½ tsp. cheese per muffin cup and then add one or two other tidbits. Use the ideas listed here as starting points to create your own flavorful fillings.

• Equal amounts kosher salt and brown sugar, with half as much pimentón (smoked paprika)

GOOD CHEESE CHOICES
• Grated Gruyère or Parmigiano-Reggiano
• Diced or grated Fontina or mozzarella
• Crumbled goat cheese
• Grated smoked Gouda or pecorino

TIDBITS TO TRY (PER MUFFIN CUP)
• Half an olive
• 3 tiny cooked cocktail shrimp
• ½ tsp. crisp crumbled bacon or sausage
• ½ tsp. chopped sautéed mushrooms
• ½ tsp. chopped sun-dried tomatoes
• ½ tsp. diced, sautéed red bell pepper

beef picadillo empanadas

YIELDS ABOUT EIGHTEEN
4-INCH EMPANADAS

The pastry for this empanada, seasoned with paprika, is a bold counterpoint to the filling.

FOR THE FILLING

- ½ **lb. lean ground chuck**
- ⅓ **cup diced white onion**
- ¼ **cup diced red bell pepper**
- ¼ **cup diced green bell pepper**
- 2 **cloves garlic, minced**
- ⅓ **cup peeled, seeded, and diced tomato**
- 1 **Tbs. drained capers**
- 2 **Tbs. green olives, minced**
- 1 **Tbs. tomato paste**
- ¼ **cup dry red wine**
- **Kosher salt and freshly ground black pepper**

FOR THE DOUGH

- 13½ **oz. (3 cups) all-purpose flour**
- 2 **tsp. table salt**
- 1½ **tsp. paprika**
- 1 **tsp. freshly ground black pepper**
- 1 **tsp. poppy seeds (optional)**
- ½ **cup plus 2 Tbs. cold vegetable shortening**
- ½ **cup ice water**
- 2 **large eggs, beaten with 2 Tbs. water, for an egg wash**

1. Make the filling: In a frying pan, cook the beef over medium heat until lightly browned, about 5 minutes. Remove from the pan with a slotted spoon and set aside. Cook the onion, peppers, and garlic in the same pan in the fat left behind until the onion is tender, about 5 minutes. Return the meat to the pan; stir in the tomato, capers, and olives. Meanwhile, stir the tomato paste into the wine until well combined. Add this to the pan and cook until the mixture has thickened slightly, about 10 minutes. Season to taste and then set the mixture aside to cool.

2. Make the dough: In a large bowl, sift together the flour, salt, and paprika. Mix in the pepper and the poppy seeds, if using. With a pastry blender or two knives, cut the shortening into the dry ingredients until the mixture resembles coarse crumbs. Add the water all at once and blend until a ball has formed. Turn the dough out onto a sheet of plastic wrap and knead gently for a few seconds. Wrap well and chill for at least 5 minutes.

3. On a lightly floured surface, roll half the chilled dough into a round that's ⅛ inch thick. (Keep the remaining dough refrigerated until ready to use.) Cut out 4-inch rounds. Spoon about 1 Tbs. of the filling slightly off-center of each round. Moisten the edges of the dough with the egg wash, fold each round in half, and seal the edges with the tines of a fork. Repeat with the remaining dough. (Alternatively, cut a smaller circle and use less filling for smaller bites, or cut two pieces of dough shaped like those left and seal them together.) Refrigerate the empanadas on greased or parchment-lined baking sheets for 30 minutes. (At this point, you can freeze the empanadas; when they're rock-hard, transfer them to a freezer bag or container. Let thaw for 1 hour before baking.)

4. Heat the oven to 375°F. Brush the empanadas with the egg wash and bake until well browned, about 30 minutes.

PER SERVING: 180 CALORIES | 6g PROTEIN | 17g CARB | 9g TOTAL FAT | 2g SAT FAT | 4g MONO FAT | 2g POLY FAT | 35mg CHOL | 350mg SODIUM | 1g FIBER

chinese pork and cabbage dumplings

YIELDS 4 DOZEN 3-INCH DUMPLINGS

You can vary this filling by substituting ground beef, chicken, turkey, or veal for the pork, and spinach, scallions, or bok choy for the cabbage. If the dough feels stiff, add a little more water 1 Tbs. at a time, but don't exceed ¾ cup total.

FOR THE DUMPLING DOUGH

  2 cups all-purpose flour

  ½ cup cold water

FOR THE PORK AND CABBAGE FILLING

  1 lb. lean ground pork

  2 Tbs. cold water

  1 Tbs. dry sherry

  1 Tbs. soy sauce

  1 Tbs. Asian sesame oil

  1 tsp. kosher salt

  1 tsp. finely chopped fresh ginger

  ½ lb. Chinese cabbage, trimmed and finely chopped (about 2 cups)

FOR COOKING AND SERVING

  2 Tbs. cooking oil (if frying the dumplings)

  1 cup water or lower-salt chicken broth (if frying the dumplings)

     Wilted cabbage leaves (if steaming the dumplings; optional)

     Ginger Scallion Dipping Sauce (recipe p. 168)

MAKE THE DUMPLING DOUGH

1. Sift the flour into a bowl. Gradually add the water, mixing with a wooden spoon until a shaggy dough forms. Turn the dough onto a lightly floured surface; knead until smooth and springy, about 5 minutes. Put the dough in a clean bowl, cover it with a towel, and let it rest at room temperature for 20 minutes.

2. Put the rested dough on a lightly floured surface and knead it for 2 minutes. Divide the dough and shape each half into a 12-inch-long cylinder that's about 1 inch in diameter. With a serrated knife, cut each cylinder crosswise into 24 rounds. Lay the rounds on a lightly floured surface and flatten with the palm of your hand to about ¼ inch thick. Sprinkle flour lightly on the pieces to prevent sticking. With a rolling pin, roll each slice into a 3-inch round about ⅛-inch thick. Pinch the edges of the rounds to make them thinner than the middle. Arrange the rounds in a single layer on a lightly floured tray or baking sheet and cover with a towel.

MAKE THE PORK AND CABBAGE FILLING

In a large bowl, combine the ground pork with the water, sherry, soy sauce, sesame oil, salt, and ginger. Add the cabbage and mix until thoroughly blended.

FILL THE DUMPLINGS

Fill each wrapper with about 2 tsp. of the filling. Fold the wrapper in half and pinch the edge in the middle of the rounded part of the half-moon. Make two small pleats on either side of the pinched middle (only on the side of the dumpling nearest you) by gathering the dough and folding it over onto itself. Point the pleats toward the middle of the dumpling. Seal the pleated and unpleated sides by pinching along the top. Cook them according to the directions that follow. Serve with the Ginger Scallion Dipping Sauce.

FOR FRIED DUMPLINGS

In a 12-inch nonstick pan, heat 1 Tbs. of the cooking oil over medium-low heat. Arrange the dumplings in the pan, pleated side up, starting from the center and radiating out, with the sides of the dumplings just touching. Cook the dumplings until the bottoms are lightly browned, about 10 minutes. Add 1 cup of water or chicken broth; cover the pan and cook over medium heat until all the liquid has evaporated, about 10 minutes. Uncover and drizzle 1 Tbs. oil around the inside edge of the pan. Fry the dumplings until the bottoms are golden brown, about 3 minutes. Loosen the dumplings around the edges with

continued on p. 168 ➤

continued from p. 166

a spatula, and then set a large serving plate over the pan. Wearing mitts to protect your hands, quickly invert the pan. Serve the dumplings fried side up.

FOR STEAMED DUMPLINGS
Arrange the dumplings, pleated side up and not touching, on a bamboo steamer lined with cheesecloth or wilted cabbage leaves. Fill a wok or a large pot with 2 inches of water and bring the water to a boil. Cover the steamer and set it on the wok. Steam over high heat for 15 minutes. Serve the dumplings in the bamboo steamer set on a large plate to catch any water that might drip. If you don't have a bamboo steamer, you can steam the dumplings on a greased, heatproof plate. Set the plate over a steam rack in the wok or a large pot. Be sure there's enough space around the edge of the plate to allow the steam to rise and circulate freely.

PER SERVING: 50 CALORIES | 2g PROTEIN | 4g CARB | 2.5g TOTAL FAT | 0.5g SAT FAT | 1g MONO FAT | 0.5g POLY FAT | 5mg CHOL | 75mg SODIUM | 0g FIBER

ginger scallion dipping sauce

YIELDS ABOUT 1½ CUPS

- **4 Tbs. Asian sesame oil**
- **4 tsp. minced fresh ginger**
- **4 Tbs. minced scallions**
- **½ cup homemade or lower-salt chicken broth**
- **6 Tbs. soy sauce**
- **4 tsp. dark Chinese rice vinegar, light rice vinegar, or cider vinegar**
- **2 tsp. granulated sugar**

This is a perfect salty, spicy sauce for fried or steamed dumplings.

In a small saucepan, heat the oil over low heat. Add the ginger and scallions. Stir for a few seconds until fragrant. Add the broth, soy sauce, vinegar, and sugar and bring to a boil. Serve at room temperature.

PER 1 TSP.: 15 CALORIES | 0g PROTEIN | 1g CARB | 1g TOTAL FAT | 0gSAT FAT | 0.5g MONO FAT | 0.5G POLY FAT | 0mg CHOL | 130mg SODIUM | 0g FIBER

how to roll out the wrappers

Individual pieces of dough are rolled to make flat rounds. You could also roll the dough flat and stamp out rounds with a cookie cutter, but then you'd have to reroll the scraps of dough.

Thinner edges make a better fold. Pinch the edges of the circle with your fingers to make them thinner.

A savory filling is at the heart of a dumpling. About 2 tsp. of filling leaves room to press together the edges, which are first brushed with water.

spiced lamb pitas with fresh mango salsa

- 1½ tsp. ground cumin
- 1½ tsp. ground ginger
- ½ tsp. ground cinnamon
- 1½ lb. ground lamb
- 1 large red onion, cut into small dice

  Kosher salt and freshly ground black pepper
- ½ cup plus 2 Tbs. Major Grey-style mango chutney, any large chunks chopped
- 1 medium-size ripe mango, peeled, pitted, and cut into ¼-inch dice
- 3 Tbs. chopped fresh cilantro
- 2 tsp. fresh lime juice; more to taste

  Pita Chips (recipe p. 87)

The combination of the fragrant meat mixture and the bright salsa will have people grabbing these with two hands.

1. Heat the oven to 450°F. Mix the cumin, ginger, and cinnamon in a small bowl. Reserve ¼ tsp. of the spice mix in a medium bowl. In a large bowl, sprinkle the remaining spices over the lamb and mix with a fork to combine.

2. Heat a 12-inch skillet over medium-high heat. Add the lamb and all but ⅓ cup of the onion. Season with salt and pepper and cook, stirring and breaking up the meat with the side of a spoon, until the lamb is fully cooked, about 9 minutes. Spoon off the fat in the pan. Stir in ½ cup of the chutney and continue to cook for 1 minute. Remove from the heat and keep warm.

3. Meanwhile, add the remaining ⅓ cup onion and 2 Tbs. chutney, the mango, cilantro, lime juice, and a pinch of salt to the reserved spices to make a salsa; stir to combine. Taste and add more lime juice if it seems sweet (it should be somewhat tangy to offset the sweetness of the meat).

4. To serve, top the pita chips with some of the lamb mixture and a bit of the salsa.

PER SERVING: 76 CALORIES | 4.5g PROTEIN | 8g CARB | 3g TOTAL FAT | 1g SAT FAT | 1g MONO FAT | 0.5g POLY FAT | 14mg CHOL | 125mg SODIUM | 0.5g FIBER

dolmathes yialantzi
(grape leaves stuffed with rice and herbs)

YIELDS 50 TO 55;
SERVES 12 TO 15

- **1** 16-oz. jar brine-packed grape leaves
- **⅔** cup plus 2 Tbs. extra-virgin olive oil
- **2** large red onions, finely chopped (about 4 cups)
- **1** cup finely chopped scallions (white and some green parts)
- **2** cloves garlic, finely chopped
- **1** cup raw long-grain white rice

    Kosher salt and freshly ground black pepper

- **½** cup each: finely chopped fresh dill, finely chopped fresh flat-leaf parsley, and finely chopped fresh mint
- **⅔** cup pine nuts, toasted
- **2½** tsp. finely grated lemon zest

    Juice of 2 lemons (about 6 Tbs.)

- **2** cups full-fat plain yogurt, preferably Greek (if not Greek, drained to thicken; see tip below)

Look for grape leaves in the supermarket; they come brined in jars that hold 50 to 60 leaves.

1. Bring a large pot of water to a rolling boil. Drain and rinse the grape leaves. In three batches, submerge them in the water to soften, 2 to 3 minutes per batch. Transfer to a colander with a slotted spoon, rinse under cold water, and drain.

2. In a 12-inch heavy skillet with a lid, heat ⅓ cup of the olive oil over medium heat. Add the onion and scallions. Turn the heat to medium low and cook, stirring occasionally, until the onion is very soft and translucent, about 12 minutes. Add the garlic and stir for 1 minute. Add the rice and cook, stirring constantly, for 3 minutes. Add 1 tsp. salt, a few grinds of pepper, and 1 cup water. Increase the heat to medium, cover, and simmer until the water is absorbed, 5 to 7 minutes. Remove from the heat and let cool. Fold in the herbs, pine nuts, and lemon zest and season with a little more pepper.

3. Set aside any grape leaves that are too small or too irregular to roll. Arrange the remaining leaves, vein side up, in rows on a large surface. Snip off any stems.

4. Pour 2 Tbs. of the olive oil onto the bottom of a large saucepan. Lay four or five of the most irregular leaves, overlapping, over the oil, covering the bottom of the pan.

5. Arrange about 1 heaping Tbs. of the rice mixture (less if the leaves are very small) across the bottom center of a leaf on the work surface. Fold the left and right sides over the filling and roll up, gently but tightly, until you have a small log resembling an egg roll. Set it seam side down in the pan. Repeat with the remaining stuffing and leaves, snuggling the rolls close together. Start a new layer when the bottom is covered.

6. Drizzle the remaining ⅓ cup olive oil and the lemon juice over the grape leaves. Sprinkle on a few pinches of salt. Cut a piece of parchment to fit tightly over the surface of the leaves and set it on top. Put a heatproof plate that fits inside the pan on top of the parchment, to weigh down the leaves and keep them from opening while cooking. Slowly pour in enough water to just cover. Bring to a boil, lower to a simmer, and cover the pot. Simmer over low heat until the leaves are tender and the rice is thoroughly cooked, 45 to 60 minutes. (By the time the leaves and rice are cooked, most of the liquid will have been absorbed.) Remove the stuffed grape leaves from the pan with a slotted spoon, cover with damp paper towels and plastic wrap, and let them cool to room temperature. (If not serving right away, refrigerate for up to 3 days and bring to room temperature before serving.) Serve with the yogurt on the side.

PER SERVING: 70 CALORIES | 2g PROTEIN | 6g CARB | 4.5g TOTAL FAT | 1g SAT FAT | 2.5g MONO FAT | 1g POLY FAT | 0mg CHOL | 280mg SODIUM | 0g FIBER

> **Rich, thick Greek yogurt is available at many supermarkets (look for FAGE Total® brand). If you can't find it, drain twice the amount of regular full-fat yogurt in a colander lined with a double layer of cheesecloth until it's as thick as sour cream, 2 to 3 hours.**

pork shiu mai

YIELDS ABOUT 5 DOZEN SHIU MAI

- **1** lb. ground pork
- **1** cup thinly sliced napa cabbage, plus extra leaves for lining the steamer
- **½** cup chopped scallions (both white and green parts)
- **¼** cup chopped fresh cilantro
- **1½** Tbs. soy sauce
- **1** Tbs. finely chopped garlic
- **1** Tbs. rice vinegar
- **1** Tbs. cornstarch; more for dusting
- **2** tsp. finely chopped fresh ginger
- **1½** tsp. Asian sesame oil
- **1** tsp. granulated sugar
- **½** tsp. freshly ground black pepper
- **1** large egg white
- **55** to 60 shiu mai wrappers or wonton wrappers

  Soy Dipping Sauce (recipe below)

Shiu mai wrappers are available in Asian markets, or else use wonton wrappers, which can be found in most supermarkets.

1. In a large bowl, stir the pork, sliced cabbage, scallions, cilantro, soy sauce, garlic, rice vinegar, cornstarch, ginger, sesame oil, sugar, pepper, and egg white.

2. Sprinkle a rimmed baking sheet liberally with cornstarch. Set a small bowl of water on the work surface. If the wrappers are larger than 3 inches across in any direction, trim them with a cookie cutter to 3-inch rounds. Otherwise, leave as squares or rectangles.

3. Working with 1 wrapper at a time, and keeping the remaining wrappers covered with plastic wrap so they don't dry out, place 1 heaping tsp. of the pork filling in the center of the wrapper. Using a pastry brush or your fingers, dab a bit of water around the edge of the wrapper to moisten. Crimp the wrapper up and around the filling, squeezing slightly with your fingers to bring the wrapper together like a beggar's pouch. Place on the cornstarch-coated baking sheet, cover with plastic wrap, and repeat with the remaining wrappers and filling until you run out of one or the other.

4. Set up a steamer with 2 inches of water in the bottom. Line the basket with cabbage leaves to keep the shiu mai from sticking. Set over medium-high heat and cover. When steam begins to escape from the steamer, remove from the heat and carefully take off the lid. Arrange the shiu mai in the steamer so they don't touch (you'll have to cook in batches). Cover the steamer and return to medium high. Steam until the pork is cooked through (cut into one to check), 5 to 7 minutes.

PER SERVING: 40 CALORIES | 2g PROTEIN | 5g CARB | 1.5g TOTAL FAT | 0g SAT FAT | 0.5g MONO FAT | 0g POLY FAT | 5mg CHOL | 80mg SODIUM | 0g FIBER

soy dipping sauce

YIELDS ABOUT 1 CUP

- **⅓** cup soy sauce
- **⅓** cup rice vinegar
- **⅓** cup thinly sliced scallions (about 3, both white and green parts)
- **2** Tbs. mirin
- **1** Tbs. Asian sesame oil
- **1** tsp. finely chopped fresh ginger

If you're not making all of the shiu mai, you won't need the full recipe; you can make a half-batch or use leftover sauce in stir-fries. Mirin, a sweet Japanese rice wine, is available in Asian grocery stores and some supermarkets.

Combine the soy sauce, vinegar, scallions, mirin, sesame oil, and ginger in a small bowl. Use within a day of making.

PER SERVING: 15 CALORIES | 1g PROTEIN | 1g CARB | 1g TOTAL FAT | 0g SAT FAT | 0g MONO FAT | 0g POLY FAT | 0mg CHOL | 440mg SODIUM | 0g FIBER

goat cheese, lemon, and chive turnovers

YIELDS 9 TURNOVERS

4 oz. (½ cup) fresh goat cheese at room temperature

¼ cup thinly sliced fresh chives

¼ cup minced yellow onion

1 tsp. finely grated lemon zest

Kosher salt and freshly ground black pepper

Flour, for dusting

1 sheet frozen puff pastry, thawed overnight in the refrigerator

The lemon zest in the filling is a nice partner to the tangy cheese.

1. Position a rack in the center of the oven and heat the oven to 400°F.

2. In a medium bowl, mash the goat cheese with a fork. Add the chives, onion, lemon zest, ½ tsp. salt, and ¼ tsp. pepper. Stir until well combined.

3. On a lightly floured surface, unfold the pastry sheet and lightly dust with flour. Use a rolling pin to roll the sheet into a 12-inch square. Cut the dough into 9 squares. Put equal amounts of the filling (about 1 Tbs.) onto the center of each square. Moisten the edges of a square with a fingertip dipped in water. Fold the dough over to form a triangle, gently pressing to remove air pockets around the filling and pressing the edges of the dough together. Use the tines of a fork to crimp and seal the edges of the turnover. Repeat this process with the other dough squares.

4. Arrange the turnovers on a cookie sheet and bake until the turnovers are puffed and golden all over, 15 to 18 minutes. Let them cool on a rack for a few minutes and serve warm.

PER SERVING: 60 CALORIES | 3g PROTEIN | 2g CARB | 4g TOTAL FAT | 2g SAT FAT | 1.5g MONO FAT | 0g POLY FAT | 5mg CHOL | 130mg SODIUM | 0g FIBER

Make Ahead

Fill and shape the turnovers up to 2 hours ahead of baking. Cover tightly with plastic or brush with melted butter before refrigerating.

Tips for Working with Frozen Puff Pastry

• We test our puff pastry recipes with Pepperidge Farm Puff Pastry Sheets, which seem to be the most widely available brand. If yours is a different brand, check that the size is similar.

• The usual recommended thawing time of 20 minutes never seems like enough, so depending on the temperature of your kitchen, allow at least 30 to 45 minutes. The sheet should be very pliable, like a thick sheet of modeling clay.

• If any moisture beads up on the sheet during thawing, blot it with a paper towel before rolling.

• Use enough flour to prevent the dough from sticking to your work surface, but brush off the excess before you fill and shape the dough.

• Sometimes cracks appear along the seams where the dough was folded. Before rolling and shaping, press the dough together to mend any weak spots.

• In some recipes, you want the flakiness of puff pastry but not the puff. To reduce puff, it's important to prick the dough all over. Use a fork with sharp tines and cover the surface of the dough completely.

• Be sure to bake the dough thoroughly so it's crisp and flaky and no longer doughy in the center. Use the recipe cooking time as a guideline and then use your own judgment.

zucchini rolls with herbed goat cheese and red pepper

YIELDS 16 PIECES

2   small zucchini, washed, dried, and ends trimmed

Kosher salt

1   small bunch fresh chives

4   oz. goat cheese, softened to room temperature

1   tsp. chopped fresh thyme

Freshly ground black pepper

Pinch cayenne

3   jarred roasted Spanish piquillo red peppers or 1 jarred roasted red pepper, cut into ¼-inch strips

The zucchini is raw in this recipe, which may sound a little strange, but it's salted ahead of time and softens to a pleasant crunch (kind of like cabbage in a cole slaw).

1. Using a mandoline, slice the zucchini lengthwise to get 16 long, thin strips each about ⅛ inch thick.

2. Line a large, rimmed baking sheet with a couple layers of paper towel. Set the zucchini on the paper towel and sprinkle both sides with salt; you'll use about 1 tsp. for all the slices. Let sit for 15 minutes to soften and remove excess water.

3. Meanwhile, trim any coarse ends from the chives. Cut 2-inch-long pieces from the tip end of the chives and reserve. Thinly slice the rest of the chives (you should have about 1 Tbs. sliced chives).

4. Mash the goat cheese with the sliced chives, thyme, ½ tsp. black pepper, cayenne, and ½ tsp. salt. Season with more salt and pepper to taste (it should be assertive).

5. Pat the slices of zucchini dry on both sides with more paper towels. Set a slice of zucchini on a clean work surface and spread with about 1 tsp. of the goat cheese (you may want to use your fingers for this). At one end of the zucchini, lay one or two strips of the red pepper and a few of the 2-inch chive sticks, positioning them perpendicular to the roll so that their more attractive end will peek out when the zucchini slice gets rolled. Beginning with the chive end, roll the zucchini up and stand the roll upright on its edges on a platter. Refrigerate for up to 2 hours before serving.

PER SERVING: 25 CALORIES | 2g PROTEIN | 1g CARB | 1.5g TOTAL FAT | 1g SAT FAT | 0g MONO FAT | 0g POLY FAT | 5mg CHOL | 150mg SODIUM | 0g FIBER

bacon-wrapped
ginger soy scallops

YIELDS 2 DOZEN

- ¼ cup soy sauce
- 1 Tbs. dark brown sugar
- 1½ tsp. minced fresh ginger
- 6 very large "dry" sea scallops (8 to 10 oz. total)
- 1 8-oz. can sliced water chestnuts, drained
- 12 slices bacon, cut in half crosswise

A riff on a timeless classic, this version includes ginger to jazz up the flavor. "Dry" sea scallops brown better, have a nicer texture and flavor, and tend to taste fresher than treated or "wet" scallops.

1. Position a rack in the upper third of the oven. Line the bottom of a broiler pan with foil, replace the perforated top part of the pan, and put the whole pan on the oven rack. Heat the oven to 450°F.

2. In a medium bowl, combine the soy sauce, brown sugar, and ginger. If the muscle tabs from the sides of the scallops are still attached, peel them off and discard them. Cut each scallop into quarters. Marinate the scallop pieces in the soy mixture for 15 minutes. Reserve the marinade.

3. To assemble, stack 2 slices of water chestnut in the center of a piece of the bacon. Put a piece of scallop on top of the water chestnuts. Wrap each end of the bacon over the scallop and secure with a toothpick. Repeat with the remaining bacon, water chestnuts, and scallops (you may not use all of the water chestnuts).

4. Remove the broiler pan from the oven and quickly arrange the bacon-wrapped scallops on the hot pan so that an exposed side of each scallop faces up. Drizzle the scallops with the reserved marinade. Bake, turning the scallops over once after 10 minutes, until the bacon is browned around the edges and the scallops are cooked through, about 15 minutes total.

PER SERVING: 80 CALORIES | 2g PROTEIN | 2g CARB | 7g TOTAL FAT | 2g SAT FAT | 3g MONO FAT | 1g POLY FAT | 10mg CHOL | 310mg SODIUM | 0g FIBER

prosciutto-wrapped shrimp with rosemary oil

YIELDS 12 PIECES

- ¼ cup extra-virgin olive oil
- 2 sprigs fresh rosemary
- 2 cloves garlic, thinly sliced
- ⅛ tsp. crushed red pepper flakes
- 12 jumbo shrimp (16 to 20 per lb.; about ¾ lb.), peeled, deveined, rinsed and patted dry

  Freshly ground black pepper
- 4 to 6 very thin slices prosciutto (about ¼ lb.)

Larger shrimp cook evenly and have a wonderful, meaty texture. If you use smaller shrimp, start checking them for doneness a couple of minutes earlier. This recipe is easily multiplied.

1. Position a rack in the center of the oven; heat the oven to 450°F.

2. Heat the olive oil, rosemary, and garlic in a small saucepan over medium-low heat until the garlic sizzles steadily and begins to brown around the edges, about 3 minutes. Remove from the heat and stir in the red pepper flakes. Divide the oil between two ramekins, with a rosemary sprig in each and let cool to room temperature.

3. Sprinkle the shrimp with a few grinds of pepper.

4. Set a flat roasting rack on a large, rimmed baking sheet.

5. Lay the prosciutto on a clean work surface, short side toward you with some space between each slice. Cut each piece lengthwise into strips about 1 inch thick. Working with one shrimp at a time, put a shrimp at the end of a strip, positioning it so that each end of the shrimp will peek out from the prosciutto when rolled. Roll the shrimp up in the prosciutto, brush on both sides with the oil from just one of the ramekins and transfer the roll to the roasting rack, seam side down. Repeat the rolling and brushing until you have rolled up all the shrimp and prosciutto.

6. Roast until the shrimp are firm to the touch and browned in places, 8 to 9 minutes. Using a clean brush, brush the shrimp with some of the remaining rosemary oil from the second ramekin (this prevents any cross-contamination), transfer to a serving platter or plates, and serve.

PER SERVING: 80 CALORIES | 7g PROTEIN | 0g CARB | 5g TOTAL FAT | 1g SAT FAT |
3.5g MONO FAT | 0.5g POLY FAT | 50mg CHOL | 240mg SODIUM | 0g FIBER

summer rolls

YIELDS 16 ROLLS; SERVES 6 TO 8; CUT IN HALF OR INTO BITE-SIZE PIECES TO SERVE MORE

- **32** medium shrimp (31 to 40 per lb.), in their shells
- **6½** oz. thin dried rice noodles
- **16** large, round rice-paper wrappers (about 8 inches in diameter); plus a few extra in case of breakage
- **20** leaves bibb or Boston lettuce, cut crosswise into 1-inch-wide strips
- **1** cup packed fresh mint leaves
- **1** cup packed fresh cilantro or basil leaves, or a mix
- **4** scallions, trimmed, cut into 4-inch-long pieces, and sliced lengthwise into thin strips

It's important to have all the summer roll elements prepared before you assemble the rolls—that is, the shrimp and rice noodles cooked and all of the vegetables for the filling prepped. Serve the rolls with the Nuoc Cham dipping sauce (below).

1. Bring a medium saucepan of water to a rolling boil over high heat. Drop the shrimp into the water and cook until they turn pink and opaque, 1 to 2 minutes. Drain in a colander and rinse with cold water until the shrimp are cool. Peel the shrimp, slice them in half lengthwise, and devein if necessary.

2. Bring a medium saucepan of water to a rolling boil over high heat. Drop in the rice noodles. Remove the pan from the heat and let stand for 8 to 10 minutes, gently lifting and stirring the noodles now and then as they soften, to cook them evenly and to keep them from clumping. Drain the noodles in a colander and rinse them with cold water to stop the cooking. You should have about 4 cups cooked noodles.

3. Arrange the noodles, rice-paper wrappers, lettuce, herbs, scallions, and shrimp around a large cutting board or tray. Have a platter nearby for the finished rolls.

4. Assemble the rolls as shown on p. 180 and serve them, cut in half or in bite-size pieces, with the Nuoc Cham.

PER 2 ROLLS: 211 CALORIES | 8g PROTEIN | 44g CARB | 1g TOTAL FAT | 0g SAT FAT | 0g MONO FAT | 0g POLY FAT | 43mg CHOL | 64mg SODIUM | 1g FIBER

Make Ahead

You can assemble these summer rolls up to 2 hours in advance as long as you cover them with a damp dishtowel and wrap them well with plastic to keep the rice paper from drying out.

nuoc cham

YIELDS ABOUT 1 CUP

- **2** Tbs. finely chopped fresh garlic
- **¼** cup granulated sugar
- **1** tsp. chile-garlic sauce (tuong ot toi)
- **6** Tbs. fish sauce (nam pla)
- **¼** cup fresh lime juice

Sweet, salty, tangy, and spicy, this is the classic Vietnamese dipping sauce.

Combine the garlic, sugar, and chile-garlic sauce in a large mortar and mash to a paste. (Or combine them on your cutting board and mash to a coarse paste using a fork and the back of a spoon.) Scrape the paste into a small bowl and add the fish sauce, lime juice, and 6 Tbs. water. Whisk until the sugar dissolves. Serve in individual bowls for dipping or refrigerate, covered, for up to a week.

PER 2 TBS.: 34 CALORIES | 1g PROTEIN | 8g CARB | 0g TOTAL FAT | 0g SAT FAT | 0g MONO FAT | 0g POLY FAT | 0mg CHOL | 1,043mg SODIUM | 0g FIBER

continued on p. 180 ➤

continued from p. 179

how to assemble the summer rolls

Fill a large skillet halfway with very warm water. Slide a sheet of rice paper into the water and press gently to submerge it until it becomes very pliable, 15 to 30 seconds. Remove the rice paper carefully, shaking gently to help excess water drain off, and lay it before you on a cutting board or tray. (If the water becomes too cool to soften the paper, reheat it briefly on the stove.)

Starting on the lowest third of the wrapper and working away from you, line up a narrow tangle of noodles (about ¼ cup), a row of lettuce strips (about ¼ cup), 5 to 7 good-size mint leaves, a row of cilantro or basil leaves, and a row of scallion strips. Leave about 1 inch of empty space along the wrapper's bottom and side edges.

Starting from the edge closest to you, roll the wrapper up and over the fillings. Stop after the first turn to tuck and compress everything snugly into the wrapper. When the first turn is good and tight, fold the right and left sides of the wrapper in onto the roll, closing off the ends, as though making an envelope.

Just above the cylinder you've already rolled, lay four shrimp halves, pink side down. Roll the wrapper tightly, all the way to the top, and press the seam closed. If necessary, dip your finger in water and run it along the paper to moisten and then press the seam closed. Set the roll, seam side down, on the platter. Continue to fill and roll up the rice paper sheets until you've made 16 rolls. (Don't let the finished rolls touch one another or they'll stick.)

stuffed mushrooms with pancetta, shallots, and sage

YIELDS ABOUT 30

- 1½ lb. cremini mushrooms (35 to 40)

- 3 Tbs. unsalted butter; more for the baking dish

- 1½ oz. pancetta, finely diced (¼ cup)

- 5 medium shallots, finely diced

- 2 tsp. chopped fresh sage

  Pinch crushed red pepper flakes

  Kosher salt and freshly ground black pepper

- ⅔ cup coarse fresh breadcrumbs

- ¼ cup freshly grated Parmigiano-Reggiano

- 2 to 3 Tbs. extra-virgin olive oil for drizzling

A drizzle of olive oil just before baking adds flavor and helps the stuffing brown and crisp.

1. Heat the oven to 425°F. Trim and discard the very bottom of the mushroom stems. Remove the mushroom stems and chop them finely, along with five of the largest mushroom caps.

2. Heat 2 Tbs. of the butter in a medium sauté pan over medium heat. Add the pancetta and cook until it starts to render some of its fat, 1 to 2 minutes. Add the shallots, sage, and red pepper flakes; cook gently until the shallots are tender, about 4 minutes. Stir in the chopped mushroom stems and ½ tsp. salt. Cook, stirring frequently, until the mixture is tender, about 3 minutes. Add the remaining 1 Tbs. butter. When it has melted, transfer the mushroom mixture to a bowl and stir in the breadcrumbs and Parmigiano. Season to taste with salt and pepper and let cool slightly.

3. Butter a shallow baking dish large enough to hold the mushrooms in one layer. Arrange the mushrooms in the dish and season the cavities with salt. Stuff each cavity with a rounded teaspoonful of the filling, or more as needed. The filling should form a tall mound. (You may have leftover filling; if you have extra mushrooms, keep stuffing until you run out of filling.) Drizzle the mushrooms with the olive oil and bake until the mushrooms are tender and the breadcrumbs are golden brown, 20 to 25 minutes. Transfer to a platter and serve warm.

PER SERVING: 35 CALORIES | 1g PROTEIN | 2g CARB | 3g TOTAL FAT | 1g SAT FAT | 1.5g MONO FAT | 0g POLY FAT | 5mg CHOL | 100mg SODIUM | 0g FIBER

Make Ahead

The mushrooms can be stuffed a day ahead and refrigerated—just let them come to room temperature before baking. Hold off on drizzling them with olive oil until just before baking.

mussels stuffed with spinach and parmesan

SERVES 4 AS AN APPETIZER, MORE AS PART OF AN HORS D'OEUVRE SPREAD

- 1 cup dry white wine
- 4 Tbs. finely chopped shallots
- 4 sprigs fresh flat-leaf parsley plus 3 Tbs. chopped parsley leaves
- 1 bay leaf
- ½ tsp. chopped fresh thyme
   Freshly ground black pepper
- 2 lb. medium mussels, sorted and cleaned
- 2 Tbs. unsalted butter or olive oil
- 2 cups lightly packed, washed, stemmed, and chopped fresh spinach
- ½ cup heavy cream
   Kosher salt
   Rock salt or aluminum foil
- ⅓ cup grated Parmigiano-Reggiano

A bed of rock salt is not only a practical way to keep mussels from rolling around during cooking, but it's a pretty way to serve them, too.

1. Combine the wine, 2 Tbs. of the shallots, the parsley sprigs, bay leaf, thyme, and ½ tsp. pepper in a pot (with a lid) large enough to accommodate the mussels when their shells have opened. Bring to a boil, add the mussels, cover, and steam until they've just opened, 2 to 3 minutes. Don't steam the mussels longer than necessary, because they'll be cooked again later. Remove the mussels with a slotted spoon and set aside. Strain the cooking liquid through a strainer lined with several layers of cheesecloth and reserve.

2. Make the stuffing: Heat the butter in a heavy-based pan. Add the remaining shallots and cook until soft, 3 to 4 minutes. Add the spinach, cover, and cook briefly until the spinach wilts. Uncover and cook until the liquid from the spinach evaporates, another 3 to 4 minutes. Add ½ cup of the strained mussel liquid and cook until the mixture is almost dry, about 5 minutes. Add the cream and cook until the mixture is almost dry, about 10 minutes. Add the chopped parsley and season with salt and a good amount of pepper.

3. Heat the broiler. Remove the mussels from their shells. Make a bed of rock salt or crumpled foil on a baking sheet (to steady the shells) and arrange as many half-shells as you have mussel meats. Put a mussel meat on each half-shell and spoon about 1 tsp. of the spinach mixture over each. Top with the grated cheese and broil until golden and bubbly, 4 to 6 minutes.

PER SERVING: 380 CALORIES | 27g PROTEIN | 12g CARB | 23g TOTAL FAT | 12g SAT FAT | 6g MONO FAT | 2g POLY FAT | 115mg CHOL | 820mg SODIUM | 1g FIBER

chicken satays with spicy peanut sauce

YIELDS 24 TO 32

- **2** boneless, skinless chicken breast halves (about 1 lb.), tenderloins removed and excess fat trimmed
- **2** Tbs. soy sauce
- **2** Tbs. fresh lemon juice
- **1** Tbs. vegetable oil
- **2** medium cloves garlic, minced
- **½** tsp. curry powder

  Kosher salt and freshly ground black pepper
- **⅓** cup crunchy natural peanut butter
- **⅓** cup unsweetened coconut milk
- **1** tsp. light brown sugar

  Pinch cayenne

  About 32 bamboo skewers, soaked in water for at least 20 minutes

You'll likely have the ingredients for this quick recipe on hand, which makes it a great "standby" appetizer.

1. With a sharp knife, cut the breasts lengthwise into ½-inch slices (you should have about six slices per breast). Cut each slice in half crosswise to make about 24 pieces total. If you have tenders, cut those in half, too.

2. In a medium bowl, combine 1 Tbs. of the soy sauce and 1 Tbs. of the lemon juice with the oil, garlic, curry powder, ½ tsp. salt, and a few grinds of pepper. Add the chicken; toss well to coat. Let the chicken marinate at room temperature for at least 15 minutes or up to 24 hours, refrigerated.

3. Meanwhile, in a small saucepan, combine the remaining 1 Tbs. soy sauce and 1 Tbs. lemon juice with the peanut butter, coconut milk, brown sugar, cayenne, and ⅛ tsp. salt.

4. Position an oven rack as close to the broiler as possible and heat the broiler to high. Thread one chicken piece onto the end of each skewer. Broil in a single layer, turning the skewers once halfway through, until the chicken is lightly browned and cooked through, about 7 minutes. While the chicken cooks, warm the sauce gently over medium-low or low heat. If the sauce seems very thick, thin it with about 1 Tbs. water. Let the chicken cool slightly and then serve the satays with the peanut sauce for dipping.

PER SERVING: 60 CALORIES | 5g PROTEIN | 1g CARB | 3.5g TOTAL FAT | 1g SAT FAT | 1.5g MONO FAT | 1g POLY FAT | 10mg CHOL | 190mg SODIUM | 0g FIBER

threading chicken, pork, or beef accordion-style

Thread the meat onto the skewers in an over-under manner.

Bunch up the meat accordion-style as you thread it and push it down the skewer.

Continue threading until you cover about 5 inches of the skewer.

spinach, sun-dried tomato, and feta purses

YIELDS 48 PURSES

1¼ cups crumbled feta
    (about 6 oz.)

1   Tbs. chopped fresh oregano

1½ tsp. chopped fresh thyme

1   tsp. (lightly packed)
    finely grated lemon zest

½   tsp. freshly ground
    black pepper

¼   lb. (½ cup) unsalted butter

1½ cups thinly sliced scallions
    (about 2 bunches)

    Kosher salt

¾   lb. baby spinach,
    well washed and dried

1   jarred roasted red pepper,
    drained, patted dry, and
    finely diced (about ½ cup)

24 sheets phyllo, preferably
    9 x 14 inches, thawed over-
    night in the refrigerator

Make Ahead

Up to a week ahead, shape the purses and freeze on a baking sheet until rock-hard before gently transferring them to an airtight container. Bake right from the freezer (don't thaw them first).

Reminiscent of spanakopita, these little pouches pack a lot of flavor in their crisp shells. To speed along assembly, you can portion out all the filling, placing 48 heaping teaspoons of it on a baking sheet or tray.

1. Heat the oven to 400°F. In a large bowl, combine the feta, oregano, thyme, lemon zest, and black pepper.

2. In a large sauté pan or skillet, melt 2 Tbs. of the butter over medium-high heat. Add the scallions, sprinkle with ¼ tsp. salt, and cook, stirring occasionally, until they soften and brown in places, about 3 minutes. Add the spinach, sprinkle with a pinch of salt, and cook, tossing with tongs until just wilted, about 3 minutes. Transfer to a colander to drain and let cool for a few minutes before thoroughly pressing and squeezing out any excess liquid. Add the spinach and the roasted red pepper to the feta mixture and combine well.

3. In a small saucepan, melt the remaining 6 Tbs. butter. Line two large rimmed baking sheets with parchment or brush them with a little of the melted butter.

4. Unroll the phyllo and stack 24 sheets on your work surface. Cover the stack with plastic wrap and a damp dishtowel. Take one sheet of phyllo off the stack and lay it on a large cutting board (recover the remaining sheets). Quickly brush it all over with some of the melted butter. Top with another piece of phyllo and brush that piece all over with butter. Repeat with one more piece of phyllo.

5. Using a sharp knife, cut the phyllo sheets in half lengthwise, then cut each half into four even pieces so that you have eight pieces about 4½ x 3½ inches each. (If you're using larger sheets of phyllo, cut them into similar size rectangles.)

6. Put 1 heaping tsp. of the feta filling in the center of each phyllo piece. Gather the corners of the phyllo together over the filling and pinch together firmly to enclose the filling. Transfer the purses to the prepared baking sheet and repeat with the remaining sheets of phyllo and filling to make a total of 48 purses in five more batches.

7. Bake the purses until the phyllo is crisp and browned all over, 15 to 20 minutes, rotating the pans halfway through to ensure even browning.

PER SERVING: 60 CALORIES | 2g PROTEIN | 6g CARB | 3.5g TOTAL FAT | 2g SAT FAT | 1g MONO FAT | 0g POLY FAT | 10mg CHOL | 115mg SODIUM | 1g FIBER

smoked salmon rolls

YIELDS 18

- ¼ **lb. cream cheese, at room temperature**
- 2 **tsp. fresh lemon juice**
- 1 **tsp. finely grated lemon zest**
- 2 **Tbs. plus 2 tsp. thinly sliced fresh chives**
  Kosher salt
- ½ **lb. thinly sliced smoked salmon (not hot-smoked)**
- ¾ **cup shaved fresh fennel**
- 1 **Tbs. finely chopped fennel fronds**

You can mix the cream cheese up to a day ahead and refrigerate it; bring it to room temperature before using. The rolls can be assembled, covered, and refrigerated up to 4 hours ahead. Let stand at room temperature for about 15 minutes before serving.

1. In a small bowl, mix the cream cheese, lemon juice, zest, chives, and ⅛ tsp. salt.

2. To assemble, lay an 8- or 9-inch-long sheet of plastic wrap on the counter. Slightly overlap slices of salmon on the plastic to create a rectangle measuring about 3½ x 7 inches. The long side of the rectangle should be parallel to the edge of your work surface. Cover with another sheet of plastic and press gently with your hands or a flat spatula to encourage the salmon to stick together. Remove the top sheet of plastic. Using a thin metal offset spatula or a butter knife, spread about 2 Tbs. of the cream cheese mixture on the salmon, leaving a ½-inch border along the long sides. Arrange about a third of the fennel shavings lengthwise on the lower half of the salmon. Sprinkle the fennel lightly with salt. Starting at the long side closest to you and using the plastic as an aid, gently roll up the salmon to enclose the filling. Gently press the roll together at the seams. Transfer the roll to a cutting board and cut the roll into six pieces. Repeat with the remaining salmon, cream cheese mixture, and fennel to make two more long rolls. You may have extra salmon or fennel. Cut each roll into six pieces.

3. Arrange the pieces on a platter, cut side up. Garnish with the chopped fennel fronds.

PER SERVING: 40 CALORIES I 3g PROTEIN I 1g CARB I 3g TOTAL FAT I 1.5g SAT FAT I 1g MONO FAT I 0.5g POLY FAT I 10mg CHOL I 310mg SODIUM I 0g FIBER

grilled steak kebab pitas with ginger and garlic dressing

SERVES 6 TO 8

- **½ cup extra-virgin olive oil;** more for brushing
- **1 Tbs. finely grated ginger**
- **1 Tbs. green Tabasco sauce** or other jalapeño hot sauce
- **2 tsp. cider vinegar**
- **1 small to medium clove garlic,** finely grated or minced
- **Kosher salt and freshly ground black pepper**
- **1½ to 1¾ lb. 1-inch-thick boneless beef strip steaks (2 to 3 steaks), trimmed and cut into 1-inch cubes**
- **6 to 8 bamboo skewers (at least 8 inches long), soaked in water for at least 20 minutes**
- **1 large red bell pepper, cored and cut into 1¼- to 1½-inch squares**
- **6 to 8 pita breads, preferably pocketless**
- **2 cups shredded lettuce, preferably a crisp variety like iceberg or romaine**

You can make more kebabs if they're only two bites each; simply use shorter skewers and only slide on two cubes of meat per skewer. Serve each with half of a pita.

1. Prepare a medium-hot grill fire.

2. In a 1-cup liquid measuring cup, whisk the ½ cup oil with the ginger, Tabasco, vinegar, garlic, ¼ tsp. salt, and ¼ tsp. pepper.

3. Thread 4 cubes of meat onto each skewer, inserting a red pepper square between the cubes. (You may not need all the skewers.) Brush the kebabs with oil and sprinkle lightly with salt and pepper.

4. Just before grilling, lightly oil the grill grate. Set the kebabs on the grill and cook, with the lid closed, turning every 2 minutes, 4 to 6 minutes total for medium rare. Warm the pitas on the grill.

5. To serve, slide each kebab off its skewer onto a pita. Top each with some of the lettuce. Whisk the dressing to recombine and drizzle over the meat and vegetables.

PER SERVING: 400 CALORIES | 20g PROTEIN | 35g CARB | 19g TOTAL FAT | 4g SAT FAT | 12g MONO FAT | 2g POLY FAT | 35mg CHOL | 540mg SODIUM | 2g FIBER

> A rasp-style grater does an amazing job of grating even the most fibrous knot of ginger into the juicy, paste-like consistency that works best for this recipe.

eggplant parmigiana rolls with pine nuts and baby arugula

4½ Tbs. plus ½ cup extra-virgin olive oil

½ medium yellow onion, cut into medium dice

1 clove garlic, chopped

3 cups peeled, seeded, and chopped fresh plum tomatoes (6 to 8 tomatoes)

Kosher salt and freshly ground black pepper

2 Tbs. pitted and very coarsely chopped Kalamata or Nicoise olives

1 Tbs. capers, rinsed and coarsely chopped if large

1 Tbs. plus ½ cup vegetable oil

1 baby (Italian) eggplant (about ½ lb.) or ½ small regular eggplant, cut into large dice (2½ cups)

2 Tbs. finely grated Parmigiano-Reggiano

2 Tbs. toasted pine nuts

2 Tbs. fresh lemon juice (from 1 lemon)

1 Tbs. thinly sliced fresh basil

3 small zucchini (about 1 lb. total)

2 cups panko

½ cup all-purpose flour

2 large eggs, beaten

5 oz. baby arugula (6 lightly packed cups)

¼ cup shaved Parmigiano-Reggiano

Inside these rolls the eggplant marries with tomato sauce and Parmigiano-Reggiano, creating the essence of eggplant parmigiana.

1. Heat 1 Tbs. olive oil in a 3-quart saucepan over medium heat. Add the onion and garlic and cook until soft and slightly browned, about 3 minutes. Add the tomatoes, ¼ tsp. salt, and a grind of pepper and simmer, stirring frequently, until the tomatoes cook down to a dry sauce, 20 to 25 minutes, reducing the heat to medium low if necessary. Turn off the heat, and stir in the olives, capers, ½ Tbs. olive oil, and salt and pepper to taste.

2. Heat 1 Tbs. each olive oil and vegetable oil in a 12-inch skillet over high heat. Add the eggplant and cook, stirring occasionally, until tender and well browned on several sides, 3 to 5 minutes. Transfer to a bowl and cool to room temperature.

3. To the eggplant, add the finely grated Parmigiano, 1 Tbs. of the pine nuts, 1 Tbs. lemon juice, the basil, and about half of the tomato sauce. Season to taste with salt and pepper.

4. Using a mandoline, slice the zucchini lengthwise about ⅛ inch thick. Select the 24 widest, longest slices and arrange them in a single layer on paper towels. Sprinkle lightly with salt and let sit until pliable, about 3 minutes—you can shingle the layers of zucchini between paper towels to save space. Pat dry. Arrange 3 slices of zucchini on a work surface, overlapping them lengthwise. Spread a heaping tablespoon of the eggplant mixture near one end of the zucchini ribbons and roll the zucchini around the filling to make a roll. Set aside, seam side down, and repeat with the remaining ingredients to make 8 rolls total. You may not need all the filling.

5. Put the panko, flour, and eggs in 3 shallow bowls. Lightly coat each roll in the flour, then dip it in the eggs, and coat in the breadcrumbs—it's fine if it isn't perfectly coated.

6. Heat the ½ cup olive oil and ½ cup vegetable oil in a 10-inch straight-sided saute pan over medium heat. Working in two batches, fry the rolls until golden brown on all sides, 2 to 3 minutes per side. As each batch finishes, transfer to a paper-towel-lined plate and sprinkle lightly with salt.

7. While the rolls cook, reheat the remaining sauce in a small saucepan, adding about ¼ cup water, or enough to thin to a wet sauce.

8. Whisk the remaining 2 Tbs. olive oil and 1 Tbs. lemon juice in a small bowl. Toss the arugula with the dressing and season to taste with salt and pepper. Serve the rolls topped with the sauce, remaining pine nuts, and shaved Parmigiano, with the salad on the side.

PER SERVING: 250 CALORIES | 5g PROTEIN | 16g CARB | 19g TOTAL FAT | 3g SAT FAT | 12g MONO FAT | 2.5g POLY FAT | 55mg CHOL | 170mg SODIUM | 3g FIBER

wild mushroom and cheese empanadas

YIELDS ABOUT 18 FOUR-INCH
EMPANADAS

FOR THE FILLING

- **1** Tbs. olive oil
- **½** small onion, diced
- **1** clove garlic, diced
- **¼** lb. button mushrooms, stemmed and diced
- **½** lb. mixed wild mushrooms, stemmed and diced
- **2** tsp. balsamic or red-wine vinegar

  Salt and freshly ground black pepper
- **½** cup grated manchego cheese
- **¼** cup roughly chopped flat-leaf parsley

FOR THE DOUGH

- **13½** oz. (3 cups) all-purpose flour
- **2** tsp. salt
- **¼** lb. (8 Tbs.) unsalted butter, chilled and cut into small cubes
- **1** egg, lightly beaten
- **3** Tbs. sherry vinegar or red-wine vinegar
- **¼** cup plus 1 Tbs. ice water
- **2** eggs beaten with 2 Tbs. water for an egg wash

Manchego is a pleasantly salty cheese that's made from the milk of sheep that graze on the plains of La Mancha in Spain. If you can't find it, substitute Parmesan or Dry Jack cheese instead.

TO MAKE THE FILLING

In a large frying pan, heat the oil over medium heat. Cook the onion until soft, about 5 minutes. Add the garlic, mushrooms, vinegar, and ¼ tsp. each of salt and pepper; cook until the mushrooms have released their water and the pan is almost dry, 20 to 30 minutes. Remove from the heat and let the filling cool completely. Add the cheese and parsley; toss well. Taste for seasoning and add more salt and pepper if needed.

TO MAKE THE DOUGH

1. In a large mixing bowl, combine the flour and salt. With a pastry blender or two knives, cut in the chilled butter pieces until the mixture resembles coarse crumbs. Add the egg, vinegar, and water; mix until well blended. Turn the dough out onto a sheet of plastic wrap and knead gently for a few seconds until you have a smooth dough. Wrap well and chill for at least 5 minutes.

2. On a lightly floured surface, roll half the chilled dough to ⅛ inch thick. (Keep the other half refrigerated until ready to use.) Cut out 4-inch squares. Spoon about 1 Tbs. of the filling slightly off center of each square. Moisten the edges of the dough with the egg wash and fold one corner over to the opposite side to form a triangle. Seal the edges with the tines of a fork. Repeat with the remaining dough. Refrigerate the empanadas on greased or parchment-lined baking sheets for at least 30 minutes. Heat the oven to 375°F. Brush the tops of the empanadas with the remaining egg wash and bake until well browned, about 25 minutes.

sips & sweets

kahlúa truffle triangles

YIELDS ABOUT 6 DOZEN
1½- TO 2-INCH TRIANGLES

FOR THE CRUST

6¾ oz. (1 ½ cups)
    all-purpose flour

3   oz. (¾ cup)
    confectioners' sugar

¼   tsp. table salt

6   oz. (12 Tbs.) cold unsalted
    butter, cut into ten pieces;
    more for the pan

½   tsp. pure vanilla extract

FOR THE FILLING

1   lb. semisweet or bittersweet
    chocolate, broken into
    squares or very coarsely
    chopped

¾   cup milk (whole or 2%)

¼   lb. (½ cup) unsalted butter,
    cut into six pieces

4   large eggs

⅔   cup granulated sugar

2   Tbs. Kahlúa® or other
    coffee-flavored liqueur

You can bake these up to a month ahead. Wrap the cooled baking pan in heavy-duty plastic wrap and freeze (no need to cut them first).

1. Make the crust: Position a rack in the middle of the oven and heat the oven to 350°F. Line the bottom and sides of a 9 x 13-inch baking pan with foil, allowing foil to overhang the long sides of the pan to act as handles for removing later. Lightly butter the foil.

2. In a food processor, combine the flour, confectioners' sugar, and salt. Process briefly to combine. Scatter the cold butter pieces and the vanilla over the flour mixture and process, using short pulses, until the dough begins to form small clumps, about 1 minute. Turn the dough into the prepared pan. Using lightly floured fingertips, press the dough into the pan in a smooth, even layer. Bake until pale golden, 22 to 25 minutes. Don't overbake or the crust will be hard. Transfer the pan to a cooling rack. Lower the oven temperature to 325°F.

3. Make the filling: In a medium bowl, melt the chocolate, milk, and butter together over a pot of barely simmering water or in the microwave. Whisk until smooth and set aside to cool slightly.

4. In a stand mixer fitted with a paddle attachment (or in a large mixing bowl, using a hand-held electric mixer), beat the eggs, sugar, and Kahlúa on medium-high speed until foamy and lighter in color, 2 minutes. Reduce the speed to low and gradually add the chocolate mixture. Stop the mixer and scrape down the bowl. Beat on medium speed until well blended, about 30 seconds.

5. Pour the chocolate batter over the baked crust and spread evenly. Bake at 325°F until the sides are slightly puffed and a toothpick inserted near the center comes out wet and gooey but not liquid, 30 to 35 minutes. Transfer the pan to a rack. As it cools, the center may sink a bit, leaving the edges slightly (about ½ inch) elevated. While the filling is still warm, use your fingertips to gently press the edges down to the level of the center, if necessary.

6. When completely cool, cover with plastic and refrigerate until very cold, at least 12 hours or up to 2 days.

7. To serve, using the foil as handles, lift the rectangle from the pan and set it on a cutting board. Tipping the rectangle, carefully peel away the foil. Using a hot knife, cut the rectangle lengthwise into 1 ½-inch strips, wiping the blade clean before each cut. Cut each strip on alternating diagonals to make small triangles. Let sit at room temperature for about 5 minutes before serving.

PER SERVING: 90 CALORIES | 1g PROTEIN | 9g CARB | 6g TOTAL FAT | 3.5g SAT FAT |
1g MONO FAT | 0g POLY FAT | 25mg CHOL | 20mg SODIUM | 1g FIBER

biscotti rustica

YIELDS ABOUT 3 DOZEN
6-INCH-LONG BISCOTTI

FOR THE DOUGH

- ½ cup dried currants
- ½ cup golden raisins
- 2 Tbs. brandy
- Grated zest of 1 lemon (about 1 Tbs.)
- ½ oz. (1 Tbs.) crystallized ginger, chopped
- 15¾ oz. (3 ½ cups) unbleached all-purpose flour
- 2 cups granulated sugar
- ¼ cup yellow cornmeal
- 1 Tbs. baking powder
- ¼ tsp. kosher salt
- 3 large eggs
- 3 large egg yolks
- 1 tsp. pure vanilla extract
- ¾ cup pine nuts, toasted until golden

FOR THE GLAZE

- 1 egg white, lightly beaten
- 1 Tbs. turbinado sugar (also sold as Sugar in the Raw® in supermarkets)

Make Ahead

Stored airtight, these biscotti will keep for about 2 weeks.

Not too sweet, these biscotti are right at home among savory appetizers.

MIX THE DOUGH

1. In a small bowl, combine the currants, raisins, brandy, lemon zest, and ginger and let stand for 20 minutes.

2. With an electric mixer fitted with the paddle attachment, combine the flour, granulated sugar, cornmeal, baking powder, and salt. In a small bowl, whisk the eggs, egg yolks, and vanilla. With the mixer on low speed, add the egg mixture to the dry ingredients until just combined and the dough looks crumbly. Take care not to overmix. Add the fruit mixture and the pine nuts, mixing just until the dough comes together (bring the dough together with your hands if it's a bit stiff). Let the dough rest for 15 to 30 minutes before shaping.

3. Meanwhile, position racks in the center and top of the oven and heat the oven to 350°F.

SHAPE THE DOUGH

Line a large baking sheet with parchment. Cut the dough in half. Using as little flour as possible on the work surface, roll each half into a log that's 16 inches long and 2 inches wide, working out the air pockets as you go. (If you're working ahead, wrap the logs in plastic and refrigerate them overnight.) Transfer the logs to the baking sheet, setting them about 3 inches apart and patting the sides to smooth and straighten.

GLAZE THE DOUGH AND BAKE THE FIRST TIME

1. Brush the tops and sides with the beaten egg white and sprinkle with the turbinado sugar.

2. Bake on the middle rack until golden brown and firm in the center, 30 to 35 minutes, rotating the sheet to ensure even baking. Set the sheet on a rack until the logs are cool enough to handle and so the dough won't compress when you cut it, about 30 minutes.

SLICE AND BAKE A SECOND TIME

1. Reduce the oven temperature to 300°F. Line two large baking sheets with parchment. With a serrated knife, saw the logs into ½-inch-thick slices, cutting on the diagonal so each slice is about 6 inches long.

2. Lay the slices flat on the baking sheets. Bake for about 15 minutes, rotating the sheets and switching their positions as needed for even baking. Turn the biscotti over. Bake until both sides are a rich golden brown, another 10 to 15 minutes. Set the baking sheets on racks, letting the biscotti cool and crisp completely on the sheets.

PER SERVING: 140 CALORIES | 3g PROTEIN | 26g CARB | 3g TOTAL FAT | 0g SAT FAT |
1g MONO FAT | 1g POLY FAT | 35mg CHOL | 50mg SODIUM | 1g FIBER

Vary the Size and Yield as You Please

The width of a log of biscotti dough will determine the length of your finished biscotti, and you can vary this according to your preference. (The thinner the slices, the bigger the yield, of course.) You can cut them as thin as ¼ inch and reduce the baking time slightly.

tenant's harbor punch

tenant's harbor punch

SERVES 10 TO 12

4 to 5 medium lemons

¾ cup granulated sugar

3 bottles (750 ml) off-dry white wine (such as Riesling Spatlese, Vouvray, or Chenin Blanc), chilled

1½ cups aquavit, preferably Norwegian, such as Linie®, chilled

2 pints fresh strawberries, hulled and halved

1 English cucumber, washed and sliced about ⅛ inch thick

4 cups sparkling water, chilled

This punch is named for a quiet, windswept point on the rocky coast of Maine. The caraway-flavored aquavit adds an unusual flavor.

1. Using a peeler, remove the zest from the lemons, avoiding the white pith. In a medium bowl, combine the lemon zest and the sugar, stirring with a wooden spoon until the sugar is fragrant and has the texture of soft, fresh snow, about 10 minutes. Add ¾ cup boiling water to the bowl and stir to dissolve the sugar. Strain the syrup and let cool.

2. Juice the lemons and strain the juice—you'll need 1 cup plus 2 Tbs. juice.

3. At least 3 hours and up to 6 hours before serving, combine the syrup, lemon juice, wine, aquavit, strawberries, and cucumbers in a large bowl or pot. Refrigerate.

4. Just before serving, pour the punch into a large chilled punch bowl or dispenser, with a block of ice. Add the sparkling water and gently stir.

PER SERVING: 290 CALORIES | 1g PROTEIN | 24g CARB | 0g TOTAL FAT | 0g SAT FAT | 0g MONO FAT | 0g POLY FAT | 0mg CHOL | 10mg SODIUM | 1g FIBER

champagne cosmo

SERVES 8

1½ cups cranberry juice cocktail, chilled

½ cup Grand Marnier®

3 Tbs. fresh lime juice

8 thin strips of lime zest (from 2 limes), each about ¼ inch wide and 3 inches long

2 bottles (750 ml) brut sparkling wine or Champagne, chilled

This festive sparkler is a Champagne twist on a Cosmopolitan.

Combine the cranberry juice, Grand Marnier, and lime juice in a small pitcher and mix well. Hold a lime strip over a tall Champagne flute, twist or tie it into a single knot to release the essential oils, and drop the zest into the flute. Repeat with the remaining zest and seven more flutes. Divide the juice mixture equally among the flutes. Top each flute with the sparkling wine (depending on the size of your flutes, you may not need all of the wine). Serve immediately.

PER SERVING: 210 CALORIES | 0g PROTEIN | 16g CARB | 0g TOTAL FAT | 0g SAT FAT | 0g MONO FAT | 0g POLY FAT | 0mg CHOL | 0mg SODIUM | 0g FIBER

classic hot cocoa

YIELDS 2⅔ CUPS; SERVES 3 OR 4

- ⅓ **cup unsweetened natural cocoa powder**
- 3 **to 4 Tbs. granulated sugar**
- **Pinch table salt**
- 2½ **cups whole milk**
- **Mini marshmallows (optional), for garnish**

This is the hot cocoa from your childhood—chocolatey but not rich enough to spoil dinner. Mini marshmallows are a delicious addition.

Put the cocoa powder, sugar, and salt in a medium saucepan. Pour in ¼ cup of the milk and whisk constantly until the mixture is smooth and free of lumps. Pour in the remaining milk and whisk to combine. Set the pan over medium to medium-high heat. Cook, whisking frequently, until hot, 4 to 5 minutes. For best flavor, do not let the cocoa boil. Serve hot, topped with mini marshmallows, if you like.

PER SERVING: 140 CALORIES | 6g PROTEIN | 20g CARB | 6g TOTAL FAT | 3.5g SAT FAT | 1.5g MONO FAT | 0g POLY FAT | 15mg CHOL | 135mg SODIUM | 2g FIBER

rich hot chocolate

YIELDS 3¼ CUPS; SERVES 4

- 2½ **cups whole milk**
- 3 **Tbs. granulated sugar (chocolates vary in sugar level, so feel free to add another tablespoon if necessary)**
- **Pinch table salt**
- 3½ **oz. bittersweet chocolate, finely chopped (about ¾ cup)**

This hot chocolate tastes rich enough to be dessert. To vary the flavor, infuse the milk with orange zest or fresh mint leaves before adding the chocolate.

Put the milk, sugar, and salt in a medium saucepan set over medium-high heat. Cook, whisking frequently, until the sugar is melted, about 2 minutes. Continue to cook until the milk nearly reaches a boil, stirring occasionally, about 2 more minutes. Turn off the heat and add the chopped chocolate to the pan. Whisk constantly until the chocolate is melted and the mixture is smooth.

PER SERVING: 260 CALORIES | 7g PROTEIN | 31g CARB | 12g TOTAL FAT | 8g SAT FAT | 4g MONO FAT | 0g POLY FAT | 15mg CHOL | 85mg SODIUM | 3g FIBER

bourbon balls

YIELDS 3½ TO 4 DOZEN

- **1 cup heavy cream**
- **¼ cup bourbon**
- **½ tsp. pure vanilla extract**
- **12 oz. bittersweet chocolate, chopped (about 2½ cups)**
- **8 oz. pecans, toasted and cooled (about 2 cups)**
- **8 oz. plain homemade or store-bought pound cake (thawed if frozen), cut into cubes (about 2½ cups)**
- **⅔ cup cocoa powder, preferably Dutch processed**
- **⅓ cup confectioners' sugar**

For some of us, it wouldn't be Christmas without these rich, potent treats.

1. In a small saucepan, bring the cream just to a boil over medium-high heat. Remove from the heat and stir in the bourbon and vanilla. Sprinkle the chocolate evenly over the cream and let sit without stirring for 5 minutes.

2. Meanwhile, pulse the pecans in a food processor until coarsely chopped. Add the pound cake and pulse until the nuts and cake are finely chopped.

3. Stir the chocolate and the cream until smooth. Pour the chocolate over the pecan and pound cake mixture in the food processor and pulse until combined. Transfer to a medium bowl and refrigerate, stirring occasionally, until firm enough to scoop, about 1 hour.

4. Sift the cocoa powder and confectioners' sugar together into a medium bowl. Line a rimmed baking sheet with waxed paper or parchment. Scoop out a heaping tablespoon of the bourbon-chocolate mixture and roll it in your hands to form a ball. Transfer the bourbon ball to the cocoa-sugar mixture, roll it around to coat, and transfer to the baking sheet. Repeat with the remaining bourbon-chocolate mixture. Sift some of the remaining cocoa-sugar mixture over the bourbon balls just to dust them. Refrigerate the bourbon balls until firm, about 2 hours. For a nice presentation, you can put them in mini muffin cups.

PER SERVING: 110 CALORIES | 2g PROTEIN | 9g CARB | 8g TOTAL FAT | 3g SAT FAT | 3.5g MONO FAT | 1g POLY FAT | 10mg CHOL | 30mg SODIUM | 2g FIBER

Cooking with Bourbon

Bourbon's smoky caramel and vanilla flavor adds a special nuance to savory and sweet dishes alike. It pairs particularly well with brown sugar, pecans, vanilla, chocolate, mint, apples, pears, peaches, ham, and pork. It's great in sauces, marinades, brines, glazes, cakes, pies, truffles, and cookies.

Bourbon whiskey, which gets its name from Bourbon County, Kentucky, is distilled from a grain mash that's at least 51% corn (but usually 65% to 80%) and may also contain barley, rye, and sometimes wheat (as in Maker's Mark® brand). The distilled liquor is then aged in new charred oak barrels from which it gets its color and smoky, caramelly undertones.

Save expensive single-barrel bourbons and small-batch bourbons for sipping. For cooking, a regular bourbon is fine.

triple-shot eggnog

YIELDS ABOUT 6 CUPS; SERVES 8

- **3** large eggs, preferably pasteurized, separated
- **½** cup granulated sugar
- Kosher salt
- **½** cup dark rum
- **¼** cup bourbon
- **2** Tbs. brandy
- **2** cups whole milk
- **1** cup heavy cream
- **½** tsp. freshly grated nutmeg, plus extra for garnish
- **½** tsp. pure vanilla extract

In this version of the holiday classic, three traditional spirits come together for a cocktail with a kick. Whisking frothy beaten egg whites into the eggnog base makes for a much lighter and less cloying drink than those found in containers at the supermarket.

1. Whisk the egg yolks in a large bowl until they just begin to turn a lighter shade of yellow. Add the sugar and a pinch of salt and whisk until thick and pale yellow. Whisk in the rum, bourbon, and brandy until well combined and then whisk in the milk, cream, nutmeg, and vanilla until blended. Chill the mixture, covered, for 4 hours or overnight. Keep the egg whites chilled separately in a medium bowl.

2. Before serving, whip the egg whites to stiff peaks with a hand-held electric mixer. Fold the whipped egg whites into the chilled yolk mixture. Serve immediately, sprinkled with a little freshly grated nutmeg, or chill for up to 4 hours. Whisk the eggnog until smooth before serving.

PER SERVING: 270 CALORIES | 5g PROTEIN | 16g CARB | 15g TOTAL FAT | 9g SAT FAT | 4.5g MONO FAT | 1g POLY FAT | 125mg CHOL | 80mg SODIUM | 0g FIBER

The risk of salmonella infection from consuming raw eggs is very low—only about 1 in 20,000 is contaminated—but you can eliminate the risk entirely by using pasteurized eggs.

the michelada

Kosher salt

½ small lime

1 12-fl.-oz. bottle light lager, such as Corona® or Modelo® Especial, chilled

2 dashes Worchestershire sauce

2 dashes soy sauce

2 dashes hot pepper sauce, such as Cholula® or Tabasco

Freshly cracked black pepper

peach melba cocktail

the michelada

This beer cocktail is simple and delicious. For an even simpler version—the Chelada—salt the rim of an ice-filled pint glass, add light lager and fresh lime juice, and enjoy.

Pour 2 Tbs. salt into a small, wide dish. Wet the rim of a chilled pint glass with the lime. Dip the rim into the salt, margarita-style. Fill the glass with ice and squeeze the lime over the ice. Fill the glass with beer and then add the Worchestershire, soy, and hot sauces. Give a pepper mill a single twist over the ice. Stir gently until the drink takes on a uniform color. Serve immediately, with the remaining beer on the side for adding to the glass as you empty it. By the time you've finished, the heat of the drink will have subsided, and you'll be ready for another.

PER SERVING: 110 CALORIES | 1g PROTEIN | 8g CARB | 0g TOTAL FAT | 0g SAT FAT | 0g MONO FAT | 0g POLY FAT | 0mg CHOL | 1,170mg SODIUM | 0g FIBER

peach melba cocktail

SERVES 1

6 fl. oz. (¾ cup) peche (peach) lambic, such as Lindemans®, chilled

2 fl. oz. (¼ cup) framboise (raspberry) lambic, such as Lindemans, chilled

1 thin slice lemon

Fruit lambic beers are tart Belgian brews fermented with wild yeasts and aged with crushed fruit or fruit juices. A mix of peach and raspberry lambics makes a drink that sounds like dessert but tastes like an aperitif.

Combine the two beers in a chilled 9-oz. Champagne flute. Gently squeeze the lemon slice over the drink and then add the slice to the drink. Serve.

PER SERVING: 130 CALORIES | 0g PROTEIN | 22g CARB | 0g TOTAL FAT | 0g SAT FAT | 0g MONO FAT | 0g POLY FAT | 0mg CHOL | 0mg SODIUM | 0g FIBER

blueberry streusel bars with lemon-cream filling

YIELDS 24 BARS

8	oz. (1 cup) unsalted butter, softened; more for the pan
13½	oz. (3 cups) all-purpose flour
1	cups old-fashioned rolled oats (not quick oats)
1⅓	cups packed light brown sugar
1	tsp. table salt
1	tsp. baking powder
1	large egg, separated
1	14-oz. can sweetened condensed milk
½	cup fresh lemon juice
2	tsp. grated lemon zest
2½	cups room-temperature blueberries (about 13 oz.), washed and drained on paper towels

Always a hit at summer picnics, these addictive squares strike the perfect balance between tart and sweet and chewy and crunchy.

1. Position a rack in the center of the oven and heat the oven to 350°F. Line a 9 x 13-inch metal baking pan with foil, leaving a 1-inch overhang on the ends. Lightly butter the bottom and sides of the foil.

2. In a large bowl, combine the flour, oats, sugar, salt, and baking powder. Using your fingers, blend the butter completely into the flour mixture. Transfer 2 cups of crumb mixture to another bowl and reserve for the topping. Blend the egg white into the remaining crumbs and then press the mixture into the bottom of the pan to form a level crust. You can tamp it with the bottom of a measuring cup to even it out. Bake the crust until it starts to form a dry top, 10 to 12 minutes.

3. Meanwhile, in a medium bowl, whisk the condensed milk, lemon juice, lemon zest, and egg yolk. Let this mixture stand for 5 minutes; it will begin to thicken.

4. Sprinkle the blueberries evenly over the hot crust and then drop spoonfuls of the lemon mixture over the blueberries. Spread gently with a spatula to distribute a little more evenly, but take care not to crush the berries; it's fine if the lemon mixture isn't perfectly even. Bake until the lemon mixture just begins to form a shiny skin, 7 to 8 minutes.

5. Sprinkle the reserved topping over the lemon-blueberry layer, pressing the streusel between your fingers into small lumps as you sprinkle. Bake until the filling is bubbling at the edges and the topping is brown, 25 to 30 minutes.

6. Let the bars cool in the pan on a rack until just warm, about an hour. Carefully lift them out of the pan using the foil overhang and transfer to a wire rack to cool completely. Remove the foil and cut into 24 bars when cool. The bars may be stored at room temperature for a few hours but otherwise should be kept in the refrigerator.

PER SERVING: 270 CALORIES | 4g PROTEIN | 41g CARB | 10g TOTAL FAT | 6g SAT FAT | 2.5g MONO FAT | 0.5g POLY FAT | 35mg CHOL | 140mg SODIUM | 2g FIBER

Buying and Storing Blueberries

You can judge some fruit with your nose, but not blueberries. Use your eyes first: Blueberries should have a lovely silvery-white bloom over the dark blue. Look for pints free of small, purplish or greenish immature berries, a sign that they were picked before their peak. Then use the "heft" test: Berries should be plump and heavy. The sure-fire way of judging blueberries is to taste a few, because sweetness is variable even within the same pint.

At home, pick through them, discarding any squishy berries that may turn moldy and infect their healthy neighbors. Store the berries in the coldest part of the refrigerator, but not in a drawer, where it's too humid. To keep them dry, don't wash them until you're ready to use them. They will keep for up to two weeks in an airtight container, although they can lose moisture during the second week and shrink slightly. For baking, this can work in your favor, because the flavor becomes concentrated. After that, it's time to freeze them. Rinse them in a colander, dry thoroughly on paper towels, and then spread them on rimmed baking sheets in a single layer until frozen solid. Once frozen, they go into plastic storage bags.

honey-nut bars

YIELDS 16 BAR COOKIES

FOR THE CRUST

	Nonstick cooking spray
½	cup whole blanched almonds, toasted
½	cup granulated sugar
11¼	oz. (2½ cups) unbleached all-purpose flour
½	tsp. baking powder
½	tsp. table salt
6	oz. (¾ cup) cold unsalted butter, cut into ½-inch pieces
1	large egg, lightly beaten

FOR THE TOPPING

¾	cup packed light brown sugar
3	oz. (6 Tbs.) unsalted butter
⅓	cup clover honey
½	tsp. table salt
2	Tbs. heavy cream
3	cups whole unsalted mixed nuts, toasted

These cookies will keep in an airtight container at room temperature for 3 to 5 days

1. Make the crust: Position a rack in the center of the oven and heat the oven to 350°F. Spray a 9 x 13-inch baking pan with cooking spray and line the bottom with parchment.

2. In a food processor, finely grind the almonds and sugar. Add the flour, baking powder, and salt and pulse to blend. Add the butter and pulse until it's the size of small peas, 5 to 6 one-second pulses. Add the egg and pulse just until the dough begins to gather into large clumps.

3. With your fingertips, press the dough into the bottom of the prepared pan and about 1 inch up the sides to form a ¼-inch-thick side crust. Using the tines of a fork, dock the crust evenly all over.

4. Bake until light golden brown on the edges and the center looks dry, 15 to 20 minutes. Cool the crust on a rack.

5. Make the topping: Bring the sugar, butter, honey, and salt to a boil in a medium saucepan over medium-high heat, stirring often. Slowly and carefully add the cream and return to a boil. Remove from the heat and carefully add the nuts, stirring to coat. Pour the nut mixture over the crust and spread evenly with a spatula. Tilt the pan to help spread the liquid to the edges and corners. Bake until the topping has just started to bubble slowly in the center, about 20 minutes. Let cool on a wire rack for 10 minutes and then run a knife around the inside edge of the pan to loosen the crust from the sides. Let the bars cool completely.

6. Invert the pan onto a flat surface and peel off the parchment. Reinvert onto a cutting board and cut into 16 bars with a sharp knife.

PER BAR: 460 CALORIES | 8g PROTEIN | 45g CARB | 30g TOTAL FAT | 11g SAT FAT | 13g MONO FAT | 4g POLY FAT | 50mg CHOL | 170mg SODIUM | 3g FIBER

orange-hazelnut olive oil cookies

YIELDS ABOUT 6 DOZEN COOKIES

- 2 cups toasted and skinned hazelnuts
- 10 oz. (2¼ cups) unbleached all-purpose flour
- 1 tsp. baking powder
- ¼ tsp. table salt
- ¾ cup plus 2 Tbs. granulated sugar
- ½ cup extra-virgin olive oil
- 2 large eggs

  Finely grated zest of 2 medium oranges (about 1½ packed Tbs.)
- 1 tsp. pure vanilla extract

Make Ahead

The unbaked logs of dough may be frozen for up to 1 month.

Reminiscent of biscotti in texture, these not-too-sweet cookies are a perfect dipper for after-dinner coffee.

1. Finely grind the hazelnuts in a food processor. In a medium bowl, whisk the hazelnuts, flour, baking powder, and salt to blend. With a hand mixer or a stand mixer fitted with the paddle attachment, beat the sugar, oil, eggs, zest, and vanilla on low speed until the sugar is moistened, about 15 seconds. Increase the speed to high and mix until well combined, about 15 seconds more (the sugar will not be dissolved at this point). Add the dry ingredients and mix on low speed until the dough has just pulled together, 30 to 60 seconds.

2. Divide the dough in half. Pile half of the dough onto a piece of parchment. Using the parchment to help shape the dough, form it into a log 11 inches long and 2 inches in diameter. Wrap the parchment around the log and twist the ends to secure. Repeat with the remaining dough. Chill in the freezer until firm, about 1 hour.

3. Position racks in the upper and lower thirds of the oven and heat the oven to 350°F. Line four cookie sheets with parchment or nonstick baking liners.

4. Unwrap one log of dough at a time and cut the dough into ¼-inch slices; set them 1 inch apart on the prepared sheets. Bake two sheets at a time until light golden on the bottoms and around the edges, about 10 minutes, rotating and swapping the sheets halfway through for even baking. Let cool completely on racks. The cookies will keep in an airtight container at room temperature for up to 1 week.

PER SERVING: 60 CALORIES | 1g PROTEIN | 6g CARB | 4g TOTAL FAT | 0g SAT FAT | 3g MONO FAT | 0g POLY FAT | 5mg CHOL | 15mg SODIUM | 0g FIBER

Skinning Hazelnuts

Toast the nuts in a single layer on a baking sheet in a 375°F oven until the skins are mostly split and the nuts are light golden brown and fragrant, about 10 minutes. Wrap the hot nuts in a clean dishtowel and let them sit for 5 to 10 minutes. Then vigorously rub the nuts against themselves in the towel to remove most of the skins.

creamy chocolate fudge

YIELDS TWENTY-FIVE 1½-INCH PIECES

- **3 Tbs. cold unsalted butter; more at room temperature for buttering the thermometer and pan**
- **3¾ cups granulated sugar**
- **1½ cups heavy cream**
- **4 oz. unsweetened chocolate, coarsely chopped**
- **3 Tbs. light corn syrup**
- **1 tsp. table salt**

The fudge will keep for 7 to 10 days stored in an airtight container at room temperature.

1. Lightly butter the face of a candy thermometer and set aside.

2. Put the sugar, cream, chocolate, corn syrup, and salt in a large (4-quart) heavy-duty saucepan and stir with a spoon or heatproof spatula until the ingredients are moistened and combined. Stirring gently and constantly, bring the mixture to a boil over medium heat, 7 to 12 minutes. Cover the saucepan and let the steam clean the sides of the pan for 2 minutes.

3. Clip the candy thermometer to the pot, being careful not to let the tip of the thermometer touch the bottom of the pot, or you might get a false reading. Let the mixture boil without stirring until it reaches 236°F to 238°F, 2 to 5 minutes. Take the pan off the heat and add the butter, but do not stir it into the mixture. Set the pan on a rack in a cool part of the kitchen. Don't disturb the pan in any way until the mixture has cooled to 110°F, 1 to 1½ hours.

4. Meanwhile, line the bottom and sides of an 8×8-inch baking pan with foil, leaving a 2-inch overhang on two opposite sides of the pan. Butter the foil. Set the pan aside.

5. Remove the thermometer from the fudge mixture. Using a hand mixer, beat the mixture on high speed until it is a few shades lighter in color and thickens enough that the beaters form trails that briefly expose the bottom of the pan as they pass through, 10 to 20 minutes. Pour the thickened fudge into the prepared pan, using a rubber spatula to help nudge it out of the pot. You can scrape the bottom of the pot but not the sides; any crystals that stick to the pot should stay in the pot. Smooth the top of the fudge with the spatula. Set the pan on a rack and let the fudge cool completely, about 2 hours. The fudge will be slightly soft the day it's made but will firm up overnight.

6. Turn the fudge out onto a clean cutting board and peel off the foil. Turn the slab of fudge right side up and cut it into 25 equal pieces.

PER SERVING: 190 CALORIES | 1g PROTEIN | 30g CARB | 9g TOTAL FAT | 6g SAT FAT | 2.5g MONO FAT | 0g POLY FAT | 25mg CHOL | 100mg SODIUM | 1g FIBER

give your homemade fudge a flavor twist

Peppermint-Chocolate Fudge
After beating the fudge, stir in ½ cup crushed peppermint candy. Sprinkle ¼ cup crushed candy over the fudge after smoothing the top.

Rocky Road Fudge
After beating the fudge, stir in 2 cups mini marshmallows and 1⅓ cups toasted slivered almonds.

Chocolate-Coconut Fudge
After beating the fudge, stir in 2¼ cups toasted sweetened coconut flakes. Sprinkle ¼ cup of the coconut over the fudge after smoothing the top.

Mocha-Chocolate Fudge
Add 2 Tbs. instant espresso or coffee to the chocolate-cream mixture and cook as directed in the recipe. After beating the fudge, stir in ½ cup cocoa nibs. If you like, after smoothing the top, lightly score the fudge into 25 pieces and place a coffee bean in the center of each piece.

chocolate-covered sandwich cookies with dulce de leche (alfajores)

YIELDS ABOUT TWENTY-EIGHT 2-INCH SANDWICH COOKIES

- **9** oz. (2 cups) unbleached all-purpose flour; more for rolling
- **9** oz. (2 cups) whole-wheat flour
- **2** tsp. baking powder
- **1** tsp. table salt
- **8** oz. (1 cup) unsalted butter, softened
- **¾** cup granulated sugar
- **1½** tsp. finely grated orange zest
- **2** 13.4-oz. cans Nestlé® dulce de leche
- **1** lb. bittersweet chocolate, chopped
- **1** pint heavy cream

These delicate shortbread cookies with a gooey dulce de leche filling and a coating of dark chocolate are a perfect holiday go-to cookie.

MAKE THE COOKIES

1. In a medium mixing bowl, whisk the flours, baking powder, and salt. In a stand mixer fitted with the paddle attachment, cream the butter and sugar on medium speed until light and fluffy, 2 to 3 minutes. Stir in the orange zest. Scrape down the bowl and paddle with a rubber spatula.

2. With the mixer on low, gradually add the flour mixture to the butter mixture. After adding the last of the flour but before it's fully incorporated, add ¼ to ⅓ cup cold water and mix just until a smooth dough forms, 1 to 2 minutes. Divide the dough into two equal pieces, form into disks, and wrap in plastic. Chill overnight.

3. Position a rack in the center of the oven and heat the oven to 350°F. Line 2 cookie sheets with parchment. Roll out the cold dough on a lightly floured surface until it's ⅛ to 3⁄16 inch thick. With a 2-inch plain or fluted round cookie cutter, cut the dough in circles—you can gather and reroll the scraps once. Bake one sheet at a time until the edges are very lightly browned and the cookies puff up slightly, 8 to 10 minutes. Cool the cookies on a rack and store in an airtight container for up to 3 days or freeze for up to 1 month, until you're ready to fill and coat them.

FILL THE COOKIES

Lay out the cookies, flat side down. Put a heaping ½ Tbs. of dulce de leche on half of the cookies. Cover each with a top cookie, flat side up.

COAT THE COOKIES

1. Put the chocolate in a small, deep, heatproof bowl. In a small saucepan over medium-high heat, bring the cream just to a boil. Pour over the chocolate and let sit for 10 minutes. Stir the mixture very gently, incorporating the cream steadily and without overworking, until glossy and completely mixed.

2. Line 2 cookie sheets or rimmed baking sheets with parchment. Pick up a sandwich cookie with a small offset spatula. Immerse in the chocolate mixture, flipping the cookie to coat completely. Pick up with the spatula and tap a couple of times on the side of the bowl to get rid of excess chocolate. With another spatula in the opposite hand, gently smooth out the top of the cookie and then run the spatula along the bottom. Transfer to the parchment-lined sheet. Repeat with the remaining cookies. Allow the coating to set at room temperature for a few hours and then serve.

3. Store in a plastic container, separating each cookie with parchment or waxed paper, in the refrigerator for up to 2 weeks or freeze for up to 3 months.

PER SERVING: 370 CALORIES | 6g PROTEIN | 45g CARB | 19g TOTAL FAT | 12g SAT FAT | 5g MONO FAT | 0.5g POLY FAT | 50mg CHOL | 160mg SODIUM | 3g FIBER

bite-size ginger cupcakes

YIELDS 36 MINIATURE
CUPCAKES

4 oz. (1 cup plus 3 Tbs.) sifted cake flour

1 tsp. ground ginger

¼ tsp. freshly grated nutmeg

¼ tsp. table salt

¼ tsp. baking soda

⅛ tsp. baking powder

3 oz. (6 Tbs.) unsalted butter, at room temperature

⅔ cup granulated sugar

½ tsp. pure vanilla extract

1 1-inch cube (¾ oz. peeled piece) fresh ginger, finely grated (plus any juice)

4 tsp. lightly packed, finely grated lemon zest

1 large egg, at room temperature

½ cup sour cream (not low-fat), at room temperature

¼ cup (about 1 oz.) finely chopped crystallized ginger; more for garnish, if you like

Lemon–Cream Cheese Frosting (recipe on facing page)

Cupcake liners make it easier to remove the cupcakes from the pan and can also make the cupcakes look more festive.

1. Position a rack in the middle of the oven and heat the oven to 350°F. Line three miniature muffin pans (with 12 cups each) with miniature paper cupcake liners.

2. Sift the cake flour with the ground ginger, nutmeg, salt, baking soda, and baking powder. Whisk to ensure thorough mixing. Using a stand mixer fitted with the paddle attachment (or a hand mixer), beat the butter in a medium bowl on medium speed until smooth, about 1 minute. Add 3 Tbs. of the sugar, the vanilla, grated ginger, and lemon zest; beat on medium speed for 1 minute. Add the remaining sugar, about 2 Tbs. at a time, beating for a few seconds after each addition. Scrape the bowl and beat for another 2 minutes. Scrape the bowl again. Add the egg and beat on medium high until very smooth, about 1 minute.

3. Add about one-third of the flour mixture and stir gently with a rubber spatula only until incorporated. Add half of the sour cream and stir until incorporated. Repeat with half of the remaining flour mixture, the rest of the sour cream, ending with the last of the flour mixture. Stir in the crystallized ginger.

4. Portion the batter evenly into the prepared muffin cups, filling each cup about three-quarters full. (Use two regular teaspoons: one to pick up the batter, one to push it off.) Don't smooth the batter.

5. Arrange the pans in the oven so that there's a bit of space between them and bake until the cupcakes are pale golden and spring back when gently pressed in the center, 17 to 20 minutes. Let the cupcakes cool in the tins on wire racks for 5 minutes and then invert the pans onto the racks to remove the cupcakes. Immediately turn the cupcakes right side up on the racks and let cool completely.

6. Spoon a heaping 1 tsp. frosting onto the center of each cupcake and spread and swirl it with the back of the teaspoon. Garnish with a thin slice or two of the crystallized ginger, if using.

PER CUPCAKE WITH FROSTING: 56 CALORIES | 0.5g PROTEIN | 7g CARB | 2.5g TOTAL FAT | 1.5g SAT FAT | 1g MONO FAT | 0g POLY FAT | 15mg CHOL | 30mg SODIUM | 0g FIBER

> **If you don't want to garnish the frosted cupcakes with chopped crystallized ginger, try a thin slice of crystallized ginger or strips of lemon zest or candied flowers.**

lemon–cream cheese frosting

YIELDS 1¼ CUPS

5 oz. cream cheese (not low-fat or whipped), at room temperature

2 Tbs. unsalted butter, at room temperature

2 Tbs. lightly packed, finely grated lemon zest

4 tsp. fresh lemon juice

½ tsp. pure vanilla extract

5 oz. confectioners' sugar (1¼ cups, spooned and leveled)

In a medium bowl, beat the cream cheese with a hand-held electric mixer on medium speed until very smooth, about 30 seconds. Add the butter and beat until smooth, about 30 seconds. Beat in the lemon zest, lemon juice, and vanilla. On low speed, gradually add the confectioners' sugar, beating until smooth. Increase the speed to high and beat for just a few seconds, until the frosting is smooth and fluffy. Don't overbeat or you may thin the frosting.

PER SERVING: 35 CALORIES | 0g PROTEIN | 4g CARB | 2g TOTAL FAT | 1.5g SAT FAT | 0.5g MONO FAT | 0g POLY FAT | 5mg CHOL | 10mg SODIUM | 0g FIBER

classic mojito

6 **large fresh spearmint leaves, plus 1 nice sprig, for garnish**

4 **tsp. superfine sugar; more to taste**

1 **lime**

Crushed ice as needed

2 **fl. oz. (¼ cup) light rum**

Cold club soda as needed

This Cuban mint and lime cocktail is pronounced moh-hee-toh. If your barware is particularly fragile, muddle the mint and sugar in a mortar or other vessel and then transfer it to the serving glass.

In a tall, narrow (Collins) glass, mash the mint leaves into the sugar with a muddler or a similar tool (like the handle of a wooden spoon) until the leaves look crushed and the sugar starts to turn light green, about 30 seconds. Cut the lime into quarters. Squeeze the juice from all 4 quarters into the glass, dropping 2 of the squeezed quarters into the glass as you go. Stir with a teaspoon until the sugar dissolves into the lime juice. Fill the glass with crushed ice and pour the rum over the ice. Top off with club soda, stir well, garnish with the mint sprig, and serve right away.

PER SERVING: 180 CALORIES | 1g PROTEIN | 13g CARB | 0g TOTAL FAT | 0g SAT FAT | 0g MONO FAT | 0g POLY FAT | 0mg CHOL | 35mg SODIUM | 0g FIBER

watermelon gin punch

SERVES 8

½ **small round seedless watermelon (about 3½ lb.), peeled and cut into large chunks**

½ **cup fresh lemon juice, strained**

½ **cup simple syrup (recipe in sidebar below)**

8 **sprigs fresh mint; more for garnish**

2 **cups Hendrick's® gin**

This refreshing pitcher drink is just the thing for a summer party

1. Working in batches if necessary, purée the watermelon in a blender or food processor and press the purée through a strainer. You'll need about 4 cups of juice—it's fine if there's some pulp in the juice. Chill.

2. Put the lemon juice, simple syrup, and mint in a 3-quart serving pitcher or a punch bowl and mash the mint thoroughly with a muddler or the back of a wooden spoon. Add about 4 cups of ice, the gin, and the watermelon juice and stir.

3. Serve in rocks glasses over ice. Garnish with mint sprigs.

how to make simple syrup

Simple syrup is the base for many a cocktail. If you have leftover syrup, store it in the fridge for up to a month.

In a small saucepan, mix 1 cup granulated sugar with 1 cup water. Bring to a boil over medium-high heat, stirring until the sugar is completely dissolved. Immediately remove from the heat and let cool. Yields about 1½ cups.

brown sugar spice cookies

YIELDS ABOUT 8 DOZEN 2-INCH
COOKIES

- 11¼ oz. (2½ cups) unbleached all-purpose flour
- 2 tsp. ground cinnamon
- 1 tsp. ground ginger
- 1 tsp. ground nutmeg
- ½ tsp. table salt
- ¼ tsp. baking soda
- ¼ tsp. ground allspice
- ¼ tsp. ground black pepper
- 6 oz. (¾ cup) unsalted butter, softened
- 1½ cups very firmly packed, very fresh dark brown sugar
- 2 Tbs. molasses
- 1 large egg yolk
- 1 large egg
- 1 tsp. pure vanilla extract
- 1 egg white
- 8 oz. (2 cups) coarsely chopped toasted walnuts

Keep a stash of this dough in the freezer so you can bake a batch at a moment's notice.

MIX THE DOUGH

Sift together the flour, cinnamon, ginger, nutmeg, salt, baking soda, allspice, and pepper. In the bowl of a stand mixer fitted with the paddle attachment, cream the butter on medium-low speed until smooth, about 2 minutes. Add the brown sugar in three additions and then add the molasses; scrape the bowl as needed. Mix for another 2 minutes. Blend in the egg yolk, egg, and vanilla, scraping the bowl again. Reduce the speed to low and add the dry ingredients in three additions, mixing just until combined. Portion the dough into thirds, wrap each third in plastic, and refrigerate until slightly firm, about 30 minutes.

SHAPE THE DOUGH

Have ready three 15-inch sheets of plastic wrap. Whisk the egg white lightly with 1 teaspoon water. Put the chopped walnuts in a long, shallow pan (like a 7x11-inch Pyrex® dish). Working with one piece of dough at a time on a lightly floured surface, roll into a log about 8 inches long. Set it on a sheet of waxed paper. Brush lightly all over with the egg white and then roll the log in the walnuts, pressing gently so the nuts adhere. The roll should lengthen to at least 9 inches. Position the log on a sheet of plastic wrap, centering it at the long edge closest to you. Roll tightly, twisting the ends firmly to seal. With your hands on either end of the log, push firmly toward the center to compact the dough. The finished log should measure about 9 inches long and 1¾ inches thick. Repeat with the remaining dough. Refrigerate until firm enough to slice, at least 2 hours, or freeze for up to 3 months.

BAKE THE COOKIES

Position racks in the upper and lower thirds of the oven. Heat the oven to 350°F. Line two rimmed baking sheets with parchment. Working with one log at a time, use a tomato knife or other small serrated knife to slice the dough into ¼-inch rounds, using a gentle sawing motion. Set the rounds 1 inch apart on the prepared pans and bake until the tops feel set and slightly firm, about 14 minutes, rotating the pans as needed. Let cool on the pans for 5 minutes. With a thin metal spatula, transfer the cookies to racks. When cool, store between sheets of waxed paper in a tightly covered container for up to a week, or freeze for up to 3 months.

keep your logs round

To keep your perfectly shaped round log from flattening out on the bottom while it chills, try these ideas:

Turn frequently Put the logs on a level shelf or flat baking sheet in the refrigerator or freezer and turn each log every 15 minutes for the first hour. As the logs chill, the bottoms will flatten from the weight of the dough. To correct this, remold the logs by rolling them back and forth a few times on the countertop.

Use a cradle If you happen to have a baguette pan, it makes a perfect cradle for chilling logs of dough. If you don't, save a few empty paper towel rolls, cut each in half lengthwise to make two cardboard troughs with rounded bottoms, and then place a log in each half for chilling. For both of these methods, after the logs have chilled for 15 to 20 minutes, turn them over once and chill until firm.

gingery plum cake

SERVES 8 TO 10

FOR THE CAKE

- 6 oz. (1⅓ cups) unbleached all-purpose flour; more for the pan
- 1 tsp. ground ginger
- ¾ tsp. baking powder
- ¼ tsp. baking soda
- ¼ tsp. table salt
- 3 oz. (6 tablespoons) unsalted butter, at room temperature; more for the pan
- 1 cup packed light brown sugar
- 2 large eggs
- 1 tsp. pure vanilla extract
- ⅔ cup (5½ ounces) sour cream

FOR THE TOPPING

- 1 plum (or pluot or ripe apricot), halved, pitted, and cut into ⅛- to ¼-inch slices
- 2 tsp. finely grated fresh ginger
- 3 Tbs. firmly packed light brown sugar
- 1 Tbs. unbleached all-purpose flour

  Whipped cream, for garnish (optional)

Apricots or pluots can also work in this recipe.

1. Make the cake: Position a rack in the center of the oven and heat the oven to 350°F. Lightly butter a 9 x 2-inch round cake pan. Line the bottom with a parchment circle cut to fit the pan and lightly flour the sides, tapping out the excess.

2. In a medium bowl, whisk the flour, ground ginger, baking powder, baking soda, and salt. In a stand mixer fitted with the paddle attachment (or with a hand mixer), beat the butter and sugar on medium high until well blended and fluffy, about 3 minutes. Add the eggs, one at a time, beating on medium speed until just blended and adding the vanilla with the second egg. Using a wide rubber spatula, fold in half the dry ingredients, then the sour cream, and then the remaining dry ingredients. Scrape the batter into the prepared pan and spread evenly. Bake for 15 minutes.

3. Meanwhile, make the topping: Combine the sliced fruit and the grated ginger in a small bowl and toss until the ginger is well distributed. Add the sugar and flour. Using a table fork, mix the ingredients to coat the fruit evenly. After the cake has baked for 15 minutes, scatter the topping evenly over the cake, working quickly. Don't worry about the fruit looking perfect—this is a rustic cake. Continue baking until a toothpick inserted in the center of the cake comes out clean, another 35 to 40 minutes.

4. Let the cake cool on a rack for 15 minutes. Run a knife around the inside edge of the pan. Using a dry dishtowel to protect your hands, lay a rack on top of the cake pan and, holding onto both pan and rack, invert the cake. Lift the pan from the cake. Peel away the parchment. Lay a flat serving plate on the bottom of the cake and flip the cake one more time so that the fruit is on top. Serve warm or at room temperature, with whipped cream if you like.

PER SERVING: 270 CALORIES | 4g PROTEIN | 40g CARB | 11g TOTAL FAT | 7g SAT FAT | 2g MONO FAT | 0g POLY FAT | 70mg CHOL | 150mg SODIUM | 1g FIBER

caramel turtle bars

YIELDS ABOUT 4 DOZEN
1½-INCH-SQUARE BARS

FOR THE SHORTBREAD CRUST

Nonstick cooking spray, vegetable oil, or melted butter for the pan

7 **oz. (14 Tbs.) unsalted butter, melted and cooled to just warm**

½ **cup packed light brown sugar**

½ **tsp. table salt**

9 **oz. (2 cups) unbleached all-purpose flour**

FOR THE CARAMEL TOPPING

2 **cups pecan halves, toasted and coarsely chopped**

1 **cup packed light brown sugar**

¾ **cup heavy cream**

¼ **lb. (½ cup) unsalted butter, cut into chunks**

½ **cup light corn syrup**

¼ **tsp. table salt**

FOR THE GANACHE

2 **oz. good-quality bittersweet chocolate, finely chopped (about ½ cup)**

6 **Tbs. heavy cream**

Crunchy pecans, chewy caramel, and chocolate. Wow.

1. Make the shortbread crust: Line a straight-sided 13 x 9-inch metal baking pan with foil, letting the ends create an overhanging edge for easy removal. Lightly coat the sides of the foil (not the bottom) with nonstick cooking spray, oil, or melted butter to prevent the caramel from sticking.

2. In a medium bowl, stir the butter, brown sugar, and salt. Stir in the flour to make a stiff dough. Press the mixture evenly into the bottom of the prepared pan. Prick the dough all over with a fork. Refrigerate the pan for 30 minutes (or freeze for 5 to 7 minutes), until the dough is firm.

3. Meanwhile, position a rack in the center of the oven and heat the oven to 325°F.

4. Bake the dough for 20 minutes, and then decrease the oven temperature to 300°F and bake until the crust is golden all over and completely set, about another 15 minutes.

5. Make the topping: Sprinkle the pecans evenly over the crust.

6. In a heavy medium saucepan, bring the brown sugar, cream, butter, corn syrup, and salt to a boil over medium-high heat, stirring until all the ingredients are melted and smooth. Let the mixture continue to boil, without stirring, until a candy thermometer registers 240°F, about 6 more minutes. Turn off the heat and immediately (but carefully) pour the caramel evenly over the prepared crust. Let the bars cool completely, about 2 hours, before garnishing with the ganache.

7. Make the ganache: Put the chocolate in a small heatproof bowl. In a small saucepan, bring the heavy cream to a boil. Remove from the heat and pour over the chocolate. Let sit for 3 minutes. Stir gently with a rubber spatula until combined and smooth.

8. Fill a zip-top plastic bag with the ganache, snip the tip off a corner, and drizzle the ganache decoratively over the caramel bars (you don't have to use all the ganache; keep the extra in the fridge for up to 5 days). Let the ganache set, 30 minutes to an hour. Carefully lift the bars from the pan using the foil sides and transfer them to a cutting board. Separate the foil from the bars by sliding a spatula between them. Cut the bars into 1½-inch squares. They will keep at room temperature for 1 week.

PER SERVING: 160 CALORIES | 1g PROTEIN | 15g CARB | 11g TOTAL FAT | 5g SAT FAT | 4g MONO FAT | 1g POLY FAT | 20mg CHOL | 45mg SODIUM | 1g FIBER

nutty chocolate shortbread wedges

YIELDS 12 OR 16 WEDGES

FOR THE SHORTBREAD

- ¼ lb. (½ cup) unsalted butter, at room temperature; more for the pan
- ½ cup granulated sugar
- ¾ oz. (¼ cup) unsweetened cocoa powder, preferably Dutch-processed
- ¼ tsp. table salt
- 1 large egg yolk
- ½ tsp. pure vanilla extract
- 4½ oz. (1 cup) unbleached all-purpose flour

FOR THE GLAZE

- 3 oz. bittersweet or semisweet chocolate, coarsely chopped (a generous ½ cup)
- 1 oz. (2 Tbs.) unsalted butter, cut into two pieces
- ½ cup (2 oz.) coarsely chopped pecans or walnuts, toasted and cooled, or chopped pistachios

Adding an egg yolk to this shortbread gives it a softer, less sandy texture.

1. Make the shortbread: Position a rack in the middle of the oven and heat the oven to 350°F. Lightly butter the bottom and sides of a 9½-inch fluted tart pan with a removable bottom.

2. In a medium bowl, combine the butter, sugar, cocoa, and salt. Beat with an electric mixer on medium speed until well blended. Scrape the bowl. Add the egg yolk and vanilla and continue beating on medium until just combined. Add the flour and mix on low speed, scraping the bowl as needed, until the dough begins to clump together, about 1 minute. Scrape the dough into the prepared pan, scattering the pieces of dough evenly. Using your fingertips (lightly floured, if necessary), pat the dough onto the bottom (not up the sides) of the prepared pan to create an even layer. Bake until the top no longer looks wet and the dough just barely begins to pull away from the sides of the pan, about 25 minutes.

3. Shortly before the shortbread is done, make the glaze: Melt the chocolate and butter on the stove or in a microwave. Stir until smooth. When the shortbread is done, transfer the pan to a rack. Pour the warm glaze over the shortbread and, using an offset spatula, spread the glaze evenly to within ½ inch of the edge. Scatter the nuts evenly over the glaze and gently press them in. Let cool completely until the glaze is set. Remove the shortbread from the tart pan and cut it into 12 or 16 wedges. Serve at room temperature.

PER SERVING: 180 CALORIES | 2g PROTEIN | 16g CARB | 13g TOTAL FAT | 6g SAT FAT | 4g MONO FAT | 1.5g POLY FAT | 30mg CHOL | 40mg SODIUM | 1g FIBER

lemon bars

YIELDS SIXTEEN 1½-INCH BARS;
2½ CUPS CURD

FOR THE SHORTBREAD

¼	lb. (½ cup) unsalted butter, at room temperature
2	Tbs. granulated sugar
1	Tbs. confectioners' sugar
½	tsp. pure vanilla extract
2¼	oz. (½ cup) all-purpose flour
2½	oz. (⅔ cup) cake flour
¼	tsp. baking powder
¼	tsp. table salt

FOR THE LEMON CURD

1	cup fresh lemon juice (from 4 to 6 lemons)
2	oz. (4 Tbs.) unsalted butter, cut into two pieces
2	Tbs. heavy cream
1	cup granulated sugar
4	large eggs
2	large egg yolks
¼	tsp. table salt
¼	tsp. pure vanilla extract

Make Ahead

Shortbread dough can be wrapped in plastic and frozen for up to 2 months. When you want to make lemon bars (or any other shortbread-based recipe), just let the dough thaw overnight in the refrigerator before proceeding.

These tangy bars will last for several days in an airtight container in the refrigerator, but they're best when fresh.

1. Make the shortbread: In a large bowl, cream the butter and both sugars with a hand mixer on medium speed (or mix by hand with a wooden spoon) until light and fluffy, about 5 minutes. Beat in the vanilla until thoroughly combined, scraping the sides of the bowl.

2. In a medium bowl, sift together both flours, the baking powder, and the salt. With the mixer on low speed, slowly blend the dry ingredients into the wet ingredients, scraping down the sides, until the flour is completely blended and the dough is homogeneous.

3. Scrape the dough from the bowl onto a sheet of plastic. Wrap well and press down to form a ½-inch-thick square. Refrigerate the dough until it's firm but still pliable, about 20 minutes.

4. Heat the oven to 350°F. Have ready two sheets of parchment, each at least 11 x 11 inches.

5. When the dough is firm, unwrap it and put it between the sheets of parchment. Roll the dough to an approximate square, slightly larger than 8 x 8 inches and about ¼ inch thick. Remove the top sheet of parchment, trim the dough with a dull knife to an 8 x 8-inch square, and put it (along with the parchment that it's on) into an 8 x 8-inch baking pan. Press the dough into the bottom of the pan, letting the excess parchment come up the sides (trim it to about 1 inch above the rim). The dough should be an even thickness all around but it needn't be perfectly smooth. Bake until the shortbread is light golden on top, 25 to 30 minutes; in a glass pan, look for a golden brown color on the bottom. Remove the pan from the oven, but keep the heat set to 350°F as you make the lemon curd.

6. Make the lemon curd: In a medium saucepan over medium heat, heat the lemon juice, butter, and cream to just under a boil; the butter should be melted. Remove from the heat.

7. In a medium bowl, whisk by hand the sugar, eggs, and yolks until combined. Whisk in a bit of the hot liquid and then gradually whisk in a bit more until it's all added.

8. Pour the mixture back into the saucepan and heat over medium heat, stirring constantly with a wooden spoon and scraping the bottom and sides of the pan to keep the eggs from scrambling. Cook until the lemon curd coats the spoon thickly enough to leave a line when you draw your finger through, 5 to 8 minutes. Remove from the heat and strain through a fine sieve. Stir in the salt and vanilla.

9. To finish: Pour the curd over the baked shortbread and smooth it evenly with a spatula, if needed. Bake until the curd has set and jiggles like firm gelatin, 15 to 20 minutes. Let cool to room temperature. Gently tug on the parchment on all sides to loosen the bar from the pan. Lift it out and onto a cutting board and let cool to room temperature. Refrigerate until the curd has completely set, at least 4 hours. Trim the sides for a cleaner look, if you like, and cut into 16 pieces.

PER BAR: 220 CALORIES | 3g PROTEIN | 27g CARB | 12g TOTAL FAT | 7g SAT FAT | 4g MONO FAT | 1g POLY FAT | 110mg CHOL | 95mg SODIUM | 0g FIBER

gingerbread biscotti

YIELDS ABOUT 24 BISCOTTI

- **10** oz. (2¼ cups) unbleached all-purpose flour; plus more for shaping
- **1¼** cups packed dark brown sugar
- **2** tsp. ground ginger
- **1¼** tsp. baking powder
- **1** tsp. ground cinnamon
- **½** tsp. table salt
- **¼** tsp. ground nutmeg
- **¼** tsp. baking soda
- **4** oz. (1 cup) pecans, coarsely chopped
- **4** oz. (½ cup) lightly packed dried apricots, coarsely chopped
- **¼** cup molasses
- **2** large eggs
- **2** tsp. finely grated orange zest (from about 1 medium navel orange)

The familiar flavors of ginger-bread work perfectly in biscotti.

1. Position a rack in the middle of the oven and heat the oven to 350°F. Line a large cookie sheet with parchment.

2. In a stand mixer fitted with the paddle attachment, combine the flour, brown sugar, ginger, baking powder, cinnamon, salt, nutmeg, and baking soda on medium-low speed until well blended. On low speed, briefly mix in the pecans and apricots. In a measuring cup, lightly whisk the molasses, eggs, and orange zest. With the mixer on low, slowly pour in the egg mixture. Continue mixing until the dough is well blended and comes together in large, moist clumps, 1 to 2 minutes.

3. Dump the dough onto an unfloured work surface. Divide into two equal piles (about 1 lb. each). Shape each pile into a log that's 10 inches long and about 1½ inches in diameter, lightly flouring your hands as needed (the dough is a bit sticky).

4. Position the logs on the lined cookie sheet about 4 inches apart. Bake until the tops are cracked and spring back slightly when gently pressed, 30 to 35 minutes. Transfer the sheet to a rack and let cool until the logs are cool enough to handle, about 20 minutes.

5. Carefully peel the biscotti logs from the parchment and transfer to a cutting board. Using a serrated knife, saw each log into diagonal slices ¾ inch wide. Return the slices to the cookie sheet (no need for fresh parchment) and arrange them cut side down. It's all right if they touch because they won't spread.

6. Bake until the biscotti are dried to your taste, about 10 minutes (for slightly moist and chewy) to 20 minutes (for super-dry and crunchy). Put the cookie sheet on a rack and let the biscotti cool completely. The biscotti will still give slightly when pressed, but will harden as they cool. When cool, store in airtight containers.

PER SERVING: 150 CALORIES | 2g PROTEIN | 26g CARB | 4g TOTAL FAT | 0g SAT FAT | 2g MONO FAT | 1g POLY FAT | 20mg CHOL | 95mg SODIUM | 1g FIBER

cardamom-honey cut-outs

13½ oz. (3 cups) unbleached
all-purpose flour; more
for rolling

1 tsp. ground cardamom

½ tsp. table salt

¼ tsp. baking soda

½ lb. (1 cup) unsalted butter,
at room temperature

¾ cup granulated sugar

¼ cup honey

1 large egg

1 tsp. pure vanilla extract

Subtle spice and honey give these cut-outs a lovely wintry flavor.

1. In a medium bowl, combine the flour, cardamom, salt, and baking soda. Whisk until well blended.

2. Using a stand mixer fitted with the paddle attachment (or in a large bowl with a hand mixer), beat the butter and sugar on medium speed until well blended and slightly fluffy, about 3 minutes. Scrape the bowl and the beater. Add the honey, egg, and vanilla. Continue mixing on medium speed until well blended, about 1 minute. Add the flour mixture and mix on low speed until the dough is well blended and comes together in moist clumps, 30 to 60 seconds.

3. Divide the dough roughly in half. On a piece of plastic, shape each dough half into a smooth 5-inch disk. Wrap well in the plastic. Refrigerate until chilled and firm enough to roll out, 1 to 1½ hours. (The dough may be refrigerated for up to 3 days or frozen for a month. Thaw overnight in the refrigerator before proceeding with the recipe.)

4. Bake the cookies: Position a rack in the center of the oven and heat the oven to 350°F. Line two or more cookie sheets with parchment or nonstick baking liners. Working with one disk at a time, roll the dough on a floured work surface to about ³⁄₁₆ inch thick. Dust with additional flour as needed. Choose one or more cookie cutters of any shape that are about 2½ inches wide and cut out shapes. Arrange the cookies about 1 inch apart on the lined cookie sheets. Gather the scraps and gently press together. Reroll and cut. Repeat with the remaining dough.

5. Bake one sheet at a time until the cookies' edges develop a ¼-inch-wide light-brown rim, 11 to 13 minutes (rotate the sheet halfway through baking for even browning). Let the cookies cool on the sheet for about 10 minutes and then transfer them to a rack to cool completely.

PER SERVING: 50 CALORIES | 1g PROTEIN | 7g CARB | 2.5g TOTAL FAT | 1.5g SAT FAT | 0.5g MONO FAT | 0g POLY FAT | 10mg CHOL | 20mg SODIUM | 0g FIBER

strawberry–mint tea
sparkling punch

sour mash
and lime tea

sour mash and lime tea

YIELDS 2 QUARTS LIME-TEA MIX;
SERVES 8

6   regular-size tea bags
    (about ½ oz. total)

1   cup granulated sugar

1   can (6 oz.) frozen limeade
    concentrate, thawed

12 oz. sour-mash whiskey
    (such as Jack Daniel's®),
    or any good bourbon
    (about 1½ cups)

    Lime wedges, for garnish
    (optional)

This is a delectable variation on a Southern Sour.

1. In a medium saucepan, bring 4 cups water to a boil. Add the tea bags, remove from the heat, cover, and steep for 15 minutes.

2. Meanwhile, put the sugar and limeade concentrate in a 2-quart heatproof container (like a large Pyrex liquid measure). When the tea is ready, remove the tea bags (don't squeeze them) and add the tea to the limeade mixture, stirring to combine. Stir in 3 cups cold water, let cool to room temperature, and then refrigerate until ready to serve.

3. To serve, pour 1½ oz. of the whiskey into each 12-oz. glass. Add 1 cup of the limeade-tea mixture to each glass. Stir to combine. Add ice and garnish with the lime wedges, if you like.

PER SERVING: 250 CALORIES | 0g PROTEIN | 38g CARB | 0g TOTAL FAT | 0g SAT FAT | 0g MONO FAT | 0g POLY FAT | 0mg CHOL | 5mg SODIUM | 0g FIBER

strawberry–mint tea sparkling punch

YIELDS ABOUT 3½ QUARTS,
ROUGHLY TWENTY 5-OZ.
PUNCH-CUP SERVINGS OR
12 COCKTAIL-SIZE SERVINGS

- **2** **pints fresh strawberries (about 1 lb.), cleaned, hulled, and halved**
- **½** **cup plus 2 Tbs. granulated sugar**
- **2** **Tbs. fresh lemon juice**
- **Kosher salt**
- **6** **regular-size mint tea bags (real tea with mint, not herbal tea), about ½ oz. total**
- **1** **liter (33.8 ounces) sparkling water, chilled**
- **Mint sprigs, for garnish (optional)**
- **Whole fresh strawberries, for garnish (optional)**

The beauty of serving this punch by the glass is that you can make a special concoction for each guest. Children will enjoy this tea with lemon-lime soda, and adults might like a splash of Champagne or an American sparkling wine.

1. Put the strawberries, 2 Tbs. of the sugar, the lemon juice, and a good pinch of salt in a food processor or blender. Process until you have a smooth purée, pour it into a container, and refrigerate until needed.

2. In a small saucepan, bring 2¼ cups water to a gentle boil. Add the tea bags, remove from the heat, cover, and steep for 15 minutes.

3. Pour the remaining ½ cup sugar into a 3-quart heatproof container (like a large Pyrex liquid measure). Remove the tea bags when they're finished steeping (don't squeeze them) and pour the tea over the sugar, stirring to dissolve the sugar. Add 6 cups cold water and stir again. Chill until cold.

4. To serve, combine the strawberry purée with the mint tea and stir well to mix completely.

5. If serving in a punch bowl, put the strawberry-mint tea in the punch bowl and slowly add the sparkling water.

6. For individual servings, fill 10-oz. stemmed glasses (wineglasses are great) two-thirds of the way with the strawberry-mint tea and top off with the sparkling water. Garnish with mint sprigs and a strawberry, if you like.

PER SERVING: 30 CALORIES | 0g PROTEIN | 8g CARB | 0g TOTAL FAT | 0g SAT FAT | 0g MONO FAT | 0g POLY FAT | 0mg CHOL | 10mg SODIUM | 0g FIBER

strawberry and champagne terrine

SERVES 8 TO 10

FOR THE CHAMPAGNE LAYER

¼ cup cold water

1 Tbs. powdered gelatin (about 1½ packets)

⅓ cup granulated sugar

1½ cups Champagne or sparkling wine

½ cup sliced strawberries

FOR THE STRAWBERRY LAYER

1 Tbs. powdered gelatin (about 1½ packets)

2 Tbs. Champagne or sparkling wine

2 pt. strawberries, rinsed and hulled

2 tsp. fresh lemon juice

3 to 6 Tbs. granulated sugar

Sliced strawberries, for garnish (optional)

This lovely terrine is made in a 6-cup loaf pan, but you can vary the look of it by using two or more smaller molds or mini loaf pans, or by alternating the Champagne and strawberry components in several layers in one pan. Just be sure that each layer is almost completely set before pouring on another. Serve the well-chilled terrine cut into thin slices.

MAKE THE CHAMPAGNE LAYER

1. Put the water in a small saucepan, sprinkle the gelatin on top, and leave to soften, about 3 minutes. Add the sugar and cook over medium-low heat, stirring to dissolve the sugar and melt the gelatin (don't let it boil). In a medium bowl, combine the gelatin mixture and Champagne. Set the bowl over ice and chill, stirring often, until it reaches the consistency of unbeaten egg whites. Carefully stir in the sliced strawberries.

2. Meanwhile, set a loaf pan in the refrigerator so that it's tilted at a 45-degree angle. (Use a wedge of cheese, sticks of butter, or something similar to prop up the pan.) Pour the Champagne mixture into the pan. Let sit until just set, about 2 hours.

FOR THE STRAWBERRY LAYER

1. In a small saucepan, soften the gelatin in the 2 Tbs. Champagne, about 3 minutes. Set the pan over low heat and heat to dissolve the gelatin. In a food processor, purée the berries with the lemon juice, add the sugar to taste, and then strain the mixture through a fine sieve. Whisk the softened gelatin into the strawberry purée.

2. Once the Champagne layer has almost set, set the loaf pan on a level surface (preferably in the refrigerator so that it won't have to be moved) and carefully pour in the strawberry purée. Refrigerate for at least 6 hours but preferably overnight.

3. To unmold the terrine, cover a cutting board with waxed paper, dip the loaf pan quickly into hot water, and invert it onto the board. Slice the terrine into ½-inch portions; garnish with sliced fresh strawberries, if you like.

PER SERVING: 90 CALORIES | 2g PROTEIN | 15g CARB | 0g TOTAL FAT | 0g SAT FAT | 0g MONO FAT | 0g POLY FAT | 0mg CHOL | 5mg SODIUM | 2mg FIBER

tiny tarts

Everyone loves pie, but it's not exactly finger food; so it's rare to find it (or to serve it) at a cocktail party. These, however, are an exception. Made in muffin tins, each tiny tartlet is a mere 2 inches across. Given their fillings—pecan, cranberry, and pumpkin—these are also a delight when presented at the end of a special dinner.

sweet tartlet dough

**YIELDS ENOUGH DOUGH
FOR 3 DOZEN TARTLETS**

10⅛   oz. (2¼ cups) all-purpose flour

⅓   cup superfine sugar

¼   tsp. table salt

1   cup cold unsalted butter, cut into ½-inch cubes

1   large egg

1   large egg yolk

1   Tbs. cold water

¾   tsp. pure vanilla extract

This buttery crust is easy to handle, can be made ahead and frozen for up to a month, and is a cinch to mold with a wooden tart tamper.

1. Put the flour, sugar, and salt in a food processor. Pulse three or four times to blend. Distribute the butter in the bowl and pulse seven or eight times. Process until the mixture resembles coarse meal, 8 to 10 seconds.

2. In a small bowl, beat the egg, egg yolk, water, and vanilla with a fork. Pour the egg mixture over the flour mixture and pulse five or six times. Process until the mixture just begins to form a mass, 8 to 10 seconds. Empty the dough onto a lightly floured surface and knead six to eight times until the dough is just smooth and malleable. Shape it into an evenly thick 6-inch square. Using a pastry scraper, score the dough at 1-inch intervals so you get thirty-six 1-inch squares. Cover the dough with plastic wrap and chill for at least 20 minutes.

3. Lightly spray 36 muffin cups (if you don't have that many tins, bake the shells in batches) with cooking spray (not necessary for nonstick tins). Using the lines as a guide, cut the dough into 36 pieces. Roll each piece into a ball in your palm. Put one ball in the center of each muffin cup.

4. If you have a wooden tart tamper, flour it lightly. Press the wider end onto a ball of dough until the dough thins out and begins coming up the sides of the cup, and then twist the tamper slightly to release it. Use the tamper's narrower end to push the dough halfway up the sides and to smooth out the dough where the sides meet the bottom. (If you don't have a tart tamper, use a narrow, flat-bottomed glass or your fingers, lightly floured, to press the dough into the cups.)

5. Rub your thumb around the rim of the dough in each cup for a clean, smooth edge. Slightly less than ¾ inch of each muffin cup should be exposed. Chill for at least 10 minutes to firm the dough and then fill the cups with any or all of the fillings on the facing page or p. 228.

pumpkin tartlets

- 1 large egg yolk
- ⅔ cup pure solid-pack pumpkin (not pumpkin pie filling)
- ⅓ cup heavy cream
- ¼ cup packed light brown sugar
- ½ tsp. finely grated orange zest
- ½ tsp. ground cinnamon
- ⅛ tsp. ground nutmeg
- ⅛ tsp. table salt

    A few dashes ground cloves

    12 muffin cups lined with Sweet Tartlet Dough (recipe on facing page)

You might want to garnish these with whipped cream and perhaps a very thin strip of orange zest, twisted into a knot.

1. Position a rack in the lower third of the oven and heat the oven to 375°F.

2. Put all the ingredients in a food processor. Pulse just until the mixture is smooth, five or six times; don't over process. Empty the filling into a liquid measuring cup with a spout and pour the filling into the dough-lined muffin cups. Bake until the pastry is golden brown, 30 to 35 minutes. Let cool for 10 minutes. Run a thin knife around the tartlets to loosen and then let them cool until they're firm enough to handle, about another 15 minutes. Using the tip of a small knife, gently lift the tartlets from the pan and set them on a rack to cool.

PER SERVING: 130 CALORIES | 2g PROTEIN | 13g CARB | 8g TOTAL FAT | 5g SAT FAT | 2g MONO FAT | 0g POLY FAT | 50mg CHOL | 50mg SODIUM | 1g FIBER

pecan tartlets

- 2 large eggs, lightly beaten
- 1 Tbs. heavy cream
- ¼ cup packed light brown sugar
- 1 tsp. all-purpose flour

    Pinch salt

- ½ cup light corn syrup
- 1 Tbs. melted unsalted butter
- ¾ tsp. pure vanilla extract

    12 muffin cups lined with Sweet Tartlet Dough (recipe on facing page)

- ¼ lb. (1 cup) broken pecans, lightly toasted in a 325°F oven for 8 to 10 minutes

This version of pecan pie is neither cloyingly sweet nor overly gooey. It's simply crunchy toasted pecans sprinkled over a mouthwatering brown-sugar filling.

1. Position a rack in the lower third of the oven and heat the oven to 375°F.

2. In a medium bowl, blend the eggs and cream. In another bowl, combine the brown sugar, flour, and salt. Stir the dry ingredients into the egg mixture, along with the corn syrup and melted butter; don't overmix. Stir in the vanilla. Transfer the filling to a liquid measuring cup with a spout and pour into the dough-lined muffin cups. Sprinkle the pecans evenly over the tops. Bake until the pastry is golden brown, 28 to 30 minutes. Let cool for 10 minutes. Run a thin knife around the tartlets to loosen and then let them cool until they're firm enough to handle, about another 15 minutes. Using the tip of a small knife, gently lift the tartlets from the pan and set them on a rack to cool.

PER SERVING: 230 CALORIES | 3g PROTEIN | 24g CARB | 14g TOTAL FAT | 5g SAT FAT | 7g MONO FAT | 2g POLY FAT | 65mg CHOL | 75mg SODIUM | 1g FIBER

continued on p. 228 ➤

continued from p. 227

gingery cranberry-pear tartlets

Crystallized ginger adds a warm note to this filling.

YIELDS 12 TARTLETS

1 cup fresh cranberries

⅓ cup granulated sugar

⅓ cup fresh orange juice

2 medium-size, slightly underripe pears (Anjou is good), about ¾ lb. total, peeled, cored, and cut into ½-inch chunks

⅓ cup golden raisins

4 tsp. minced crystallized ginger

A few drops of pure vanilla extract

12 muffin cups lined with Sweet Tartlet Dough (recipe on p. 226)

1. In a 3-qt. saucepan, cook the cranberries, sugar, and orange juice over medium heat just until the berries begin to pop. Reduce the heat to a simmer, partially cover, and cook for 5 minutes. Add the pears, raisins, and ginger. Cook over low heat with the lid askew until the pears are translucent, stirring gently if necessary, 10 to 12 minutes. Uncover and continue cooking until the liquid is syrupy and has reduced to about 2 Tbs., about 2 minutes. Remove from the heat and gently stir in the vanilla (avoid crushing the pears). Let cool to room temperature; the mixture thickens as it stands.

2. Position a rack in the lower third of the oven and heat the oven to 375°F. Spoon the filling into the dough-lined muffin cups. Bake until the pastry is golden brown and the fruit is bubbling, about 30 minutes. Let cool for 10 minutes. Run a thin knife around the tartlets to loosen and then let them cool until they're firm enough to handle, about another 15 minutes. Using the tip of a small knife, gently lift the tartlets from the pan and set them on a rack to cool.

PER SERVING: 140 CALORIES | 1g PROTEIN | 22g CARB | 6g TOTAL FAT | 3g SAT FAT | 2g MONO FAT | 0g POLY FAT | 25mg CHOL | 20mg SODIUM | 1g FIBER

Make Ahead

You can freeze the baked tartlets for a month. Reheat them in a 325°F oven until warm.

sweet ruby

SERVES 1

- **1 fl. oz. (2 Tbs.) ruby port, such as Warre's® Warrior Special Reserve**
- **¾ fl. oz. (1½ Tbs.) Amaretto di Saronno®**
- **2 dashes Angostura bitters**

Ruby port and amaretto liqueur make this a great post-meal warmer: It's sweet, complex, and rich, but very easy to make.

Combine the port, amaretto, and bitters in a chilled mixing glass or cocktail shaker. Fill the glass almost to the top with ice. Stir with a long spoon until well combined, about 10 seconds. Strain into a chilled rocks glass over fresh ice and serve.

PER SERVING: 130 CALORIES | 0g PROTEIN | 14g CARB | 0g TOTAL FAT | 0g SAT FAT | 0g MONO FAT | 0g POLY FAT | 0mg CHOL | 0mg SODIUM | 0g FIBER

eve's black heart

SERVES 2

- **8 fl. oz. (1 cup) dry hard cider (such as Crispin® brut or Farnum Hill™ semi-dry), chilled**
- **1 14.9-fl.-oz. can Guinness draught, chilled**
- **1 fl. oz. (2 Tbs.) Calvados**

Similar to a Black Velvet, which is made with Guinness® and Champagne, this beer cocktail has a double hit of apples from both hard cider and apple brandy. Hence, the name, derived from Eve's penchant for the forbidden fruit.

Divide the cider between two chilled pint glasses. To float the Guinness on top of the cider, pop the tab on the can, let it foam up, and then pour the beer slowly over the rounded back of a tablespoon measure held over each glass, stopping when almost full. Gently pour 1 Tbs. of the Calvados on top of each drink.

PER SERVING: 180 CALORIES | 1G PROTEIN | 17g CARB | 0g TOTAL FAT | 0g SAT FAT | 0g MONO FAT | 0g POLY FAT | 0mg CHOL | 10mg SODIUM | 0g FIBER

pistachio meringues with toasted coconut

YIELDS ABOUT 40 KISSES

- 3 oz. (¾ cup) confectioners' sugar
- ½ cup superfine sugar
- Pinch of table salt
- 4 large egg whites, at room temperature
- ½ tsp. cream of tartar
- ¼ tsp. pure vanilla extract
- ⅓ cup unsalted pistachios, chopped medium finely
- ⅓ cup shredded unsweetened coconut, lightly toasted
- 3 Tbs. finely chopped pistachios for garnish (optional)

Secrets to Success

A few tips guarantee great results.

- Don't try to make meringues if your kitchen is very humid (humidity keeps them from crisping).
- Begin with your ingredients at room temperature for best volume, and be sure the beaters and bowl are grease free and dry.
- Keep beating. Don't stop beating your egg whites and sugar until you have beautiful, glossy, firm peaks.

These lighter-than-air delights are as much fun to make as they are to eat. If you can't find superfine sugar, finely grind granulated sugar in a food processor; measure after grinding. If you don't have a pastry bag, simply spoon the meringues into free-form shapes. Another plus: you can flavor these as you please. And though super delicate, meringues will keep, stored airtight, for weeks.

1. Position racks in the upper and lower thirds of the oven. Heat the oven to 175°F. Line a large heavy baking sheet with parchment. Sift together the confectioners' sugar, superfine sugar, and salt.

2. Using a stand mixer fitted with the whisk attachment (or in a large bowl with a hand mixer), beat the egg whites and cream of tartar. Begin mixing on medium-low speed until frothy. Increase the speed to medium high and beat until the whites form soft peaks. Continue beating while gradually sprinkling in the sifted sugars. When all the sugar is added, increase the speed to high and whip until firm, glossy peaks form. Add the vanilla and the ⅓ cup pistachios and beat just until blended, about 10 seconds.

3. Spoon about half of the meringue into a large pastry bag fitted with a large (#8) star tip. Pipe shapes as you like—see the photos on the facing page (for kisses, about ½ inch wide and about 2 inches from tip to base)—onto the prepared baking sheet, about ½ inch apart. If the tip gets clogged with a nut, use the back of a small knife or spoon to pry open the points of the star tip slightly and the nut will wiggle out. Sprinkle the toasted coconut over the meringues along with a dusting of pistachios, if you like.

4. Bake the meringues until dried and crisp but not browned, about 3 hours. Turn off the oven (leave the door shut) and let the meringues sit in the oven for about 1 hour. Remove them from the oven and gently lift the meringues off the parchment. Serve immediately or store in an airtight container for up to a month.

piping primer

To pipe, squeeze gently with the hand that holds the top of the bag. Use your other hand to guide the tip. (You may want to practice on a sheet of parchment.) This meringue makes lovely little cookies in a variety of sizes and shapes. If you're aiming for consistency, use a template and a pencil to draw circles or other shapes on the parchment to guide your piping.

KISSES Hold the bag perpendicular to the pan and squeeze gently from the top of the bag. Lift the bag straight up while releasing pressure to let a peak form.

LADYFINGERS Gently pipe ladyfinger shapes with even pressure, lifting the tip slightly as you finish.

chocolate espresso torte

- **5 oz. semisweet chocolate, chopped**
- **3 oz. unsweetened chocolate, chopped**
- **¼ lb. (8 Tbs.) unsalted butter, cut into pieces; more for the pan**
- **4 eggs, at room temperature**
- **½ cup sugar**
- **¼ cup brewed espresso or double-strength coffee, cooled to room temperature**
- **1 Tbs. sifted, finely ground espresso beans (from about 1 heaping Tbs. whole beans)**
- **¼ tsp. salt**
- **¼ cup all-purpose flour; more for the pan**

This extremely deep, rich, and dark cake tastes great with whipped cream.

1. Heat the oven to 350°F. Butter an 8-inch cake pan and line the bottom with kitchen parchment. Butter the parchment and lightly flour the pan, shaking out the excess.

2. In a small, heavy-based saucepan over medium heat, melt the chocolates and butter, stirring frequently. Set aside. Using the whisk attachment of a stand mixer, whip the eggs, sugar, brewed espresso, ground espresso beans, and salt on medium-high speed until thick and voluminous, at least 8 minutes. Turn the mixer to low and mix in the butter-chocolate mixture. Turn off the mixer. Sift the flour over the batter and fold until all the ingredients are fully incorporated. Pour the batter into the prepared pan and bake until a skewer inserted in the center of the cake comes out clean, 25 to 30 minutes. Cool in the pan on a rack for 10 min. Set a plate over the torte and carefully invert the torte onto the plate; peel off the parchment. Flip the torte back onto the rack to cool completely before slicing.

PER SERVING: 270 CALORIES | 4g PROTEIN | 24g CARB | 20g TOTAL FAT | 12g SAT FAT | 6g MONO FAT | 1g POLY FAT | 110mg CHOL | 90mg SODIUM | 2g FIBER

Brew a Strong Cup of Coffee

To get the most flavor when using brewed coffee in a recipe, use espresso or regular coffee at double strength. For example, most coffee makers suggest using 1 rounded teaspoon for every 6 ounces of water, so for baking use 2 rounded teaspoons. (Keep in mind that when making espresso, the amount of water called for, whether instant or whole beans, is only about 3 ounces, not the 6 ounces used for regular coffee.) For instant coffee, use twice the powder for the amount of water that's called for.

sparkling sidecar

SERVES 1

- **1 fl. oz. (2 Tbs.) chilled orange liqueur, such as Combier® or Cointreau®**
- **½ fl. oz. (1 Tbs.) Cognac**
- **4 fl. oz. (½ cup) chilled cava, such as Segura Viudas® Brut Reserva; or as needed**
- **Lemon twist, for garnish**

This festive take on a Sidecar cocktail (which typically contains Cognac, orange liqueur, and lemon juice), features Spanish cava in place of the traditional citrus juice.

Combine the orange liqueur and Cognac in a coupe or Champagne flute. Top with the cava, squeeze a lemon twist over the glass, drop it in, and serve.

PER SERVING: 220 CALORIES I 0g PROTEIN I 15g CARB I 0g TOTAL FAT I 0g SAT FAT I 0g MONO FAT I 0g POLY FAT I 0mg CHOL I 0mg SODIUM I 0g FIBER

bourbon hot toddy

SERVES 1

- **2½ fl. oz. (5 Tbs.) bourbon**
- **1 fl. oz. (2 Tbs.) honey**
- **3 small lemon wedges**
- **3 whole cloves**

While a hot toddy can't cure a cold or the flu—as it was thought to do when the drink was invented in the late 19th century—it sure can soothe the soul.

1. Put a kettle of water on the stove to boil.

2. Put the bourbon and honey in a coffee mug. Squeeze the juice from two wedges of lemon into the mug. With a knife, poke 3 holes in the rind of the remaining lemon wedge and push the cloves into the holes. Pour 4 fl. oz. (½ cup) boiling water into the mug and stir well to dissolve the honey. Add the clove-studded lemon wedge and let steep for a couple of minutes before drinking.

PER SERVING: 290 CALORIES I 0g PROTEIN I 36g CARB I 0g TOTAL FAT I 0g SAT FAT I 0g MONO FAT I 0g POLY FAT I 0mg CHOL I 0mg SODIUM I 0g FIBER

hot buttered rum

YIELDS ABOUT ¾ CUP BUTTER, ENOUGH FOR 10 TO 12 DRINKS

- ¾ cup lightly packed dark brown sugar
- ½ cup (8 Tbs.) unsalted butter, at room temperature
- 1 tsp. pure vanilla extract
- ½ tsp. ground cinnamon
- ¼ tsp. ground cloves
- ¼ tsp. freshly grated nutmeg
- ¼ tsp. ground allspice
- 2½ to 3 cups high-quality dark rum, preferably Gosling's®

    Whipped heavy cream, for garnish

Dark brown sugar and a dollop of whipped cream give this buttered rum a deep, rich flavor. The trick to this recipe is to use the best-quality rum you can find. The spiced butter is also delicious spread onto fresh, crusty bread.

1. In a small bowl, mash the sugar, butter, vanilla, cinnamon, cloves, nutmeg, and allspice with a fork until well combined. The spiced butter can be made ahead and refrigerated for up to 3 weeks. Bring the butter to room temperature before using.

2. Bring a kettle of water to a boil; you'll need ½ cup of water for each drink. Fill mugs or heatproof glasses with hot tap water to warm them. Once the water in the kettle boils, empty the warm mugs and fill each with ½ cup boiling water and ¼ cup rum. Stir a generous tablespoon of the spiced butter into each mug until melted. Garnish with a small dollop of whipped cream.

PER SERVING: 250 CALORIES | 0g PROTEIN | 14g CARB | 10g TOTAL FAT | 7g SAT FAT | 3g MONO FAT | 0g POLY FAT | 30mg CHOL | 10mg SODIUM | 0g FIBER

orange-scented mulled wine

YIELDS ABOUT 6 CUPS; SERVES 8

- 10 cloves
- 3 3-inch cinnamon sticks
- 2 star anise
- 1 whole nutmeg, cracked with the side of a chef's knife into a few pieces
- 1 tsp. coriander seeds
- ½ tsp. whole black peppercorns
- 2 bottles (750 ml) or one bottle (1.5 l) medium-to full-bodied fruity red wine, such as Merlot, Shiraz, or Zinfandel
- 1 clementine or tangerine, washed and cut in half crosswise (seeded if necessary)
- ⅓ cup granulated sugar; more to taste
- ¼ cup brandy
- 1 Tbs. Grand Marnier (optional)
- ½ tsp. pure vanilla extract

This traditional cold-weather drink is just what its name implies (to mull means to warm and spice): wine, usually red, infused with sugar, citrus, and spices, served warm. A seasonal clementine adds a sweet fruit note.

1. Toast the cloves, cinnamon, star anise, nutmeg, coriander, and peppercorns in a medium (4-quart) saucepan over medium heat, stirring occasionally, until aromatic, 1 to 2 minutes. Transfer the spices to a 6 x 6-inch piece of cheesecloth and set the pan aside to cool slightly. Gather the corners of the cheesecloth and tie with butcher's twine to make a sachet.

2. Put the wine, clementine, and sugar in the slightly cooled pan along with the sachet. Heat the wine mixture uncovered over low heat for 1 hour to infuse it with the spices. Do not let the mixture boil.

3. Using a pair of tongs, gently and carefully squeeze the juice from the clementine or tangerine into the wine mixture. Discard the juiced citrus halves and the sachet. Stir the brandy, Grand Marnier (if using), and vanilla into the wine and taste. Add more sugar if needed—use just enough to smooth out the flavors but not so much that it actually tastes sweet. Serve hot.

PER SERVING: 220 CALORIES | 0g PROTEIN | 15g CARB | 0g TOTAL FAT | 0g SAT FAT | 0g MONO FAT | 0g POLY FAT | 0mg CHOL | 10mg SODIUM | 0g FIBER

Make Ahead

If you want to infuse the wine a day before serving it, go right ahead. Just make sure to remove the spice sachet before storing it for the night. Gently reheat the wine in a medium pot over low heat and then add the brandy, Grand Marnier, and vanilla.

hot buttered
rum

orange-scented
mulled wine

chocolate-glazed chocolate–hazelnut cookies

YIELDS 6 TO 7 DOZEN 2¾- TO 3-INCH COOKIES

- 5 oz. (1 cup) whole hazelnuts, toasted
- 1½ tsp. instant espresso powder
- 3 oz. bittersweet or semisweet chocolate (not unsweetened), broken up or coarsely chopped
- 5⅓ oz. (⅔ cup) unsalted butter, slightly softened
- ¾ cup granulated sugar
- 1⅛ oz. (⅓ cup) unsweetened Dutch-processed cocoa powder
- 1 large egg
- 1½ tsp. pure vanilla extract
- ¼ tsp. table salt
- 8¼ oz. (1¾ cups) unbleached all-purpose flour
- Butter or nonstick spray for the baking sheets
- Chocolate Glaze (recipe on facing page)

The cookies will keep, refrigerated, for up to 5 days. Remove them from the refrigerator about 10 minutes before serving; if the cookies stand unrefrigerated for longer than about an hour, the chocolate surface may begin to dull.

1. In a food processor, process the hazelnuts and espresso powder until they're ground to the consistency of a nut butter, 2 to 3 minutes.

2. Melt the chocolate in a microwave or on the stove. Set aside to cool until warm.

3. In a large bowl, beat the butter, sugar, cocoa powder, and hazelnut mixture with a stand mixer (use the paddle attachment) or a hand-held mixer on medium speed until very well blended and fluffy, 1½ to 2 minutes; scrape the bowl as needed. Add the egg, vanilla, and salt; beat until completely blended and smooth, about 1½ minutes. On low speed, mix in half of the flour and then the melted chocolate just until evenly incorporated. Mix or stir in by hand the remaining flour until evenly incorporated. Set aside for 10 minutes; the dough will firm up slightly.

4. Cut the dough into thirds. Set each third between sheets of parchment or waxed paper. Roll out each portion to ⅛ inch thick; check the underside and smooth any wrinkles. Stack the rolled pieces (paper still attached) on a tray. Refrigerate until firm, about 45 minutes, or for several hours (or freeze for about 20 minutes to speed chilling).

5. Position a rack in the center of the oven and heat the oven to 350°F. Butter several large baking sheets or coat with nonstick spray. Working with one piece of dough at a time and keeping the remainder chilled, gently peel away and then replace the top sheet of paper. Flip the dough over. Peel off and discard the second sheet of paper. Cut out the cookies using a 2½- to 2¾-inch fluted round, oval, or other cutter. (If the dough softens too much to handle easily, transfer the paper and cookies to a tray, and refrigerate until firm again.) Using a spatula, carefully transfer the cookies to the baking sheets, arranging them about 1½ inches apart. Reroll the dough scraps. Continue cutting out the cookies until all dough is used; refrigerate as necessary if it becomes too soft to handle.

6. Bake the cookies one sheet at a time (keep the rest refrigerated) until they feel dry and almost firm when pressed in the center, 7 to 10 minutes. Let cool on the sheets for 3 or 4 minutes before transferring to racks to cool completely. Prepare the cookies for glazing by freezing them for at least 20 minutes or up to several hours. (You can also freeze the cookies at this point, tightly wrapped, for up to 2 months.) To glaze the cookies, follow the directions in the sidebar on the facing page.

chocolate glaze

16 oz. bittersweet or semisweet chocolate (not unsweet-ened), broken up or coarsely chopped

1 Tbs. corn oil or other flavor-less vegetable oil

Since the finished cookies are stored in the refrigerator, you don't need to temper the chocolate

1. Line several small trays or baking sheets with aluminum foil. Combine the chocolate and oil in a medium metal bowl. Set the bowl over a saucepan containing about an inch of barely simmering water and stir with a spatula until melted. Turn off the burner under the saucepan but leave the bowl over the hot water to keep the chocolate warm; stir the chocolate occasionally. (Replace the water in the pan with hot water as it cools off during the dipping process, but be careful not to splash water into the chocolate.)

2. To glaze the cookies: Working with only about five or six cookies at a time (keep the remainder frozen), dip the cookies in the chocolate glaze.

to glaze, just tilt, dip, and scrape

With the bowl tipped so that the chocolate pools on one side, hold a cookie verti-cally and dip until half is submerged in the chocolate. Lift the cookie out and shake off excess chocolate. Gently scrape the bottom of the cookie against the side of the bowl to remove excess chocolate from the bottom surface.

Arrange the dipped cookies on the foil-lined sheets, spacing them slightly apart. When a pan is full, refrigerate it for 30 minutes so the chocolate can firm up. Then peel the cookies from the foil, pack them in airtight containers, and return them to the refrigerator.

Chocolate and Hazelnuts

Throughout Europe, chocolate and hazelnuts are a classic pair. The combination appears frequently in Italian cakes, in various frozen desserts called semifreddo, and in a hazelnut-chocolate confection known as gianduia. Gian-duia originated in Italy, but it's enormously popular throughout Switzerland, Germany, and Austria as well, turning up in an array of bonbons, truffles, and other candies. The Swiss, Germans, and Austrians also use chocolate and chopped or ground hazelnuts in all sorts of tortes, puddings, pastries, and cookies.

lemon-lime butter wafers

YIELDS ABOUT 8 DOZEN
2¼-INCH COOKIES

- **10** oz. (2¼ cups) unbleached all-purpose flour
- **½** tsp. table salt
- **½** lb. (1 cup) unsalted butter, softened
- **1** Tbs. finely grated lemon zest (from about 1 large lemon)
- **1** Tbs. finely grated lime zest (from about 1 large lime)
- **1¼** cups granulated sugar
- **1** Tbs. fresh lemon juice
- **1** Tbs. fresh lime juice
- **1** Tbs. pure vanilla extract

Be sure the butter is softened at room temperature but still firm. Starting with butter that's too soft will result in dough that's tricky to shape into logs.

MIX THE DOUGH

Sift the flour and salt into a medium bowl. In the bowl of a stand mixer fitted with the paddle attachment, beat the butter and both zests on medium low until well blended, about 2 minutes. Add 1 cup of the sugar in a steady stream and mix for another 2 minutes until well blended. Blend in the lemon juice, lime juice, and vanilla. Reduce the speed to low and add the flour mixture in two additions, mixing just until blended.

SHAPE THE DOUGH

Have ready two 15-inch sheets of plastic wrap. Put the remaining ¼ cup sugar in a long, shallow pan (like a 7 x 11-inch Pyrex dish). Shape one half of the dough into a log about 10 inches long and roll gently in the sugar to thoroughly coat. Position the log on a sheet of plastic, centering it on the long edge closest to you. Roll tightly, twisting the ends of the plastic firmly to seal. With your hands on either end of the log, push it firmly toward the center to compact the dough. The finished log should be about 9 inches long and 1½ inches thick. Repeat with the remaining dough. Refrigerate the logs until firm enough to slice, about 2½ hours, or freeze for up to 3 months.

BAKE THE COOKIES

1. Position a rack in the center of the oven and heat the oven to 375°F. Line two rimmed baking sheets with parchment.

2. Working with one log at a time, use a sharp, thin-bladed knife to cut ⅛-inch-thick rounds. Set the rounds 1 inch apart on the baking sheets and bake one sheet at a time until lightly browned around the edges, about 10 minutes, rotating the sheet as needed for even browning. Let cool on the pan for about 5 minutes before transferring the cookies to racks with a thin-bladed spatula. When cool, store layered between sheets of waxed paper in airtight containers for up to a week, or freeze for up to 3 months.

> Logs of slice-and-bake cookie dough can be stored in the refrigerator for up to 3 days. For longer storage, put the logs in airtight, zip-top bags and freeze for up to 3 months. To thaw the logs, put them in the refrigerator overnight. Any unused dough may be frozen again.

oatmeal-cranberry cookies

**YIELDS ABOUT 6 DOZEN
2¼-INCH COOKIES**

- ⅓ cup orange juice
- ½ cup dried cranberries
- 1¾ cups old-fashioned oatmeal
- 5¾ oz. (1¼ cups) unbleached all-purpose flour
- 1 tsp. ground cinnamon
- ½ tsp. baking soda
- ½ tsp. table salt
- 6 oz. (¾ cup) unsalted butter, slightly firm
- 1 tsp. finely grated orange zest
- ¾ cup very firmly packed, very fresh dark brown sugar
- ¼ cup granulated sugar
- 1 large egg
- 1½ tsp. pure vanilla extract

A hint of orange zest and flecks of cranberry give classic oatmeal cookies a twist.

MIX THE DOUGH

1. In a small saucepan, heat the orange juice until very hot. Add the cranberries; let steep off the heat until softened, about 15 minutes. Drain the cranberries, pat dry on paper towels, and coarsely chop into ¼-inch pieces.

2. Put the oatmeal in a food processor and pulse eight to ten times to just break up the oatmeal. Remove ½ cup and transfer to a long shallow pan (like a 7 x 11-inch Pyrex dish). Add the flour, cinnamon, baking soda, and salt to the food processor and pulse with the remaining oatmeal eight to ten times just to blend the ingredients. Don't over process; the oatmeal should remain coarse.

3. In the bowl of a stand mixer fitted with the paddle attachment, beat the butter and orange zest on medium low until well blended, about 2 minutes. Add both sugars and mix for another 2 minutes. Blend in the egg and vanilla, scraping the bowl as needed. Reduce the mixer speed to low. Add half of the dry ingredients, then the cranberries, and then the remaining dry ingredients. Mix just until combined.

SHAPE THE DOUGH

Have ready six 15-inch sheets of plastic wrap. Portion the dough into thirds. Drop spoonfuls of dough onto each sheet and use the plastic to roll and shape the dough into logs about 8 inches long. Refrigerate the dough to firm it slightly, about 30 minutes. When chilled, roll one log at a time in the reserved oatmeal. Reroll each log tightly in a clean sheet of plastic wrap, twisting the ends firmly to seal. With your hands at either end of the log, push firmly toward the center to compact the log so it measures about 7 inches long and 1½ inches thick. Refrigerate the logs until firm enough to slice (they must be very well chilled), about 4 hours, or freeze for up to 3 months.

BAKE THE COOKIES

Position racks in the upper and lower thirds of the oven. Heat the oven to 350°F. Line two rimmed baking sheets with parchment. Working with one log at a time, use a tomato knife or other small serrated knife to slice the dough into ¼-inch-thick rounds, using a gentle sawing motion. Set the rounds 1 inch apart on the prepared pans. Bake the cookies until set on top and lightly browned around the edges, about 15 minutes, rotating the pans as needed for even browning. Let cool on the sheets for about 5 minutes before transferring the cookies to racks. When cool, store between sheets of waxed paper in an airtight container for up to a week, or freeze for up to 3 months.

METRIC EQUIVALENTS

LIQUID/DRY MEASURES	
U.S.	**METRIC**
¼ teaspoon	1.25 milliliters
½ teaspoon	2.5 milliliters
1 teaspoon	5 milliliters
1 tablespoon (3 teaspoons)	15 milliliters
1 fluid ounce (2 tablespoons)	30 milliliters
¼ cup	60 milliliters
⅓ cup	80 milliliters
½ cup	120 milliliters
1 cup	240 milliliters
1 pint (2 cups)	480 milliliters
1 quart (4 cups; 32 ounces)	960 milliliters
1 gallon (4 quarts)	3.84 liters
1 ounce (by weight)	28 grams
1 pound	454 grams
2.2 pounds	1 kilogram

OVEN TEMPERATURES		
°F	**GAS MARK**	**°C**
250	½	120
275	1	140
300	2	150
325	3	165
350	4	180
375	5	190
400	6	200
425	7	220
450	8	230
475	9	240
500	10	260
550	Broil	290

CONTRIBUTORS

Katherine Alford is the test kitchen director at the Food Network and is a judge on the network's show *Ultimate Recipe Showdown*.

Pam Anderson is a contributing editor to *Fine Cooking* and the author of several books, including, *Perfect One-Dish Dinners, All You Need For Easy Get-Togethers*. She blogs weekly about food and life at www.threemany-cooks.com

Jennifer Armentrout is senior food editor at *Fine Cooking*.

John Ash is the founder and chef of John Ash & Co., in Santa Rosa, California. He teaches at the Culinary Institute of America at Greystone and is a cookbook author. His latest, *John Ash: Cooking One on One*, won a James Beard award in 2005.

Jessica Bard is a food stylist, food writer, and recipe tester who teaches cooking classes at Warren Kitchen and Cutlery in Rhinebeck, New York.

Paul Bertolli is a writer, artisan food producer, and award-winning chef in the San Francisco Bay area of California.

Ethel Brennan is a writer and food and prop stylist from San Francisco, California.

Georgeanne Brennan is an award-winning cookbook author who lives in Northern California, where she offers seasonal cooking classes from her garden.

Bill Briwa is a chef-instructor at the Culinary Institute of America Greystone campus in California.

Lew Bryson is an award-winning drinks writer. He lives outside of Philadelphia.

Viviana Carballo is a food consultant and recipe developer. She also writes a weekly food column for the *Orlando Sentinel*.

Greg Case was a pastry chef at Dean & DeLuca in New York City and Hammersley's Bistro in Boston before setting out on his own. He owns the G. Case Baking Company in Somerville, Massachusetts.

Joanne Chang is the pastry chef and owner of Flour Bakery + Café, which has two locations in Boston and one in Cambridge; she is also chef and co-owner of Myers + Chang in Boston.

Melissa Clark is a food writer and the author of 29 cookbooks. Her latest is *In the Kitchen with A Good Appetite*, based on her *New York Times* Dining Section column.

Andy Corson is a fulfillment systems coordinator at The Taunton Press and is also baker-owner of American Artisan Food & Bakery in Newtown, Connecticut.

Rosetta Costantino is a cooking instructor in the Bay Area of California.

Dave Crofton is the chef and co-owner of One Girl Cookies bakery in Brooklyn, New York.

Carrie Davis lives and celebrates the Jewish holidays in Toronto, Ontario, Can., where she also teaches art to high school students.

Mitchell Davis is the vice president of the James Beard Foundation in New York City. He blogs about food at www.cookandeatbetter.com.

Tasha DeSerio is a cooking teacher and food writer, and the co-owner of Olive Green Catering in Berkeley, California. She is the co-author of *Cooking from the Farmer's Market*.

Abby Dodge, a former pastry chef, is a widely respected baking expert as well as a popular food writer and instructor. She studied in Paris at La Varenne and is the author of seven cookbooks, including her latest, *Desserts 4 Today*, as well as *The Weekend Baker*, an IACP Cookbook Award Finalist.

Stephen Durfee is a Pastry Instructor at The Culinary Institute of America and was the pastry chef at The French Laundry in Yountville, California.

Kay Fahey, a former restaurateur, lives in Reno, Nevada, and writes about food.

Keri Fisher is a food writer and cookbook author who cut her teeth at restaurants in Florida and Boston.

Janet Fletcher is a Napa Valley food writer and the author of *Fresh from the Farmers' Market* and *Cheese & Wine: A Guide to Selecting, Pairing, and Enjoying*.

St. John Frizell is a food, drink, and travel writer whose work has appeared in *Oxford American*, *Edible Brooklyn*, and *Edible Manhattan*, as well as on epicurious.com. He is the owner of the café-bar, Fort Defiance, in the Red Hook neighborhood of Brooklyn, New York.

Joyce Goldstein is one of the foremost experts on Mediterranean cooking in this country. She is an award-winning chef, prolific cookbook author, and cooking teacher.

Bonnie Gorder-Hinchey has over 25 years of experience as a food scientist developing products and recipes for companies including General Mills, Nestle, and Starbucks. She owns Creative Cuisine and is an adjunct professor at The Art Institute of Seattle, where she teaches culinary classes as well as classes in nutrition and general science.

Aliza Green is a cookbook author, journalist, and chef. She lives near Philadelphia, Pennsylvania.

Gordon Hamersley is chef-owner of Hamersley's Bistro in Boston, Massachusetts.

Lisa Hanauer is a former chef-restaurateur who now writes about food and teaches preschool. She lives in Oakland, California.

Kate Hays is the chef-owner of Dish Catering in Shelburne, Vermont. She is also a recipe tester, recipe developer, and food stylist.

Susanna Hoffman is an anthropologist and food writer. Her most recent book is *The Olive and The Caper: Adventures in Greek Cooking*.

Martha Holmberg is the former editor in chief of *Fine Cooking* and a food writer and cookbook author.

Barbara Hom is executive chef at the Sheraton Hotel Petaluma in California.

Sarah Jay is a former executive editor of *Fine Cooking* and the proprietor of www.paellapans.com.

Sara Jenkins is the chef and owner of Porchetta in New York City and the co-author of *Olives and Oranges: Recipes and Flavor Secrets from Italy, Spain, Cyprus and Beyond*.

Steve Johnson is chef-owner of Rendezvous in Central Square, Cambridge, Massachusetts.

Eva Katz has worked as a chef, caterer, teacher, recipe developer and tester, food stylist, and food writer. She is a member of the Program Advisory Committee at the Cambridge School of Culinary Arts in Massachusetts.

Diane Kochilas is a well-known Greek food expert and author who consults on Greek food and wine to restaurants and manufacturers.

Allison Ehri Kreitler is a *Fine Cooking* contributing editor. She has also worked as a freelance food stylist, recipe tester, developer, and writer for several national food magazines and the Food Network.

Paula LeDuc is an event planner and caterer in Northern California.

Ruth Lively trained at La Varenne in France, was the editor of *Cooking from the Garden*, and was senior editor at *Kitchen Gardener*.

Lily Loh, a cookbook author, teaches healthy Chinese cooking classes in California.

Leslie Mackie is chef-owner of Macrina Bakery & Café in Seattle.

Deborah Madison is the founding chef of Greens restaurant in San Francisco and the author of 11 cookbooks and numerous articles on food and farming. She writes and gardens from her home in Galisteo, New Mexico.

Nancie McDermott writes cookbooks and teaches cooking classes around the country. A North Carolina native who spent three years as a Peace Corps volunteer in Thailand, she covers both the cuisines and cultures of Asia and the traditional cooking of the American South.

Perla Meyers is an award-winning author of nine cookbooks. She also teaches workshops around the country and at her own school in Connecticut.

Susie Middleton, the former editor and current editor-at-large for *Fine Cooking* magazine, is a chef, food writer, and recipe developer. She is the author of the cookbook *Fast, Fresh & Green*.

Greg Patent was a national spokesperson for Cuisinarts, Inc., hosted a TV series on The Learning Channel, and teaches cooking classes all over the country. He is also an award-winning cookbook author and co-host of the "The Food Guys," a Montana Public Radio show.

Liz Pearson is a food writer and recipe developer based in Austin, Texas.

Randall Price was resident chef/instructor and director of the test kitchens at La Varenne's Chateau du Fey and cooks for private clients in Paris and the Auvergne.

Nicole Rees, author of *Baking Unplugged* and co-author of *The Baker's Manual* and *Understanding Baking*, is a food scientist and professional baker.

Peter Reinhart is the author of eight books on bread baking, including *Peter Reinhart's Artisan Breads Every Day*. He is the chef on assignment at Johnson & Wales University in Charlotte, North Carolina.

Adam Ried is a cooking columnist, cookbook author, recipe developer, and tester of all things kitchen-related. His latest book, *Thoroughly Modern Milkshakes*, came out in the summer of 2009.

Tony Rosenfeld, a *Fine Cooking* contributing editor, is also a food writer and restaurant owner based in the Boston area. His second cookbook, *Sear, Sauce, and Serve*, will be out spring 2011.

Tania Sigal is a food writer and chef/restaurant owner/caterer in Miami.

Maria Helm Sinskey is a chef, cookbook author, and the culinary director at her family's winery, Robert Sinskey Vineyards, in Napa Valley, California. She is a frequent contributor to *Food & Wine, Bon Appetit*, and *Fine Cooking* magazines. Her most recent cookbook, *Family Meals: Creating Traditions in the Kitchen* was a 2010 IACP Cookbook Award Winner.

Molly Stevens is a contributing editor to *Fine Cooking*. She won the IACP Cooking Teacher of the Year award in 2006; her book *All About Braising* won the James Beard and International Association of Culinary Professionals awards.

Craig Stoll is chef and co-owner of Delfina and Pizzeria Delfina in San Francisco, California.

Alan Tangren, a food writer, was a pastry chef at Chez Panisse and collaborated on *Chez Panisse Fruit* with Alice Waters.

David Tanis is head chef at Chez Panisse, as well as the author of *A Platter of Figs and Other Recipes*.

Adem Tepedelen is an award-winning beer and spirits writer who lives in Victoria, British Columbia.

Fred Thompson is a food writer, food stylist, and culinary developer. He is the author of eight cookbooks, including *Barbecue Nation* and *Grillin' with Gas*.

Sue Torres is the chef-owner of Sueños restaurant in New York City.

Jerry Traunfeld is the chef and owner of Poppy in Seattle and the former executive chef of The Herbfarm in Woodinville, Washington. He was the recipient of the James Beard Award for Best Chef Northwest in 2000.

He is also the author of *The Herbfarm Cookbook* and *The Herbal Kitchen: Cooking with Fragrance and Flavor*.

Rori Trovato is a cookbook author, food stylist, cooking teacher, and caterer.

Carole Walter is a master baker, baking instructor, and award-winning cookbook author. Her book *Great Pies & Tarts* was sited by the James Beard Foundation as one of The Baker's Dozen 13 Essential Bakery Books of the Past 40 Years.

Alice Waters is the founder and proprietor of Chez Panisse in Berkeley, California.

Annie Wayte was the executive chef of Nicole's and 202 in New York City. Her first cookbook is *Keep It Seasonal: Soups, Salads, and Sandwiches*.

Kathleen Weber is a bread baker and owns Della Fattoria bakery in Northern California.

Bruce Weinstein and Mark Scarbrough are award-winning cookbook authors, columnists, and contributors to national food publications. Their work has appeared in *Eating Well, Cooking Light, The Wine Spectator*, and *The Washington Post*, among others. Their latest book is *Real Food Has Curves: How to Get Off Processed Food, Lose Weight, And Love What You Eat*.

Laura Werlin is one of the country's foremost cheese experts whose specialty and passion is American cheese. She is the James Beard award-winning author of four books on the topic, including *Laura Werlin's Cheese Essentials*.

Peggi Whiting is the only Caucasian female sushi chef trained in Japan. She is the founder and *sensei* of the Seal Sama Teriyaki Sauce line.

Barbara Witt is the former owner and executive chef of a nationally acclaimed Washington, D.C., restaurant, a private chef, and the author and coauthor of several cookbooks.

Su-Mei Yu is the chef-owner of Saffron restaurant in San Diego, California. She is also an award-winning cookbook author. Her latest book is *The Elements of Life, A Contemporary Guide to Thai Recipes and Traditions for Healthier Living*. She is the founder of The Organic Cooking Academy by Su-Mei Yu in Mae Rim, Thailand.

Daphne Zepos is owner of the Essex Street Cheese Company in Brooklyn, New York. Visit her website at essexcheese.com

PHOTO CREDITS

INDEX